David W. Semple

Crusading with Knights Templar Under the Banners of Allegheny Commandery, No. 35

David W. Semple

Crusading with Knights Templar Under the Banners of Allegheny Commandery, No. 35

ISBN/EAN: 9783337285968

Printed in Europe, USA, Canada, Australia, Japan

Cover: Foto ©ninafisch / pixelio.de

More available books at **www.hansebooks.com**

To the Right Eminent Grand Commander,
Officers and Sir Kni

GREE

It having come to my knowledge, by petition duly signed, direct

that ALLEGHENY COMMANDERY, No. 35, Knights Templar, under

the honor of the Orders of Knighthood, and aiding the cause of

I hereby Grant Permission *Unto E. Sir* LEE

to appear in public in **FULL TEMPLAR UNIFORM, OR FATIGUE**

TO ESCORT THE MEMBERS OF TH

and to leave this State for a blending of Knightly sentiments and enjoyme

to present and make known to our Illustrious Frater, Right Em

of the State of New York, and other Illustrious Companions

the friendly and Knightly regards and good intent of the Pennsylva

Fraternal Love *may forever exist between us, and that* Peace and

And further, *our Sir Knights comprising said Command*

Templar in your jurisdiction.

Given under our hand, *as witness our signature, and*

attested by the signature of our Grand Recorder, in the City of Meadville,

establishment of the order of Knighthood in Pennsylvania.

By order of

RDERS,
NNSYLVANIA.

of the Grand Commandery of New York,

NG:

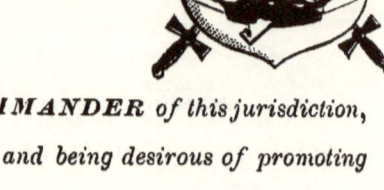

s RIGHT EMINENT GRAND COMMANDER of this jurisdiction,
template visiting your jurisdiction, and being desirous of promoting
edge and Humanity:

Commander, Officers and Sir Knights of Allegheny Commandery, No. 35,
mplar, as they may wish, on July 1, 2, 3 & 4, A. O. 780, A. D. 1878,
O EUROPE TO NEW YORK CITY,
the Sir Knights Templar of your jurisdiction, and with Knightly courtesy
nander of the Grand Commandery of the Knights Templar
composing the Grand Commandery of the State of New York,
ts Templar for your continued prosperity and well being, trusting that
nity may ever prevail throughout the world, in this Christian Order.
, are hereby commended to your Knightly consideration, and to all Knights

e seal of the Grand Commandery of Knights Templar of Pennsylvania, and
s 27th day of June, A. D. 1878, A. O. 780. Being the 80th year of the

muel B. Dick Grand Commander.

and Recorder.

CRUSADING

WITH

Knights Templar,

UNDER THE BANNERS

OF

Allegheny Commandery, No. 35,

ALLEGHENY CITY, PA.

DURING 1878.

BY DAVID W. SEMPLE.

PITTSBURGH:
PUBLISHED BY WM. P. BENNETT, 94 FIFTH AVENUE.
1879.

COPYRIGHTED, ACCORDING TO LAW, BY
DAVID W. SEMPLE AND WILLIAM P. BENNETT,
IN THE OFFICE OF THE LIBRARIAN OF CONGRESS.

To

THE "CRUSADERS" OF

Allegheny Commandery, No. 85,

Knights Templar,

OF

ALLEGHENY CITY, PENNSYLVANIA,

THIS VOLUME IS

RESPECTFULLY DEDICATED.

CONTENTS.

LETTER OF CREDENCE.... ....Frontispiece

PREFACE,... 5

ORGANIZATION OF, AND PREPARATION FOR, THE CRUSADE,................... 7

INTRODUCTION—

Introduction of Author and "Quartette."—The Pilgrims.—Preparing to Leave.—The Excursion to New York. 29

LETTER NUMBER ONE—

The Pilgrims at Sea.—Celebration of Our Glorious Day of Independence.—Notorious Interruption of Religious Services.—A Truly Loving Couple.—Nine Days in a World of Our Own,... 47

LETTER NUMBER TWO—

The Pilgrims Landed at Queenstown.—Their First Trouble on Ireland's Green Sod.—Attempts at Smuggling.—Reception in Cork.—In Trouble Again in a Barber Shop.—A Row with a Hotel Proprietor.—Blarney Castle.—Shandon Church.—Incidents by the Way,.......... 72

LETTER NUMBER THREE—

The Pilgrims at Killarney.—One of the Gems of Irish Scenery.—Amusing Scenes in Genuine Irish Life.—A Pleasant Ride through the Gap of Dunloe, and on the Lakes.—Incidents by the Way,.................... 105

CONTENTS.

LETTER NUMBER FOUR—

Killarney to Dublin.—Knights Templar transposed into Knights of Submission.—Full Account of the Impressive Ceremonies of Initiation, as well as the Grand Ennobling Principles of the Order.—In Dublin.—Incidents by the Way, ... 139

LETTER NUMBER FIVE—

Dublin to Enniskillen.—Londonderry.—The Giant's Causeway, and Belfast.—Riding on an Irish Locomotive.—A Grand Day spent with a Glorious People.—A Gala Day with True Friends, and the Ladies of Enniskillen.—Incidents by the Way, ... 166

LETTER NUMBER SIX—

Up the River Clyde.—In and Around Glasgow.—The Grand Reception by St. Mungo Encampment, and others. —Purchase of a Clothing House.—Trouble with Gents' Furnishing Goods.—A Day spent with Friends.—Separation of "Carlisle" from the remainder of the "Quartette."—Arrival in Edinburgh.—Incidents by the Way, ... 207

LETTER NUMBER SIX—CONTINUED—

Edinburgh.—Presentation of Bills to the Trio of the "Quartette."—Reception and Banquet by the Provincial Grand Lodge.—Melrose and Abbottsford.—Recherche Banquet at Leeds.—To London.—The Doctor and "Carlisle," now Two Poor and Weary Pilgrims, Traveling Alone.—Incidents by the Way, ... 238

LETTER NUMBER SEVEN—

A Saturday Night's Ride to Paris.—The Two Pilgrims in Paris.—Meeting of Friends in Cologne.—Accident on the Rhine.—Bingen.—Mayence.—Heidleberg.—Bale.—Lake Lucerne.—Brunig Pass and Brienz Valley. —Interlaken.—Berne.—Martigny to Chamouny.—Over the Tête Noire.—Geneva.—To London.—Incidents by Way, ... 263

CONTENTS.

LETTER NUMBER EIGHT—
    London and its Sights.—The Unfortunate Loss of a Watch.—Pilgrims Turn their weary feet Homewards.—" Carlisle " and the Doctor badly used up on the Homeward Voyage.—Particularly " Carlisle."—Arrival Home.—Incidents by the Way,.............................. 314

LETTER NUMBER NINE—
    Extracts from Letter Written by the Captain-General, W. C. Moreland, Esq., while doing the Italian Section, with part of the Crusaders.—Description of Scenery and Art,.. 341

CONCLUSION,.. 349

IN MEMORIAM,... 367

Preface.

PERHAPS in no country, where the rites and ceremonies of that ancient and honorable institution known to the world as Freemasonry are observed, is there any society, whether public or secret, which carries upon her banners a higher prestige or a more honorable name, than does the Commandery of Knights Templar stationed in Allegheny City, Pa., known as Allegheny Commandery, No. 35.

From the outer world, as well as within the broad fold of Templarism, come most gratifying words of commendation as to her composition, her character, and her tacit following of the signs she bears upon her banners and upon her arms.

Knowing full well the trust graciously bestowed would be carefully guarded and preserved, permission of the Grand Commandery of our grand Old Keystone State was granted to Allegheny Commandery to pay a fraternal visit to fraters of our mother country, and we trust egotism may not be laid at our door, when we make the assertion that the Grand Commandery can have no regret at the confidence reposed, and No. 35 of her subordinate Commanderies, has yet, for the first time, either at home or abroad, to bring to her fair name a single tinge of color or shame.

Though a series of correspondence has followed the "Second European Crusade of Allegheny Commandery," that could but be done in a condensed form and limited manner, and that the Second Pilgrimage may be more conveniently followed, we endeavor to place before our readers in these pages, as accurate an account as possible of the Crusade, and laying aside the dull, monotonous method usually pursued in "Travels Abroad," we prefer giving the actual daily occurrances met with by us all, rather than the prosy and wearisome descriptions of Castles, centuries old; and ivy-covered stones, *said to be* started 2000 years B. C., and which have been written up and described times without number and without end.

If we can in your hands spend an hour pleasantly with you, and if we can take you with us from city to city, and country to country, our aim is accomplished, and that we may endeavor to do so in a manner more simple than a continuous chapter of incidents, we care rather to talk with our reader in the shape of correspondence.

THE AUTHOR.

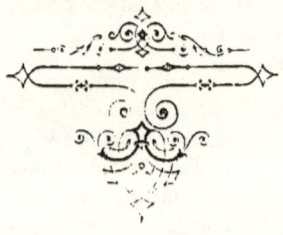

Organization of, and Preparation for
THE CRUSADE.

THE first "Crusade" by any Masonic body in modern days, was made during 1871, by ALLEGHENY COMMANDERY, KNIGHTS TEMPLAR, when forty-one Sir Knights left friends and home, not on a crusade of warfare against the blindness and superstitions of any clan or religious sect; not upon the test of steel against steel, valor against valor, arm against arm; but upon the most sublime pilgrimage man can ever undertake, that of carrying "Peace and Good Will to Man," of laying aside the sword; and the fraters of the New World grasping with "fraternal good will and brotherly love," the hands of the fraters of the Old.

As those forty-one Sir Knights bade adieu to Allegheny City; as they steamed down the bay towards the broad Atlantic; as they reached the farther shore, and Great Britain's Templars received, with open arms, those of America, how the world looked on! And truly, never was a better example given to the gaze of the eager eyes which watched, than of man meeting man, friend meeting friend, brother meeting brother with hand full of welcome in its fraternal grasp, and heart full of love in its every pulsation.

With each succeeding year was the Commandery invited and importuned to pay a second visit to Europe, and accordingly a resolution was offered that Allegheny Commandery make a Second European Pilgrimage, which was unanimously passed, and arrangements were at once commenced that placed the matter in definite shape to carry out this resolution. A committee being duly appointed and negotiations at once entered into with E. M. JENKINS, Esq., a member of Allegheny Commandery, by the way, and a person widely and favorably known to the traveling public of the United States, in fact of the world.

That the Committee labored industriously at their work, is shown more fully in the following circular, issued *sixty* days after the offering of the resolution in the Commandery:

Allegheny Commandery,

No. 85,

KNIGHTS TEMPLAR.

OFFICE OF THE RECORDER,

GEO. C. JOHNSTONE, *Rec.*

Allegheny, Pa., August 20th, 1877.

Dear Sir Knight:
This Commandery, which made a highly successful tour during the Summer of 1871, propose, at the earnest solicitation of a number of prominent Sir Knights, to make, during 1878, a

SECOND PILGRIMAGE TO EUROPE.

To that end a resolution was offered and unanimously adopted at the June conclave, and for the purpose of making all necessary arrangements, a Committee consisting of the following Sir Knights was appointed, viz:

Sirs B. F. HORNER,
P. Em. C. WILLIAM H. SLACK,
EDWARD COATES,
P. Em. C. JOSEPH H. ELTON, and
GEO. C. JOHNSTONE.

The Committee have been occupied in the performance of this duty, for several weeks past. They have consulted the wishes of those who have already decided to accompany the Commandery, among them several who made the first pilgrimage in 1871. They have been in written and personal communication with Sir E. M. Jenkins, a member of the Commandery, but now a resident of New York, whose experience and judgment will be recognized, and as a result announce the following:

The Commandery will take its departure from New York the last week in June or the first week in July, 1878,—the exact date to be hereafter announced. One of the best steamers of a first class line, probably a Cunarder, will be selected for their accommodation. The Commandery will land at Queenstown, the following being the adopted

ROUTE:

Queenstown to Cork; Blarney Castle; Mallow; Killarney; Gap of Dunloe; Lakes of Killarney; Dublin; Drogheda; Dundalk; Enniskillen, Londonderry; Port Rush; Giant's Causeway; Belfast; Glasgow; Loch Lomond; Loch Kathrine; Frossachs; Stirling; Edinburgh; Melrose; Abbottsford; Carlisle; Leeds; Sheffield; Liecester; Bedford; London; Flushing; Antwerp; Brussells; Rotterdam; Amsterdam; Utrecht; Cologne; the Rhine, by day steamer; Wiesbaden; Frankfort-on-the-Main; Darmstadt; Heidleburg; Baden-Baden; Strasburg; the Black Forest; Schaff-hausen; Zurich; Lucerne; the Rhigi; Lake Lucerne; Alpnacht; Brunig Pass; Brientz; Giesbach; Illuminated Waterfall; Interlacken; Berne; Lausanne; Lake Leman; Bouveret; Martigny; Tete Noir; Chamouix; Geneva; Macon; Dijon; Fontainbleau; Paris; Rouen; Dieppe; Newhaven; Brighton; London; Oxford; Warwick; Stratford-on-Avon, Chester; Liverpool; New York. Time occupied about seventy-five days, allowing a week each in London and Paris, and an amply sufficient time at each other place.

THE ENTIRE COST WILL BE $500,00 GOLD, EACH.

This will include Ocean Passage, Rail Road, Steamboat and Diligence Travel, Hotel Accommodation at each city,—*all first class*. It will also include Omnibuses for transfer between Hotel and Rail Road Stations; Jaunting Cars to Blarney Castle and Giant's Causeway; Boats and Ponies at Killarney; Wagonettes at Melrose for Abbottsford. Meals and accommodations to be in accordance with the custom of each country visited, viz.: In Ireland, Scotland and England, Meat Breakfast, Table D'Hote Dinner, Bedroom, Lights and Attendance. One hundred pounds baggage allowed free in Great Britain and Ireland; sixty-six pounds on the Continent. Porterage is also included, and the service of a competent Conductor, who will accompany the party all through the tour, who will act as Guide and Interpreter, and also as Superintendent of Traveling Arrangements, and who will pay all bills for sight seeing, who will assist in the formation of small Carriage Parties, and engage such local guides at points needed, as the members of the party may wish, the expense of which will be borne by those requiring them, as the sum quoted does not include carriage hire, or fees for sight seeing, and such small expenses as cannot be controlled by the conductor.

Some of the members of the Commandery desire to have the company of ladies. It is therefore determined that those who wish may be accompanied by their wives. The accommodation on the Steamers selected will be *outside rooms*, three persons in each room; or *inside rooms*, two persons in each room. An outside room can be given to two persons, u[on payment of $36.00 in gold, each, which will include ocean passage both ways.

A contract with E. M. Jenkins has been made to the above effect. It is expected that Sir Knight Jenkins will accompany the Commandery, and take charge of the traveling arrangements.

The Committee, in determining the above route, have been governed to some extent by the experiences obtained on the *first pilgrimage* of Allegheny Commandery in 1871. They have stricken from the programme all the unnecessary features of the former pilgrimage, while retaining those the most pleasant. Having a vivid recollection of the heat, dust and fleas of Italy, they have determined to omit that country this year, though a route will be laid out and a plan arranged for those who desire to take it. The route, as adopted, though very similar to that taken in 1871, is still quite different.

The Grand Commandery of Pennsylvania have already granted permission to Allegheny Commandery to make this Second Pilgrimage, and previous to their departure will issue a Letter of Credence, as the following extract from the minutes of said Grand Commandery attest :

Whereas, In the year 1870, this Grand Commandery granted permission to Allegheny Commandery, No. 35, to travel abroad and visit Commanderies in Europe, and a Letter of Credence was issued for that purpose by the Grand Commandery of Pennsylvania ; the Sir Knights were received with credit, honor, and great distinction throughout Great Britain or wherever this Letter of Credence was presented. It is well known that the Pilgrims from America conducted themselves while abroad with honor and dignity, which reflected credit upon Templar Masonry in America : Therefore,

Resolved, That this Grand Commandery grant permission to Allegheny Commandery, No. 35, to make a Second Crusade to Europe, for the purpose of visiting the Exposition in Paris, next year, and to visit Commanderies in Great Britain, and that a Letter of Credence be issued similar to the one issued in 1870.

While the Commandery will keep its organization intact, during its absence, still it is not the intention of the Eminent Commander to make "hard and fast" rules, which will interfere with the pleasure of the members. Certain proper orders will be issued for the government of those participating, which it is believed will be observed without inconvenience to anyone, the principal being to remind each member he is a Knight Templar, *and a Member of Allegheny Commandery*. Should any fail to remember this, he will have refunded to him the balance of his unexpended fare, less 10 per cent., and told to depart in peace.

While the object of this pilgrimage is pleasure, sight-seeing and relaxation from business, still the Commandery expects to meet many of its fraters, some of whom they had the gratification of meeting in 1871, and they hope to be prepared to return some of the compliments received during that year.

Each Sir Knight will be required to provide himself with the uniform and complete equipments known as "Crusader's Uniform," Allegheny Commandery; particulars can be obtained by addressing the Recorder.

A limited number of Knights Templar from other Commanderies, accompanied, if they visit, by their wives, will be cordially and heartily welcomed to join this pilgrimage. The names of such Sir Knights will be duly presented to Allegheny Commandery, for Honorary Membership. You are invited to make one of the number.

It is expected that those who decide to go will pay to Sir Hon. ALFRED SLACK, Treasurer of Allegheny Commandery, a deposit of One Hundred Dollars, previous to January 1st, 1878, the money thus deposited being used to secure steamship accommodations. This deposit is not necessarily to be forfeited, in case of withdrawal, as no difficulty is apprehended in finding a substitute. The balance of the amount due will be required to be paid thirty days before departure. Any further information desired will be given by addressing the undersigned.

GEORGE C. JOHNSTONE,
Recorder.

The above circular being mailed to a number of Sir Knights, members of a limited number of Commanderies, necessarily resulted in quite a heavy work in the line of correspondence; and right here we may be permitted to add, by way of parenthesis, not only as an individual member of Allegheny Commandery, but on behalf of that body as a whole, that we take it as an opportune moment to congratulate Allegheny Commandery upon her selection of a Sir Knight to fill one of her most responsible positions, requiring judgment, care and prudence, that of Recorder, so efficiently and ably filled by Sir Knight Geo. C. Johnstone, a worthy gentleman, a capable officer, and an honorable Knight of the Temple.

Some little conception may be formed of the work necessary to be performed, incidental to moving a Commandery on such a pilgrimage, when we name but a few of the cities from which were received letters of inquiry in answer to the foregoing circular, and the amount of correspondence occurring in replying to all sorts of questions made concerning the tour.

Letters came from Rochester, Elmira, Ithica, Syracuse, Albany and New York City, N. Y.; Lancaster, Emilie, Philadelphia, Coatesville, Shippensburg, Sharon, Altoona, Greensburg, Bellefonte, Columbia, Harrisburg, Scranton, Williamsport, and Clearfield, Pa.; Versailles, Richmond, Paris, Cynthia, Ky.; Winooski, Burlington, Vt.; Cincinnati, Canton, Cleveland, Chillicothe, Hamilton, Dayton, O.; Staunton, Wheeling, Halltown, W. Va.; Davenport, Dubuque, Keokuk, Burlington, Muscatine, Iowa; Dover, Del.; Rock Island, Chicago, Ills.; West Joplin, St. Joseph, St. Louis, Mo.; Elkhart, Logansport,

Evansville, South Bend, Ind.; Black Hawk, Denver, Col.; Georgetown, Washington, D. C.; Kansas City, Kan.; Little Rock, Ark.; San Francisco, Cal.; Savannah, Ga.; etc., etc. Of course from so many varied sources, as to any business house, the letters seeking information would be concise, " boiled down " and to the point; while others would begin with their " sit me down with pen in hand, etc.," giving the pedigree of themselves, " their sisters. their cousins, and their aunts," and many were quite a fund of amusement.

One letter from a very nice, rather aged gentleman, (now deceased, poor fellow!) contained an obituary notice of his wife, written by himself, her age at death, etc.; as well as a complete history of himself, his age, his height, his weight, how many children, their ages, sexes and general physical make up.

However the requisite number was speedily attained to make the pilgrimage, and the following supplementary circular was issued:

SECOND PILGRIMAGE TO EUROPE.

THE EMINENT COMMANDER DESIRES TO GIVE THE SIR KNIGHTS FURTHER INFORMATION ON THE SUBJECT:

Since the issue of the Circular from the Recorder's Office, under date of August 20, 1877, so many applications have been received for permission to join, both by our own membership and those of other jurisdictions, that the SECOND PILGRIMAGE is now a fixed fact.

The following arrangements have now been completed: The Commandery will leave Pittsburgh on Monday Evening, July 1st, next, for New York, and will sail by a Cunard Steamer, on Wednesday, July 3d, landing at Queenstown in Ireland. The Route in Europe is as follows:

ROUTE:

Queenstown to Cork; Blarney Castle; Mallow; Killarney; Gap of Dunloe; Lakes of Killarney; Dublin; Drogheda; Dundalk; Enniskillen; Londonderry; Port Rush; Giant's Causeway; Belfast; Glasgow; Loch Lomond; Loch Kathrine; Trossachs, Stirling; Edinburgh; Melrose; Abbottsford; Carlisle; Leeds; Sheffield; Liecester; Bedford; London, Flushing; Antwerp; Brussells; Rotterdam; Amsterdam; Utrecht; Cologne; the Rhine by day Steamer; Wiesbaden; Frankfort-on-the-Main; Darmstadt; Heidelberg; Baden-Baden; Strasburg; the Black Forest; Schaff-hausen; Zurich; Lucerne; the Rhigi; Lake Lucerne; Alpnacht; the Brunig Pass; Brientz; Giesbach; Illuminated Waterfalls; Interlacken; Berne; Lausanne; Lake Leman; Bouveret; Martigny; *Tete Noir;* Chamouix; Geneva; Macon; Dijon; Fontainbleau; Paris; Rouen; Dieppe; Newhaven; Brighton; London; Oxford; Warwick; Stratford-on-Avon; Chester; Liverpool; New York. Time occupied, about seventy-five days, allowing a week each in London and Paris, and an amply sufficient time at each other place. The return will be made in a Cunard Steamer; the Steamship Tickets will be good to return for a year.

Those who wish to extend their tour to Italy, will be permitted to do so, and the following additional arrangements have been made with Sir Knight E. M. Jenkins: To leave main party at Geneva; to be supplied with a conductor, (if there be ten in the party,) and go via Mount Cenis Tunnel to Turin; Milan; Verona; Venice; Padua; Boulogne; Florence; Rome; Naples; Vesuvius; Pompeii; Pisa; Genoa; Turin; and back to Paris, London, Liverpool and New York. To occupy three weeks longer, and to cost $140, in gold, more, which includes all hotel expenses, gondolas in Venice, carriages for three days' sight-seeing in Rome, with Companion Shakspere Wood for guide, carriages and ponies for Pompeii and Vesuvius.

The accommodations on board the Steamships, at Hotels, and on the Railroads, are first class in every particular. The Rooms on the Ocean Steamers are to be occupied by three persons; but smaller rooms for two persons may be obtained at no increased expense. Should two persons wish to occupy a large outside room, the additional charge will be $36 in gold, each, for the journey both ways. The Steamship accommodations must be secured by the middle of February, and it is intended to engage and pay for twenty rooms, by that time; hence it is important that those who intend participating in this pilgrimage, pay at once to the Treasurer of Allegheny Commandery, Sir Alfred Slack, the advance payment necessary to secure these rooms. The balance of the amount can be arranged by the 1st of June, in a manner to be announced.

The Pilgrimage Party will be limited to the number necessary to fill twenty rooms, which in no case will exceed fifty, and may fall below that number.

By order of Em. Commander,

GEO. C. JOHNSTONE,
Recorder.

B. F. HORNER,
W. H. SLACK,
EDWARD COATES,
JOS. H. ELTON,
JOHN HEATH,
GEO. C. JOHNSTONE,
Committee.

Final arrangements for the Crusade, so far as the other side of the ocean was concerned, being thus completed, the following letters were received, showing our fraters across the Atlantic were anticipating our visit:

ENNISKILLEN, IRELAND, March 7, 1878.

Dear Sir and Brother:

Kindly drop me a line by return mail, saying what day the Allegheny Commandery will positively leave New York and reach Enniskillen. If you have a dated itinerary to spare, I would be glad to have it.   *   *   *   *   Hoping to meet you all well and hearty on your arrival.

Fraternally and faithfully yours,

O. TERNAN.

GEO. C. JOHNSTONE, Esq.,
Allegheny City, Pa.

LEEDS, ENGLAND, March 26th, 1878.

Dear Sir Knigh':

I have heard through E. M. Jenkins' agents here, that your Commandery purpose to pay Leeds a visit this summer, and as you would not object, perhaps, to meeting your brethren on this side the water, I have written to our E. C. to-day, informing him, and no doubt he will call a meeting to see what we can do; our numbers are only small, but I doubt not we shall be able to give you an English welcome. With fraternal regards to yourself and the other Sir Knights, believe me,

Fraternally yours,

† W. J. BECK, P. E. P.

Sir GEO. C. JOHNSTONE,
Allegheny City, Pa.

In the meantime the efficient Committee, in whose hands were the arrangements, had been perfecting and completing the same, so that on June 1st, 1878, their arduous and well managed labors were ended, the books being closed with thirty-eight persons forming the party.

The following kind letter was then duly received from a Commandery whose "fame has spread both far and wide," and from gentlemen of whom it is entirely worthy, and of whom we shall have occasion to speak later on. The words contained therein speak kindly and directly as though coming from the heart sincerely:

HEADQUARTERS

Palestine Commandery,

No. 18, K. T.

Masonic Temple,
6th Ave. & 23d St.

NEW YORK, June 8th, 1878.

To the Eminent Commander, Officers and Sir Knights of Allegheny Commandery, No. 35, K. T., Stationed at Allegheny City, Pa.:

B

Dear Fraters:

We are well aware that you are to make a Pilgrimage to Europe, leaving this port on July 3d, next, and wishing you to leave these shores in the most pleasant manner, we therefore, as a Commandery, should like to meet you on your arrival in our city, on Tuesday, July 2d, and escort you to your hotel.

Palestine, No. 18, desires to become better acquainted with the Sir Knights of Allegheny, No. 35, and we trust this may be the means of so doing it.

Trusting that you will accept of our escort, and if you will give us full particulars as to the time of your arrival here, we will make all proper arrangements for receiving you.

We remain,
    Courteously and fraternally yours,

ATTEST,   † GEORGE W. SKELLEN,
 JAMES A. RICH,   *Em. Commander.*
 Recorder.

This hearty and kind invitation, coming as it did, so manifestly an evidence of fraternal good will and esteem, was unanimously accepted on the part of Allegheny, No. 35, by means of the following letter:

Allegheny Commandery,
No. 35, K. T.

ALLEGHENY CITY, Pa., June 12, 1878.

To the Eminent Commander, Officers and Sir Knights of Palestine Commandery, No. 18, K. T., Stationed at New York, Greeting:

Dear Fraters:

Your official communication has been duly received. Knowing well the reputation the Sir Knights of Palestine Commandery, No. 18, have ever enjoyed of being "Good Sir Knights, and True," those composing the membership of Allegheny Commandery, No. 35, will deem it one of the most pleasant features of their Second Pilgrimage to Europe, to meet and greet, personally, the members of your

Commandery, and as you have to this end so kindly intimated, we cheerfully accept the tender of your Commandery as escort on our arrival in New York.

We leave Pittsburgh on Monday evening, July 1st, at 6 P. M. via Pennsylvania Rail Road, arriving at Jersey City about 7:15 A. M. July 2d.

We remain ever,
Courteously and fraternally yours,

ATTEST, LEE S. SMITH,
GEO. C. JOHNSTONE, *Em. Commander.*
Recorder.

And the following answer was received:

HEADQUARTERS

Palestine Commandery,

No. 18, K. T.

Masonic Temple,
6th Ave. & 23d St. NEW YORK, June 20, 1878.

GEO. C. JOHNSTONE,

Recorder Allegheny Commandery, No. 35, K. T.

Dear Sir Knight:

Your courteous letter of 12th inst., accepting our escort, was duly received. We have also received your circular giving particulars of route, etc., and we will therefore arrange our plans accordingly for the 2d proximo.

Please state the *exact* time you will leave your headquarters, the Grand Central Hotel, on July 3d, to go on board the S. S. "Russia." Your reply by Monday morning next, will greatly facilitate our orders and plans.

Yours, fraternally and courteously,

JAMES A. RICH,
Recorder.

The following orders were then issued from the Commandery, in accordance with all previously arranged plans:

HEADQUARTERS

Allegheny Commandery,
No. 35, K. T.

MASONIC HALL, ALLEGHENY CITY, PA., June, 15, 1878.

SPECIAL ORDER No. 1.

I. In accordance with Resolution of the Commandery, the Report of Committee of Arrangements for Excursion to New York, will accompany this order.

II. The members of Allegheny Commandery, as well as those of Pittsburgh No. 1, Tancred No. 48, and all others who desire to participate in escort, will assemble at Asylum, at 4 P. M., sharp, on Monday, July 1st, in full Templar uniform. It will be necessary to complete formation and assign Sir Knights to their positions before leaving the Asylum.

III. On arrival in New York the Command will be received by Palestine Commandery No. 18, stationed in New York, and escorted to hotel.

IV. After escorting the Crusaders to steamer in New York, July 3d, the escort will return to hotel where it will be disbanded. It will be necessary for Sir Knights to take with them a full suit of citizen's clothing.

V. Sir Knights who cannot accompany escort to New York, and desire participating in parade before starting can do so; their baggage will be taken to depot, that they may change their dress there.

VI. Band will report at depot at 5:00 P. M. sharp, to Captain-General of Commandery.

By order of LEE S. SMITH,
ATTEST, *Em. Commander.*
GEO. C. JOHNSTONE, EDWARD COATES,
Recorder. *Capt.-General.*

Allegheny Commandery,

No. 35, K. T.

Masonic Hall, Allegheny City, Pa.,
Sir Knight: June, 1878.

At the stated conclave of the Commandery, held April 26th, it was resolved that the Commandery go to New York, as escort to Members of this and other Commanderies who accompany Allegheny Commandery on its Second Pilgrimage to Europe in July next.

The Committee of Arrangements for the Excursion, issued the following Information, viz:

The Commandery will go via P. R. R., on special train, leaving Union Depot at 6 P. M., Monday, July 1st. Baggage will be taken from Masonic Hall, Allegheny, and Library Hall, Pittsburgh, to depot, (free of charge,) by kindness of Sir John W. Haney, of Pittsburgh Commandery, No. 1.

Members of Pittsburgh, No. 1, Tancred, No. 48, and all visiting Sir Knights, are courteously invited to join with us on this occasion.

Fare to New York and Return, $12.50,

Tickets good for 15 days. Any Sir Knight wishing to remain longer can have his ticket endorsed by Thomas E. Watt, Esq., who will accompany Commandery to New York.

Tickets for European party good until return. Quarters have been secured at Grand Central Hotel, New York, at $2.50 per day.

Sleeping-car rates as usual. In order that sufficient accommodation may be provided, those intending to participate and desiring sleeping-car berths, will notify Sir William H. Bown, Chairman Committee, No. 136 Wood Street, immediately, and by paying him they will be secured.

Tickets will be sold to friends of Sir Knights desiring to go to New York on this train.

Tickets may be had at Union Depot, of Thomas E. Watt, General Ticket Office, corner Fifth Avenue and Smithfield Street; also at the Asylum, at regular Conclave, June 28.

In order to arrange for special train, it will be necessary to know soon how many are going. You will please notify George C. Johnstone, Recorder, No. 11 Boyle Street, Allegheny, immediately. Lunch will be provided on train.

WILLIAM H. BOWN,
GEO. W. SPENCER,
THOMAS M. WHITE,
Committee.

All arrangements on the part of the Commandery for the Crusade being complete, we awaited the receipt of our "Letters of Credence" from the Grand Commandery of Pennsylvania, as well as permission from that body, and the Grand Commandery of the State of New Jersey, to pass through the two named States as a body of Knights Templar, which came duly to hand, to-wit:

LETTER OF CREDENCE.

Allegheny Commandery, No. 35,

MASONIC KNIGHTS TEMPLAR, ALLEGHENY, U. S. OF A.

1878.

To the Most Eminent and Supreme Grand Master:

The Grand and Subordinate Officers and Sir Knights of all Encampments, Preceptories and Priories of the Royal, Exalted, Religious, and Military Order of Masonic Knights Templar, in England and Wales, and Jurisdiction thereunto belonging; as well as to those of Scotland, Ireland, and in whatever country wherein the symbol of the Cross has been displayed upon the banners of Templarism, to advance the moral, intellectual, and religious knowledge of our Christian order,

PEACE, UNITY, AND FRATERNAL LOVE.

BE IT KNOWN, That Allegheny Commandery, No. 35, of the City of Allegheny, Pennsylvania, deriving a charter from the Grand Commandery of Knights Templar, of the State of Pennsylvania—

in their associate capacity as a Subordinate Commandery, having made all the necessary arrangements for an excursion through Europe, and to visit all Encampments, Preceptories, and Priories, on their designated route—it is eminently proper on such an occasion that the Right Eminent Grand Commandery of Knights Templar should present a Letter of Credence to such valiant and magnanimous Knights of Allegheny Commandery, No. 35, as may participate in the excursion.

A list of these Sir Knights is appended, to which they have affixed their signatures. It is more particularly required from this Grand Commandery, as Pennsylvania was the first State in the American Union which organized a Grand Encampment, in Philadelphia, in 1797, from Sir Knights who came to this State from the mother country, and brought with them the rites and ceremonies of our chivalric and Christian Order. Hence it is right and proper that the glorious old Keystone State should be the first Grand Commandery in America to send to our mother country one of her subordinate Commanderies, fully equipped, to visit the home, the altars, the asylums, the historic memorials ; nay, the graves and monuments of our Templar fathers. This fact of itself should, and we trust ever will, render more stable and lasting the fraternal intercourse which should exist between the brethren of two countries descended from a common origin and bound together by the same ties.

In the exalted character of Knights Templar, therefore, we affectionately and fraternally commend each and every one of the members and Sir Knights of Allegheny Commandery, No. 35, as Master Masons, who have worked on the Square—as Royal Arch Masons who have wrought on the Triangle at the rebuilding of the Second Temple, and brought to light treasures of inestimable value—and as Sir Knights, who as Pilgrim Penitents in our Asylums, have not only visited the Sepulcher, but knelt around the Sacred Delta and beheld the cross of our ascended Redeemer.

These Sir Knights go from among us, for a season, as our immediate representatives, and we pray you, as officers and Sir Knights, to extend to our beloved subordinates, the Sir Knights of Allegheny Commandery, No. 35, and those associated with them from other States and other Commanderies, those fraternal greetings, and that disinterested friendship and unbounded hospitality which ever has, and we trust, ever will continue to adorn, distinguish and characterize our magnanimous Order, based upon brotherly love, friendship, and the Christian religion.

Throughout their perilous voyage by sea and land, the officers of the Right Eminent Grand Commandery, its subordinates, and the individual Sir Knights will feel it to be their duty to pray, Immanuel, God with us, to have the illustrious Knights of Allegheny Commandery, No. 35, and those associated with them in His most holy keeping, and in due time, return the Sir Knights in peace and health to their families, their friends, their brothers, and their Asylums, in which fond and loving hearts will greet them as weary, wayworn pilgrims, who, having performed their pilgrimage, desire to rest and offer their prayers and meditations at the shrine of their Redeemer.

Given under our hands and seal of the Grand Commandery of Knight Templar of Pennsylvania, at the City of Meadville, Crawford County, this tenth day of June, 1878, A. O. 760, A. E. O. P. 81.

SAMUEL B. DICK, R. E. G. Com.
J. P. S. GOBIN, D. G. Com.
DE WITT C. CARROLL, G. Generalissimo.
GEO. W. KENDRICK, Jr., G. Capt.-Gen.
B. FRANK BRENNEMAN, G. Senior Warden.
CHAS. W. BATCHELOR, G. Junior Warden.
RICHARD MUCKLE, G. Treasurer.

SEAL.

ATTEST.

CHAS. E. MEYER, *Grand Recorder.*

The Grand Commandery of Pennsylvania issues the enclosed Letter of Credence to the following Knights, Members of ALLEGHENY COMMANDERY, NO. 35, KNIGHTS TEMPLAR, STATIONED AT ALLEGHENY, PENNSYLVANIA, and those associated with them from other Commanderies:

LEE S. SMITH, E. C.

WILLIAM H. SLACK, P. E. C.

DAVID W. SEMPLE,

Rev. W. B. WATKINS,
No. 1, Pennsylvania.

JESSE L. STACKHOUSE,
No. 4, New Jersey.

ROBERT MORRIS,
Kentucky.

JAMES MILLIKEN,

J. F. BEILSTEIN,

JAS. C. RAFFERTY,

GEO. S. HAINES,

J. D. LANDIS, C. G.
 No. 34, Pennsylvania.

A. O. BAKER,
 No. 54, Pennsylvania.

WILLIAM C. MORELAND,
 No. 48, Pennsylvania.

GEO. S. EYSTER,
 Potomac, W. Va.

JOHN HEATH,
 No. 35, Pennsylvania.

R. R. CARSON, E. C.
 Logansport, Ind.

JOHN AMSDEN, P. E. C.
 Versailles, Kentucky.

ROBERT J. BAXTER,
 No. 16, St. Louis.

WILLIAM FULLERTON,
 No. 2, Colorado.

EDWARD F. CLINTON,
 No. 2, Colorado.

O. H. BRUSIE,
 South Bend, Indiana.

ED. L. SCHRODER,
 York, Pa.

W. C. IRWIN,
 No. 12, Ohio.

JOS. W. SMITH,
 No. 7, Pennsylvania.

WALTER E. HAGUE,
 No. 35, Pennsylvania.

ALFRED SLACK,
 No. 35, Pennsylvania.

Accompanying these Letters of Credence, a copy of which was given to each Crusader, was the following to the Right Eminent Grand Commanders of Knights Templar, Jurisdictions of New Jersey and New York, to pass through their jurisdiction as a body of Knights Templar:

Grand Commandery, Knights Templar,

AND APPENDANT ORDERS OF THE STATE OF PENNSYLVANIA.

To the Right Eminent Grand Commander,
 Officers and Sir Knights of the Grand Commandery of N. Jersey,

GREETING:

It having come to my knowledge, by petition duly signed, directed to me as *Right Eminent Grand Commander* of this Jurisdiction, that *Allegheny Commandery, No. 35,* Knights Templar, under our command, contemplate visiting your jurisdiction, and being desirous of promoting the honor of the Order of Knighthood, and aiding the cause of *Virtue, Knowledge and Humanity,*

I HEREBY GRANT PERMISSION unto Em. Sir LEE S. SMITH, Commander, Officers and Sir Knights of Allegheny Commandery, No. 35, to appear in public in full Templar uniform, or fatigue dress of Knights Templar, as they may wish, on July 1st, 2d, 3d and 4th, A. O. 760, A. D. 1878, to escort the members of the Pilgrimage to Europe to New York City, and to leave this State for a blending of knightly sentiments and enjoyment with the Sir Knights Templar of your jurisdiction, and with knightly courtesy to present and make known unto our Illustrious Frater, Right Eminent Grand Commander of the Grand Commandery of the Knights Templar of the State of New Jersey, and other Illustrious Companions, Sir Knights, composing the Grand Commandery of the State of New Jersey, the friendly and knightly regards and good intent of the Pennsylvania Knights Templar, for your continued prosperity and well being, trusting that *fraternal love* may ever exist between us, and that *peace* and *unity* may forever prevail throughout the world in this Christian Order.

AND FURTHER, our Sir Knights comprising said Commandery, are hereby commended to your knightly consideration, and to all Knights Templar in your jurisdiction.

GIVEN UNDER OUR HAND, as witness our signature, and the Seal of the Grand Commandery of Knights Templar of Pennsylvania, and attested by the signature of our Grand Recorder, in the City of Meadville, this 27th day of June, A. D. 1878, A. O. 760, being the 80th year of the establishment of the Order of Knighthood in Pennsylvania.

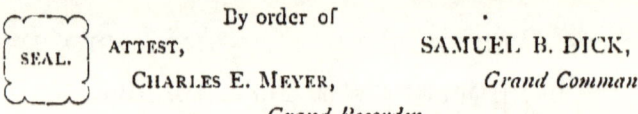

{ SEAL. } By order of
ATTEST, SAMUEL B. DICK,
CHARLES E. MEYER, *Grand Commander.*
Grand Recorder.

With a similar authority to the Right Eminent Grand Commander of the State of New York, Allegheny Commandery, No. 35, was, in every way, as a body, prepared for her "Second European Pilgrimage;" and, apropos of our preparation, the following General Orders of Palestine Commandery, No. 18, of New York, were issued to the members of that command, so that every detail had been arranged to make the departure of Allegheny, No. 35, a success in every particular.

HEADQUARTERS OF THE EMINENT COMMANDER
353 WEST 24TH STREET.

Palestine *Commandery*

No. 18, *K. T.*

MASONIC TEMPLE, SIXTH AVE. & 23D ST.

ORDER No. 2. NEW YORK, June 27, 1878.

Sir Knight:

In accordance with our letter to Allegheny Commandery, No. 35, K. T. (tendering them an escort, on their arrival in this city, on their way to Europe, and which they have accepted,) you are ordered to assemble at the ferry, foot of Cortlandt Street, N. R., on the morning of Tuesday, July 2d, promptly, at 9¾ A. M., in full uniform for escort duty.

A delegation of six Sir Knights, (to be appointed at our next regular conclave, July 1st,) will cross the ferry to Jersey City, and meet the Sir Knights of Allegheny, No. 35, and those of Pittsburgh, No. 1, and Tancred, No. 48, who accompany the Crusaders.

When the delegation and our visiting Knights reach this side, the line of march will move through Cortlandt Street to Broadway, through Broadway to the Grand Central Hotel. On arrival at the hotel the Commandery, as a body, will be dismissed for the day.

It is especially ordered that all Sir Knights will be prompt at Cortlandt Street Ferry, on Tuesday morning, at the specified time, to answer the roll call, and to receive their numbers in line, by which they will be designated. If the weather proves stormy, the *full fatigue* dress will be worn.

It is the express desire of the Eminent Commander, that as many Sir Knights of our Commandery as can possibly do so, will parade, as he is desirous of having a full representation of our Command.

Every Sir Knight who can, will be present at 7½ o'clock, *promptly*, on Monday, 1st prox.

ATTEST, † GEO. W. SKELLEN,
JAMES A. RICH, *Em. Commander.*
Recorder.

The arrangements being wholly completed, the first day of July was awaited patiently, each of those participating in the crusade being now busily engaged in arranging their business matters, and individually preparing for departure.

Introduction.

Introduction of Author and the "Quartette."—The Pilgrims.—Preparing to Leave.—The Excursion to New York.

AT the very outstart of this volume, and at the threshold of our work, our condemnation may be written, our doom may forever be sealed, so far as book-work may be concerned, for an apparent evidence of egotism, but we feel that a certain feeling of friendship should exist between the reader and the writer, and that all should become acquainted with the "poor and weary pilgrims" about departing on their wayfaring tour; hence, we trust that in thus introducing ourselves, our most severe critics may lean charitably towards us, when we state the fact, that under no circumstances can we permit our hours spent far into the night, the waking in the mornings with bleared eyes, sunken and expressionless in appearance, with visions of ghosts and hobgoblins flashing like wild-fire through our brain—to use a description frequently read of poor and lowly authors, who, for a meager pittance, in some lowly corner or garret, grind out page after page of intellectual food for the hungry mind, knowledge for the learning and studious, or trash for the young or lower minds—we say we cannot permit such an opportunity to pass, without introducing ourselves to our reader, and to each Sir Knight with whom we may thus become acquainted; therefore we humbly ask that pardon, which we feel will readily be granted by all, at least those who have been taught the invaluable lessons of charity and brotherly love, we having thus frankly confessed judgment in this case.

By occupation we wearily tread the path of life as—pardon our bashfulness—an editor; earning our livelihood wielding the pencil for a journal, not of the kind that says, "Good morning" to us at the breakfast table, to be read by *pater familias*, with glaring headlines of 50,000 majority for the opponent of our political views, and which causes us to throw down the innocent paper violently, with still the last bite of toast in process of mastication, jam our hats on wrong side foremost, and pass out at the door, muttering something about Maine, Ohio or Pennsylvania gone Republican, Democratic or Greenback again. No; not a political journal, nor even one that drops in during the sombre hours of the evening, with foreign news twelve to twenty-four hours old, clippings from other papers and titbits of romance from the monthlies, with choice bits of mild gossip and light scandal; no, neither such as these, but of such an one as goes into the hands of smiling maidens and pretty creatures of the fair sex, with pages of cuts from the latest imperative orders from dame fashion, which regal mistress causes the fair reader and looker on to beseech papa to open his heart and pocket-book to give daughter the wherewithal to purchase sufficient material to make a costume copied from pattern No. 12, &c.

An editor is supposed by all who are not editors to be a portion of a race of people entirely different from their brethren in humanity—a sort of peculiar personage, who lives, moves and has his being in the most simple kind of manner, a sure dead-head on all *free* excursions; every pocket bulged out with rail road and street car passes; with the doors of theatres and opera houses wide open to allow him to enter therein; picked up bodily and carried by sheer force, and entirely in opposition to his will, into Congress and into power; one who knows everything, can stand any amount of abuse and fears no living thing; and on behalf of the editor, without denying or affirming the common belief, we would say that the latter clause is about the only thing on this earth an editor has to be thankful for, namely, he is allowed considerable freedom about his own office, his home or upon the street, for as a rule the multitude fear the editor, for he is the ghoul of his jurisdiction, particularly if he be the editor-in-chief, the city editor and proprietor, for these three form the grand trinity of newspaperdom with one noble head the—fighting editor.

When we bring to the notice of loving parents and kind guardians the fact that away up flights of stairs, in some secluded nook or corner, gazing upon busy and begrimmed humanity below, or 'neath the dim light of lamp or gas, sits the editor, scratching his cranium, as his brain ekes out that, which in his opinion is to please mankind generally, only to find that within twenty-four hours after his pencil has left his article, some terribly offended personage presents himself at the door of the sanctum, armed in a manner a lava bed or Ute chief would envy, and cry for b-lud; or when we recall the fact that perhaps the strawberry short-cake, furnished by some church festival—for notice—is the only morsel he has had for days to drive away the dull gnawing at his vitals, we would say, give your boy the education of a lawyer, doctor, dentist, machinist, counter-hopper, roller, puddler—anything in this world, but do not we pray you entice the young man into a situation where he is not only in great danger of starving, but of being thrashed daily, and under no circumstances allow him to take to the craft, unless you go over him with a tape line and by exact measurement find him to be six feet one inch high, chest forty-two to forty-five inches, his arm above elbow twenty-four inches, with six inches of a "sliding scale" at that point, well skilled in the manly art, an expert with the sword, and a crack pistol shot. With qualifications such as these, the chances are, with a fine education thrown in, ninety-nine to one hundred he will be able to drag out a weary existence on this mundane sphere amid struggling humanity.

We have thus, perhaps lengthily, told of our occupation, but we considered it necessary, for had we not filled the afore-described bill and made a success of it, how could we possibly have gathered together sufficient resumption money to go on a " Crusade ? "

We take pleasure now in introducing first, three gentlemen who accompanied the " Crusade " and who with the author formed what we shall know through our work as the " Quartette."

Lee S. Smith, Esq., a gentleman engaged in business, in the centre of the busy home of enterprise in the city of much smoke, alias Pittsburgh, alias Iron City, &c., &c., in whose office are case after case filled with front teeth and back teeth, upper teeth and lower teeth, eye teeth and stomach teeth, wisdom teeth, molar teeth,—and— teeth, and—well, yes, and—teeth. Preceding his name is the title of doctor, a title he honestly deserves, and hereafter we shall know him with the " Quartette " as the Doctor.

Major William C. Moreland, a gentleman well-known to the citizens not only of Pittsburgh, Allegheny City and their vicinity, but throughout the whole State of Pennsylvania, as a gentleman of the highest culture ; gifted with a flow of language and oratory such as the Almighty gives to but an infinitessimally small number of the human race ; a gentleman who takes the platform before the largest audiences possible to be assembled, and with his vivid powers of description, his elegantly rounded periods, holds the vast multitude in perfect silence, until the pulsation of a heart could almost be heard aloud; a gentleman well know to the bench and bar of Allegheny County, and who has made the rooms of the court house ring and the ears of many "twelve good men and true" tingle with his eloquence—is the third person we wish our readers to become acquainted with, and as a member of the "Quartette" shall know him as the Major.

And now to complete the four, whose acts and deeds "have spread both far and wide," we have the pleasure of introducing Colonel Samuel McConihe, an officer in the United States army, a particularly fair and handsome gentleman, who fought, bled, died and came to life again during our civil war, and now stationed in that far western territory where many men think and feel they are happy with anywhere from six to sixty wives and countless children; a gentleman whose pleasant acquaintance we shall ever remember with a positive and lasting pleasure. Thus is completed with the Colonel, Major, Doctor and "Carlisle" a perfect and happy Quartette.

PREPARING TO LEAVE.

As the day neared for the departure, we find registered the following persons, making the subjoined

ROSTER:

Em. Sir LEE S. SMITH, *Em. Commander.*
Em. Sir JOHN AMSDEN, *Generalissimo.*
Sir WM. C. MORELAND, *Captain-General.*
Sir DAVID W. SEMPLE, *Recorder.*

Em. Sir GEO. S. EYSTER, *Treasurer.*
Em. Sir WILLIAM H. SLACK, } *Prelates.*
Em. Sir ROBERT MORRIS,
   Sir WM. FULLERTON, *Senior Warden.*
   Sir JAS. C. RAFFERTY, *Junior Warden.*
   Sir J. D. LANDIS, *Sword Bearer.*
Em. Sir O. H. BRUSIE, *Standard Bearer.*
   Sir ROBERT J. BAXTER, *Warder.*
Sir Knights JAMES MILLIKEN,
      GEORGE S. HAINES
      J. F. BEILSTEIN,
      EDWARD F. CLINTON,
      A. O. BAKER,
      JESSE L. STACKHOUSE,
      EDWARD L. SCHRODER,

AND AS MEMBERS OF THE PARTY:

Col. S. M'Conihe, of Salt Lake City, Utah; Dr. Wm. M. Herron, Misses Mary and Nannie Herron, Miss Lillian B. Patterson, Mrs. William H. Slack, Mrs. E. C. Rafferty, and Frank E. Heath, Esq. of Allegheny City, Pa.; Dr. A. Dudley, of Salem, Mass.; Mrs. E. L. Schroder, of York, Pa.; Mrs. J. T. Mifflin and Mrs. W. T. Frohock, of Philadelphia, Pa.; H. C. Levis, Esq., of Mt. Holly, N. J.; Wm. E. Corey, Esq., of Kearney, N. J ; C. D. Boynton and Miss Ella M. Carr, of Jersey City, N. J. Miss Susan M. Leverich, of Bridgeport, Conn.; Jacob Laucks, Esq., of Womelsdorf, Pa., and E. W. Parker, Esq., of Little Rock, Ark.

The first day of July finally came round and all were on the *qui vive*—friends hurrying hither and thither, packing satchels and trunks; and just here let us add, it is one of the most pleasant features of leaving home on an extended tour.

It is such an enjoyable affair after having been puffing and tugging with your collar loose at the back, projecting itself away up over your ears, pulling at a strap, endeavoring to close the gaping sides of a trunk or satchel, you have it at last securely fastened, and with a sigh of relief you say, "Well, there's a good job done;" you seat yourself to cool off (we beg our readers to remember that this time is the first of July;) you see something white below the table or bed on which you have had your things, and you discover you have forgotten to put in your collars or some handkerchiefs, and of course they must go in.

An air from "Pinafore" or a bar of the "Sweet Bye and Bye" are of course the first things which come to your recollection, and with a cheerful smile you proceed to unbuckle your hard-earned pull; your satchel flies open with a dull thud; you place in a corner the articles you have innocently overlooked; and go to work again on the satchel. Now you cannot close it; you sit down on it or call in your wife or the landlady to sit down on it; you place your left foot against it, the veins in your forehead and neck begin to swell; your face alternately becomes purple and red; you wear paper collars: a button hole bursts; you stoop to take a better hold, away goes a suspender button, and still the abominable arrangement will not fasten; you begin to feel a little mad now, and of course it helps things amazingly to heave the satchel a fearful kick, touching up a tender corn or bunion on your right foot; then you look at it and around it, and lo! the poor little innocent tab-like arrangement that is in your linen, for holding smoothly down the elegantly laundried shirt-front, has doubled up and in some manner unexplainable, gotten out over the edge, and prevents the lid of the satchel or trunk from being fastened; you open it to remove the obstruction, when out slides some collars, a necktie, a pair of hose, or something of the kind; pleasantly replacing them, you get up smiling, aye, may be, singing aloud a verse of some old familiar Sunday school, or revival, or camp-meeting hymn, and with cheerfulness depicted on every feature, you go at the pulling process again, only to break a strap or to have a buckle give way, and the reaction brings you up standing, striking your head against some sharp point or corner, but heeding not any of these seeming little annoyances, the tune you are humming goes on quite as cheerfully as ever. All this we say is exhilarating in the extreme, and would lead a person to wish they were going away every day in the week.

EXCURSION TO NEW YORK.

But every mortal thing comes to an end sometime, and as with all others so does the pleasantry of packing;

and as according to our orders it is now almost 4 P. M. and the hour of departure is almost at hand; we must say "Good bye" now to dear and loved ones, and although it is surnamed the "ocean ferry" and little is now thought of the dangers of travel by sea, yet there is scarcely anything more touching to a man's heart if he is the possessor of a happy home, than to gather around him his loving wife, and his little ones upon his knee, and hear those tender words, affectionately said, "Good-bye, husband," and "Bye-bye, papa dear," from the loving children as their tender arms encircle the father's neck; and as he turns at the doorstep to snatch a last fond kiss from those who are dearer than all the world to him. None but those having such homes and passed through such scenes, can appreciate the father's feelings, as he leaves, on looking into his little one's eyes so beautiful, sparkling and clear, containing the big tear now ready to roll out and over, and hurriedly thinks himself home again, to see those eyes once more all sunshine and gladness, or that he is now looking into them for the last time on this earth; despite the anticipated pleasures of the trip and the excitement attendant, it is with sad heart he goes forth from home.

At 5 P. M. we find the Asylum of Allegheny Commandery all bustle and excitement, baggage being checked—and here it is but due to a worthy Sir Knight, an honorary member of Allegheny Commandery, that to his kindness much trouble was avoided to the "Crusaders," by having voluntarily proffered his wagons and services in checking baggage directly from the Asylum to the steamer, and transporting the same to the depot. As Allegheny Commandery is under obligations for many such acts of kindness upon the part of the same gentleman, all will know to whom we refer, our worthy frater, Sir John W. Haney, of Pittsburgh Commandery, No. 1.

The hour of starting is 5:30 P. M., and with military promptness—an escort kindly tendered us by Pittsburgh Commandery, No. 1, and Tancred, No. 48, both turning out some fifty swords each—were in waiting for us at our Asylum.

The lines were soon formed, consisting of about one hundred and fifty Sir Knights, and the commands: *Officers*, POSTS! *Commandery, forward*, MARCH!! were given, when as a piece of machinery, with steady and measured tread, light of foot and heart, Allegheny Commandery stepped off from her Asylum on her second European Crusade.

As we left our quarters we were handed a package by an old time friend, Joseph H. Elton, Esq., with whom we shook hands regretfully, as we should like to have had him along with his old command, and although he gave seemingly good and sufficient reasons for not going we are prone to believe he inwardly reflected that thirty-eight persons were a good many to laugh at one man, a couple of days out from New York.

It was a lovely summer evening, and as the Commandery moved down Federal Street, headed by the band of the Commandery, under the leadership of Prof. Thomas F. Kirk, playing the "Child of the Regiment." all along the route, on the sidewalks, in the windows, were crowds giving a farewell cheer to the pilgrims as they passed, showing, as came forth the hearty "Good-bye Lee, Will, James," &c., that they bore with them the good wishes for a safe voyage and return of their fellow citizens.

At the Union Depot we find a special train awaiting us, made up of luxurious sleeping-coaches, placed at our disposal by Thos. E. Watt, Esq., of the Pennsylvania Rail Road Company, and after a hearty shake all round, "all aboard" was cried out by the conductor; and at 6 o'clock sharp, amid the loud cheers from our friends, and music from the band, we were out of the depot, soon leaving the good old Smoky City behind, and traveling over the road at the rate of forty miles an hour.

It would be superfluous on our part to describe the main division of the Pennsylvania Rail Road, with its "Pack-Saddle," Johnstown, Cresson, Horse Shoe, Kittanning Point, &c. Suffice it to say we soon reached Altoona, where we made a combined attack upon the supper table, spread specially for us in the dining-room of the Logan House, which we will say is the only place on the Pennsylvania Rail Road where the weary traveler can obtain what the common run of humanity would call a meal.

Leaving Altoona we sought our berths and with

George C. Johnstone as our bed-fellow, we sought rest in laying down, but so far as sleep was concerned, were out about two dollars and fifty cents worth, for in talking over matters in general we did not notice the time pass so rapidly, and were surprised to hear the porter say, "time to get up, gentlemen," which of course we did, and prepared to go into the restaurant at Philadelphia, and go through the *form* of eating at least—we will not say a word about this place, for those who have been there know what it is, and those who have not can try it once and judge for themselves.

Leaving Philadelphia we sped lively from the United States into "New Jersey," and at 10 A. M. arrived at Jersey City, where we found a detachment of six Sir Knights in waiting to receive us from Palestine Commandery, No. 18, of New York, under command of Sir Horace H. Brockway, Generalissimo of Palestine Commandery.

The Command was again formed and marched on board the ferryboat and conveyed to Cortlandt Street, on the New York side. Arrived at Cortlandt Street, the Knights of Palestine Commandery under the command of Em. Sir George W. Skellen, the Eminent Commander, and Sir Thomas B. Rand, the Captain-General of that Commandery, were found, drawn up in line awaiting us, and bearing the burning heat of the sun with commendable and exemplary patience; and after exchange of courtesies by the respective officers, the Sir Knights of Palestine at once assumed the duties of escort, and both bodies under the banners of their respective Commanderies, and headed by the band of the Seventy-first Regiment, moved up Cortlandt Street and into Broadway.

Once on the great thoroughfare of the metropolis, the sidewalks were speedily filled with people, who accompanied the Sir Knights on their march to the Grand Central Hotel.

The march up Broadway to the stirring music of the band was exceedingly pretty and gained special attractiveness by the maneuvres of the escorting Knights, who frequently left the ordinary style of marching in company form, and fell into the cruciform and triangle form. All along the route the occupants of the stores and warehouses crowded to the windows to see the unexpected pageant, and when the Knights drew up in front of the hotel the crowd had grown to very considerable proportions.

The Command was then halted and filing into the corridor of the hotel, and the "Pilgrims" were drawn up in line on the northern side, when the escort went by at a quick pace, giving their guests a marching salute. Doubling back again they drew up in line on the southern side, when Eminent Commander Skellen stepped between the lines, bade Eminent Commander Smith and the Sir Knights of Allegheny Commandery welcome to the city in the name of Palestine Commandery, and also wished a pleasant voyage to such as were about to depart for Europe. Eminent Commander Lee S. Smith, fittingly replied to the warm and feeling remarks of Em. Sir Skellen, after which personal congratulations were exchanged; and the warm grasp of the hand, the friendly and knightly welcome to each and all of us by the Sir Knights of Palestine Commandery made us feel perfectly at home, and in five minutes were surrounded by as warm friends—though we had never met before—as almost any we could claim in Allegheny City.

The bodies as bodies, were then dismissed for the day, to answer roll-call at headquarters at 8 P. M., the day being spent mostly in the quiet of our rooms until the hour for assembling had arrived, when our escort again visited our quarters, where an informal meeting and reception was held and a most delightful evening spent in old reminiscences of our former pilgrimage, and we feel assured that that evening will ever be remembered as one of the most pleasant occurrences experienced in our " Crusade."

Pleasant and happy addresses were made by Em. Sir George W. Skellen, who, by the way, is a gentleman we shall always remember for his genuine good-heartedness and kindness; but we must not, cannot mention one unless we speak of all who were there on that evening, for all alike proved themselves to be " good men and true," and everything in their power was done to make our visit to the metropolis as pleasant as it was.

Remarks were kindly made by Sir James A. Rich,

the genial and gentlemanly Recorder, and by Past Grand Commander of the State of New York, Em. Sir Ellwood E. Thorne, who made some very beautiful and touching remarks; requesting the Sir Knights ever to bear in mind the Cross, the emblem of their Christian order, as on them and their doings the eyes of the curious and the world would gaze, and asked the Great Jehovah to take the "Crusaders" under His special care and keeping, and then briefly referring to the death of Sir Knight Bell, of Glasgow Scotland, also an honorary member of Allegheny Commandery, closed by bidding us a hearty and knightly "farewell."

These remarks were replied to by our Captain-General and our friend Sir William C. Moreland, who with his wonderful God-given power as an orator, in the wonderfully beautiful language of which he possesses an exhaustless store, held all within his hearing as though spell-bound, and until the palpitations of the hearts of those present could almost be heard, and scarcely an eye but was dimmed with a tear—an evidence we ever consider noble, as nothing so truthfully tells the heart of man or woman as the tear which comes unforced—as he referred to the life of a Christian and Sir Knight of the Order of the Temple; and indeed we felt as it were a feeling strongly savoring of pride, as round after round of applause came forth, to know that we had such talent with us to control entirely, almost for half an hour, the nigh unto breathless attention of so fine and cultivated a body of gentlemen and Sir Knights as were there assembled.

During the social exchanges of the evening a very pleasant and unexpected little episode occurred, which added much to the already full enjoyment of the occasion.

Major Moreland arose, and on behalf of a few friends in the "Crusade," presented Em. Commander Smith, in a few appropriate words, with a very fine U. S. signal glass, which we can say was most worthily bestowed, for never did any body of men leave home with a head carrying so honorably the respect and esteem of all, not only under his official charge, but of all our citizens generally—a gentleman whose name stands far above any reproach—than Em. Sir Smith, who was in every way worthily qualified to lead a body bearing the good name of Allegheny Commandery. The gift was a complete surprise to the recipient, and was received in a few neat remarks in return, and thus was a pleasant evening, happily spent, when, owing to the early hour of sailing the following morning (7 A. M.,) the tender of an escort was respectively declined, and we were bade "adieu" by the Sir Knights of Palestine Commandery, and a "sky-rocket" (a new arrangement to us at that time,) and which we immediately appropriated, despite the fact that Palestine had a patent on the same, and warned us to that effect, so that our friends in Allegheny and Pittsburgh are at any time liable to hear such a clatter of fireworks as will lay the "great and glorious Fourth" completely in the shade, and not have their insurance rates advanced either.

We must say truly, that Allegheny Commandery has journeyed hither and thither, made many pilgrimages, and will require to make quite a number more, before her members will be more cordially received, more courteously treated, and more hospitably entertained, than were the " Crusaders " by the Sir Knights of Palestine, and we trust the acquaintance formed between No. 18 and No. 35 may be long, lasting, and continued, and that the " sky-rocket " may go forth frequently on the banks of the Ohio in honor of Palestine's visits to Allegheny.

After a good night's rest we were called at 4:30 A. M. to make ready for sailing from the Cunard wharf, in Jersey City, and at 5 A. M. breakfasted, paid our bills, and boarded the coach in waiting to take us thither. We should like to, in fact we almost feel it our duty to speak of our stay at our hotel, but we will pass it by, we will only say, that Allegheny Commandery *owns* a fine coach and span of horses in New York, the use of which we fraternally extend to any visiting Sir Knights when in New York City; this tender we freely leave open to all, without reserve.

Our friends accompanied us to the steamer, and again the ceremonies of handshaking were indulged in, and we find ourselves at 6:45 A. M., on Monday, July 3d, on board the *British and North American Royal Mail Trans-Atlantic Steam Ship* " Russia," and if there is anything in a name, we were in for all the benefit we could derive from that.

Letter No. 1.

ON BOARD R. M. S. S. "RUSSIA," AT SEA.

The Pilgrims at Sea.—Celebration of Our Glorious Day of Independence.—Notorious Interruption of Religious Services.—A Truly Loving Couple.—Nine Days in a World of Our Own.

HAVING found our baggage all safely stowed away in our rooms, we returned to the deck of the steamer to take a last look into the faces of our fraters and friends upon the dock; the last bell had rung for all to leave the ship who were not going out with her; all was hurry and bustle and activity, orders being passed from captain to officers, and from officers to sailors; making preparations to cast loose the lines which held the steamer to the dock.

On every hand were little groups—husbands parting from wives, wives from husbands, parents from children, and friends from friends; a merry laugh here mingled with a sob there; making the near surroundings very pathetic.

"All ashore!" "Heave away that aft line!" were

shouted from the bridge, and in a few moments the lines were cast off, the bell in the engineer's room was heard to tingle, the machinery was set in motion, the water at the stern commenced to boil and gurgle, and we were now truly away.

Out upon the head of the pier had gathered our friends, and as we glided slowly out, loud and lusty were the cheers that went up from those on the pier to those on the steamer, and a " Good bye, George!" or a " Good bye, James," " Good bye, Ed.," was heard all along the side of the steamer, which continued until the ship had made her long and graceful curve, turning her pretty sharp prow toward the narrows; then the faces became dim, until we could see and recognize only the white straw hat of our genial and jovial friend, A. M. Rambo, Esq., and the last person recognizable being our old friend, George C. Johnstone, from whom we parted with regret; the red cross upon his cap, that noble and glorious emblem of the magnanimous order of Knights Templar, pointed him out as he stood at his post waving his handkerchief, and soon the crowd upon the dock was only an apparent mass of small pieces of waving rags, and no one could be distinguished.

What a beautiful morning! as we slowly and quietly dropped down the bay; yet, as the sun cast his reflection upon the waters, we looked not with envious eyes back to the city we were fast leaving, for there was every indication the good citizens of New York would that day be running around with grape leaves in their hats, mopping off their fevered brows with four-quarter bandanas, chewing ice and running about promiscuously, and generally in search of "schooners" without masts.

But how nice, cool and pleasant with us; the stiff breeze coming up the bay was a cheerful stranger to meet; and we now were seated away forward, taking in the scenery, beautiful as it is, passing pretty Staten Island and down under the guns of forts Hamilton, Wadsworth and Richmond. We passed the Hook, and giving our pilot a bushel or so of postal cards, letters, &c., we put him in his little boat, and immediately put to sea, closely followed by the "Perierre," of the French line, and met her sister ship, the "Amerique," coming in.

Having now passed far away from any view of land, we begin to meditate upon our situation, and it is only now we realize the fact that we are on board a "Cunarder." What! a "Cunarder?" Yes, and the commodore ship of the line, the "Russia." There is a singular fact in connection with this steamer, and that is: prior to the placing of the "Scythia," "Bothnia" and "Gallia," in this line, we never met any person—not one—who had been to Europe and had crossed in a Cunard boat, but had crossed in the "Russia." "Been to Europe, Mr. Smith?" "Yes, sir; just returned. Came over in the 'Russia.'" "Been to Europe, Mr. Jones?" "Yes, sir; arrived in New York one week ago, in the 'Russia,'" and so on *ad infinitum*. We have yet for the first time to meet one who had ever crossed in the "Samaria," "Java," "Calabria," "Parthia," or "Olym-

D

pus;" and beyond all question of doubt, the "Russia" has carried more trans-Atlantic passengers to the square inch than any other boat or boats combined to the square mile. Having frequently noticed the afore-stated fact, we now realize that we are *at last* making *one* trip across the ocean in true pomp and style, on board a pompous and stylish steamer, belonging to a line having a long name, and that had *never* lost a life. (Sailors' lives not counted.)

We felt ourselves grow considerably when we thought of all these things; any former experience of ours in a nautical way being confined exclusively to more humble and common lines, such as the "City of Boston," or "City of Baltimore," of the Inman, and the "Columbia," "Cambria," "Anglia," "Australia" and "California," of the Anchor Line; and we are now prepared to be lifted from our narrow, contracted ideas of what a steamship is, into all the grandeur of a floating palace.

Without commenting, let us rather attempt a description of an *humble* boat of an *humble* line, and then make a tour of the one we are now on. The "Circassia" say, of the Anchor Line, has, first, a flush deck—meaning a deck covered over and solid, the entire length and breadth of the ship, making a grand promenade. On this deck, amidships, are a smoking room, a handsome ladies' saloon, and away above, as the roof to these large and commodious rooms, is what is called the "hurricane deck," being on a level with the officers' bridge; and on this is built a round tower with glass windows, so that in times of wet and stormy weather, passengers can enjoy, if they wish, the "billowing, tumbling waves." From the main deck you pass down a magnificent stairway, bronze statuary holding aloft large lamps, and from this stairway you pass round into your staterooms or into the saloon.

The saloon is the whole width of the steamer, say forty to forty-two feet, and maybe as long. The ceiling in the centre is open, in which are growing the most luxurious tropical plants and beautiful flowers, while surrounding this in a circle is the music room, a piano and a pipe organ at either end; libraries filled with elegantly bound standard works of history, science and fiction.

The staterooms are on a level with the saloon, large and commodious, luxuriantly upholstered and fitted up; electric bells in every room, so that a steward or stewardess can be called in a moment; no tin pails and rattling basins, but running water from a spigot can be had at any time. On board are a very large lavatory, barber shop, and every possible luxury the ocean traveler could possibly desire, either for comfort or necessity. It will be observed, as stated, the staterooms are all directly underneath the main deck, so that those rooms are always above water, and it has to be a pretty rough day when the portholes cannot be kept open, and freshen the rooms with good, pleasant air. Hastily described, these are a few of the comforts of so *common* a boat as the "Circassia," with one other important addition: *two* persons *only* are ever placed in a single room.

Now let us look about us and see our commodore ship, and about the simplest manner possible to describe her, is to say she has not one of these conveniences. You go down a ladder from the quarter deck to the main deck, and then pass down two stairways to the "first floor," where instead of good clear daylight, you have lamps and foul air from closed portholes, and three, or even four, in a room. Ladies can have their choice, go down two stories to their rooms, or stay on deck through rain and fog. Gentlemen can suit themselves, give up the filthy practice of smoking, or hug the smokestack, or sit down in the hatchway and enjoy their fragrant Havanas, and finally, if the "Russia" is a commodore ship we would like to try a liner.

Of one thing we can freely speak in terms of praise; never will more perfect discipline be seen on land or sea, nor a more gentlemanly man, or more watchful captain, than Commodore Cook of this steamer. He is never seen gadding and gossiping around with ladies and passengers in general, always by himself, and always on duty, taking a peep at the compass or a squint at the sails.

Having now been down to our room—we say *down* with emphasis—and having made the rounds of the steamer, and having put on our overcoats we are fully prepared for the wind or the blast, or neither, of our sea voyage. Our party numbering thirty-eight, we are assigned to what is termed the fore saloon, a very cosy room too, away forward of the smokestack, and just sufficiently large to accommodate us, and by this method we are the better enabled to become acquainted with each of our traveling companions, and of course the first day is sufficient to decide who are to be "crowds" on the voyage.

Of course among so many as we have on board, we have a large assortment of dispositions; young men fresh from college, young ladies from "Bosting," old gentlemen from the country, doctors, lawyers, ministers, politicians, priests, merchants, school teachers, music teachers, philanthrophists, philosophers, astronomers, and generals, colonels, captains, by the score.

Thursday, July 4th, the great and glorious day of our American Independence, we were all up early and moving round as lively as crickets. The day was dull, foggy, yet withal not disagreeably so; the water as smooth as the Allegheny or Ohio rivers. None but were at least, as Gough would say, "com-for-a-ble,"—not a single person sick, tables all full, and all working out bravely their passage money. No signs whatever of having a laugh at the expense of another; in fact we despaired, from the healthy appearance and hearty appetites of all, of seeing, as Judge Kirkpatrick describes them, running to the side of the steamer and lustily yelling, "New York! New Yoruk!! New Yorruk!!!"

After dinner we met in our saloon for the purpose of commemorating in some way the one hundred and second anniversary of our Natal Day. The meeting was called to order by Prof. William H. Slack, who nominated Lee

S. Smith for president, and D. W. Semple for secretary, both of which nominations proved the appreciation of our party for superior talent, when some one loudly moved the nominations close, and it is needless for me to say, dear reader. the election was unanimous. Messrs. Robert Morris, L. L. D., of Lagrange, Ky.; Edward Clinton, of Colorado; Dr. A. M. Milligan, Chaplain of the Western Penitentiary, in Allegheny City; J. B. Amsden, of Kentucky, and George S. Eyster, of West Virginia, were elected vice-presidents.

Although with two hundred and seventy-five passengers on board, yet our little party was the only one to show any remembrance of our nation's birthday, and we are now patiently waiting our appointment to some $17,500 foreign mission—say to the court of St. James—by the President, as an appreciation of our loyalty. Prof. Slack stated the object of the meeting, which was opened by a fervent prayer by Dr. Milligan, and the singing of the " Star Spangled Banner " by Prof. Slack, and a hearty chorus by all in the party, which we are sure frightened away at least all the little fishes, if not the larger ones, which might be swimming along in the wake of the steamer, waiting for those persons to come to the side and yell " New Yorruk!! " and which was rendered so heartily, and with such a strong good will as to at once awaken enthusiasm, and to fire up everyone to make the meeting a rousing one.

Major Moreland was called on, and well he warmed up in his oratory for he had a glorious subject and as gloriously did he acquit himself; and as he finished his remarks, he was applauded and cheered until the clapping of hands and roars from hundreds of voices might have been heard at Sandy Hook, and rendering the fog whistle utterly useless.

" My Country 'Tis of Thee," was then sung, and Dr. Milligan made an able and stirring address. Sir Robert Morris, the noted traveler and lecturer, was the next speaker, and feeling a " leetle onpleasant " about where the vest fits the tightest, made only a few brief remarks, but exceedingly well put, of many persons going abroad as " traveled monkeys." Rev. Dr. Deere, of Michigan, spoke at some length, pointedly and ably; then came " Columbia the Gem of the Ocean," followed by the beautiful duet, " Larboard Watch," by Prof. Slack and Dr. Lee Smith who has an elegant deep basso voice, (particularly for crying, "Steward, some more prunes and crackers!") Other songs were then sung, and Dr. Smith recited beautifully, " Wounded," and our pleasant evening was closed with " In the Sweet Bye and Bye," and the Fourth of July, 1878, was numbered with the past. Foggy all day, sea very calm and at noon had made three hundred and fifty miles.

Friday, the 5th, was clear and beautiful, and if such were possible, the sea smoother than ever; the "Perierre" again in sight, as well as a steamer having fair winds with her, was making rapid way to New York. Not a " ripple on the wave," and it was a most amusing sight to see some of our party poke their fingers in the arm-holes of their vests, and strutting about the deck, loudly boast, "Oh! I'm not going to be sick!" "Why, I went round Cape Hatteras in a gunboat once," or "Went up the Kiskiminetas or Schuylkill river in a skiff and never missed a meal." Among those so boasting and so strutting was the D. D., (not Doctor of Divinity but Doctor of Dentistry.)

We gazed with the utmost satisfaction upon the Doctor, the Major, the Colonel, and others, as they rolled indiscriminately into soups, pies, "roly-poly" and "sich like," and seeing them progressing thusly, we couldn't stand the dull monotony any longer, so we set to work to get up a little toss, which by the little clouds no larger than a man's hand away off on the horizon, we concluded we would have, and we did have it, as we will soon see. This day was pleasantly passed with a shuffle-board, euchre, whist, attempts at reading, etc., and at noon had added three hundred and twenty miles more to our log.

Saturday, July 6th, was clear and pleasant; meeting occasionally or passing a sailor or two; the party walking in heavily to rich dinners, and getting an excellent "ready on" for the following day. All were going round with broad grins and pleasant smiles, coming up cheerfully, cracking jokes at one another, and oh! how jolly they all felt as they said, "Good morning" or "Good night, Doctor," "Good night, Carlisle," &c., and with what an immense feeling of satisfaction every one would come up from dinner and "pull down his vest."

The Doctor did that; the Major did that, and several others, and all retired that evening just "feeling elegant." Ahem! Made three hundred and six miles to-day.

Sunday, July 7th. I awakened from a most refreshing sleep, and heard some kind of somnambulism in my room; the sea was gurgling up and over the porthole in a very violent manner. I looked over my bunk to find my room-mate, the Doctor, had vacated. James Rafferty, another room-mate, lay in his upper berth making some kind of mumbling remarks about " Federal Street—Allegheny—home." On looking over the side I found something come bumping around my bed on the sofa, the Doctor's valise diving wickedly into the sides of my two-story Saratoga; friend Rafferty's Knight of Templar cap running around fearful of being jammed between trunks and evidently searching for its owner; one leg of my pantaloons chasing the other wildly up and down ; a cent running after a pocket-book, or the pocket-book trying to capture the escaped cent; umbrellas playing leap frog with canes, and everything in the room, in fact, having a jolly good game of "tag," and the vessel bobbing round like a cork. I said, "Well, James, how do you feel?" " Oh, 'Carlisle,'" says James, "if I only was at home; Ugh! Ugh!!" That was enough; I knew how James felt; I had been there on more than one occasion. Finally I arose feeling, so far, tip-top, and after skirmishing round for a little while and bracing myself between two trunks, I succeeded in laying hands on the drunken water-pitcher, and having performed the necessary ablutions, proceeded on deck to find but a few persons there and it almost eight o'clock. The first person we meet is the Doctor, and with "Good morning, Doctor," we greet him " how are you this morning?" "Oh, I am not sick at all, Carlisle," says he, " but I am not well by a large majority."

Of this we were perfectly satisfied before inquiring, but the Doctor takes everything good-naturedly and philosophically, and enjoyed the laugh on him all in good part. Now and again, up comes some straggler, among whom was the Major, or the Absolom of our party, his raven locks just as neat, pretty and curly as ever ; but, oh! horrors, what a face! Not usually lengthy, now distended six inches further than customary, and after a hasty rush to the side to see if he can observe any barnacles on the ship's side, "fesses up" like a man, "that he is sick and don't care a continental who knows it."

Then away forward coming towards us is our friend Baxter, from St. Louis, now and then stopping to see if phosphorescence can be seen in daylight. The vessel is rolling fearfully and it is with difficulty one can navigate the deck, and it was a most amusing sight to see our musical professor coming along the deck at an angle of about forty-five degrees, a lady on either arm, his portly figure only half visible from carrying waterproofs, wraps, gum cloaks, nubias, shawls, in fact a general assortment of dry goods, and in addition to these, of course, every lady must have her book and smelling-bottle, and umbrella, and crocheting, and lace work, and knitting, &c., all of which Professor S. was carrying gracefully and smiling as cheerfully as ever, his countenance as bright and happy as though leading the Allegheny " Quartette " to musical glory, or the good people of a certain church in Allegheny in 8's, 7's and 4's, for so far our genial friend has not been under the weather, he being an old tar, and crusaded with our fraters in '71. And we might add here that we do not see how many of our party would have gotten along without him, for he was as a ministering angel unto many, proving himself exceedingly kind and attentive, going down into the staterooms of this one and that one, putting in a kind word here or prodding another one there with his inevitable cane, until they they were compelled to get out on deck, take in some of the good fresh air, and be made well. But then he, like us all, has his faults, being mortal as us all, and we do unquestionably vote him the most selfish man on board the vessel in one particular; notwithstanding the fact that he is accompanied by his better-half, yet he monopolized the entire company of the young ladies of our party at the table, to the evident displeasure of our young friends from West Virginia, New Jersey and Pennsylvania, for they were debarred the pleasure of doing the agreeable; but the boys had the inside track on him when the stars began to twinkle and the moon shone o'er the sea.

To return to Sunday, a broad smile would have been " smoled " could the reader have seen our manly and gallant Em. Commander, who had bravely faced the enemy in our late civil war and led whole armies to battle, and shot down poor starving prisoners with cold hearted pleasure, (in the "Drummer Boy of Shiloh," on the stage of one of our Pittsburgh theatres,) his noble six feet of manhood laying prostrate on the deck, meek and helpless as an innocent little lamb, pleading with "Carlisle" to go down and interview the steward on the subject of a sour orange, and laboring under a bad attack of the "Ugh's!" and our famed orator, the Major, beside him, with not exactly an attack of the "Ugh's!" but correspondingly as bad of the "Oh! my's!" He who is our pride, our gallant Captain-General, as sick as his superior officer.

Then there is our friend from St. Louis, the sickest man I ever saw in my life, threatening to commit suicide by jumping overboard, and his face as long as a politician's affidavit. But he was cured this morning. He was treading along the deck, swaggering with every lurch of the ship, his hand about the centre of his body, (we trust only to pull down his vest;) but through it all the best natured and kindest hearted person possible. He went away forward and engaged the ship's carpenter in conversation, mistaking him for the Doctor, related to him his feelings. The carpenter said he could soon fix him up. Our friend wanted to know how, of course, and discovered his mistake in the person he was addressing, when Mr. Carpenter brought forth some pine boards, a saw and some nails, and drawing hastily a coffin on one of the boards, said he could make *one* like that in about *five* minutes. Sunday was an awful day on our friend from St. Louis. He succumbed to the pleadings of the Doctor for a "sour orange," and, on returning from the interview with the steward, (in fact we were now steward *de facto* ourselves,) we found our friend B—— from Indiana was in reality a philosopher. He was evidently near-sighted at that moment, and was intently looking down through a scupper-hole, and replied on our inquiring what he was doing there, and with his face so close to the opening, "that he was simply meditating upon the mysteries of naval architecture; that they would make holes in the sides of the vessel, and wondering why the sea did not come up through and sink the vessel." Then a few steps further on we met our friend C——, from Colorado, large tears coursing down his cheeks from his large blue eyes, doubtless thinking tenderly of home, and we did not stop him to inquire the cause of his sadness, fearing that we should start afresh the fountains of grief.

Many were the amusing scenes of this Sunday—the few persons at the table grabbing for a runaway soup-dish, an escaping plate or cup, or a harum-scarum tumbler or goblet that wanted to carry on its own course regardless of the liberties and rights of others. The Commandery was but poorly represented at table so far as quantity was concerned; the officers having fallen in the good fight, and we presume that their feelings were that they did not care at that time whether all the Grand or Subordinate Commanderies in Christendom went to wreck or not; at least judging from the woeful, distressed and sorrowful faces of the Em. Commander and Captain-General.

Speaking of the table, one of the most amusing scenes occurred this day we have had the pleasure of seeing for many a day. At our table, and near us, sat a gentleman from "Bosting," who "could n't for the world, you know, see how any one could wear clean or white linen in so vile a place as the City of Pittsburgh," and this gentleman of "culchah" has been seasick almost all the voyage, at least he has been troubled with "considerable nausea," particularly so on this day, and was beyond all question of doubt the best "feeder" within our knowledge. So, to use a very vulgar expression, which, under the circumstances, we ask our reader to pardon, a gentleman from Brooklyn and "Carlisle" set up a base job on him.

We got him down to the dinner table, which is as a rule particularly rich and fine on Sunday; made friends with him, sympathizing deeply with him in all of his miserable feelings, and having gained his confidence, proceeded to prescribe several specific remedies for that abomination of abominations, sea sickness. We told him his only reason for his being so afflicted was insufficiency of eating,—he in the meantime, at all previous meals, going directly through the bill of fare as the boys of to-day do through a commercial college, and adopting the tactics of our friend from Indiana—philosophy, we *philosophized* with him thusly: That to fill a steamer but three-quarters full in each of her holds, it stood plainly to reason that on putting to sea in that condition her cargo in time of rough weather would rattle around regardlessly, and give her officers considerable trouble. On the same principle precisely was it with a man in sea sickness; that if he ate but little, leaving a vacuum in nature's receptacle, and did not pack himself tight, his cargo would necessarily flop around at will, and this constant churning was the whole and only cause of all this terrible nausea and state of un-com-for-a-ble-ness; and to this *philosophy* he entirely succumbed, perhaps on its vast strength, perhaps on its general principles; and we referred our argument to the several medical and clerical gentlemen opposite us, viz.: Dr. Wm. M. Herron, Dr. Bittinger and Dr. A. M. Milligan, whom any fair minded person would consider a committee of good authority on either physical or spiritual matters, and of course they could not but agree with us in our argument; adding that all the Isaac Newton's were not passed from among us.

So to-day we sent him almost unto death's door, insisting upon him punishing the following list, which he did, and it is a fact, too: Two large plates of maccaroni soup, (now anyone knows that maccaroni soup is a sure cure for sea sickness,) then a large piece of baked salmon and three potatoes, (more good cure,) roast beef, roast turkey, salmon pie, and palmed off a pork chop for a mutton chop, some more potatoes, corn, spinach, and some cucumbers, (now we advise all seasick persons to eat cucumbers. Oh! they are a sure remedy!) And all these we assisted him to in large doses ; some he did not wish to touch, but having the gentleman's welfare and health at heart, we felt it our duty as a brother man to make him a well man. Then we gave him about half an apple pie, a lemon tart, a raspberry tart, some rice, jam and custard, all on his plate at one time, (these items have never been known to fail in effecting a speedy and certain cure!) The next course we gave him almonds, filberts, raisins, figs, oranges, and a green apple; and begged to suggest that all that was necessary now to settle his sea sickness forever, was a good cup of strong coffee, (and if these things would n't fetch a man nothing under the sun would!) While the coffee was being brought, we suggested as a capital thing to settle the stomach for the night, was the taking of a Welsh rarebit and a bottle of porter just before retiring, which he said he would take that evening. We noticed a peculiar gagging sensation was being carried on by our friend, and just before the coffee was served, we mentioned the fact of many persons crossing the ocean frequently without having the least unpleasant sensation until reaching the coast of Ireland, when we had known the ship to rise and fall anywhere from *forty* to *seventy-five* feet, and you should have seen the gentleman get up and leave that table when he heard the "*seventy-five*" feet. Never waited on coffee or said a word, but seizing his shawl and cap, was out the door like a streak of lightning, amid roars of laughter from our fellow passengers, and that was the last meal he ate at that table on that voyage.

Amid all these passing scenes, we would not have the reader suppose that Allegheny Commandery, on leaving home, would forget or neglect her devotions, and as there was to be church in the large saloon, the Commandery was called together by orders at 10 A. M. to answer roll call and to attend divine service at 10:30 A. M., and the following surviving Sir Knights answered to their names: Past Em. Com. William H. Slack and your humble servant, "Carlisle." Just think of it! Here were two members of No. 35, now all that were left of the good old Commandery, to go down to worship; therefore being at once E. C., Generalissimo, Capt.-Gen, Treas., Recorder, and line officers and privates, at one and the same time. The Professor and "Carlisle" accordingly linked arms and wended their way down the ladder and to the house of devotion. Dr. Abercrombie, of New Jersey, read the service, and Dr. Peabody, ex-president of Yale College, preached the sermon, which was one hour and fifteen minutes in duration, and would have been an admirable theological address to students.

But even in the temple of solemnity we are prone to enter the house and portals of mirth and merriment, for while the services were being read by Dr. Abercrombie, a most amusing thing occurred, and one we shall never forget so long as we live. In the beautiful Episcopalian service, where the responses are given and chants rendered by a trained choir, and precisely at those parts, for instance, "Good Lord, deliver us," was being responded, a couple of distressed parties were out at as many scup-

E

per-holes, and were evidently gargling their throats for some affection therein, and vociferously yelling, "Oh! dear!" "Oh, my!" "Ugh!" "New Yorruck!" and similar expressions, and fitting in so perfectly at the points they did, a titter was started in the worshiping congregation, and even our worthy minister smiled rather audibly. After service we made earnest endeavor to find out who it was. The Doctor declared it was the Major and the Major as earnestly declared it was the Doctor. Personally I am satisfied it was the Doctor, for a Methodist minister was at one scupper-hole, and I am certain the Doctor went to the other through sympathy and kind feeling towards one of the same faith and creed, and besides we have since then discovered that the Doctor mustered up his courage to come down and sit with the balance of the Commandery, but the aforesaid scupper-hole was as far as he reached on his pilgrimage, for the spirit was willing but his stomach most fearfully weak.

We would kindly say a word here to husbands, that you need have no fear of sending your wives to Europe whenever they may desire to make such a trip, for they will suffer from no lack of attention whatever; and to wives, that they need have no fear either that their husbands, going from their homes, will lose or forget their customary gallantry.

We have on board a lady who claims to be the wife of a minister, (let us trust that she is *mistaken*, to put it mildly,) from ———, and a celebrated lawyer, (in his own estimation,) from ———, who were fun for the million. We happen to have several attorneys on board who *actually* do hail from ———, and they unanimously tally in their report that they never before heard of such a man as Dr. ———. Well, this gentleman—this celebrated lawyer—was some six feet tall, wore a Dutch cap over his right eye, and taking him in generally, we have frequently in our daily walks in life seen many much more handsome men.

She, Mrs. Minister, was fully four feet nine inches, and we have also seen at times ladies who might be termed more beautiful than she, and even be telling the truth; while between the two it was about five parts to five parts as to affectation to hear them discussing the "solah" system, etc., as in the evening they cosily sat nigh unto each other, a warm robe giving its warmth to both at the same time.

This Sunday evening Prof. Slack and "Carlisle," at about 11 P. M., concluded to go up on deck, after having been reading for an hour or so in the saloon, and obtain a little fresh air before retiring to our beds of ease 'neath eider-down quilts, and we were fully repaid for our intentions. Having opened the package mentioned earlier in this work, we found our friend Joseph H. Elton had known our failings and put us up a box of fragrant and choice Havanas, and lighting one we meandered towards the main deck. On reaching there all was still and silent as the grave, no signs of life visible save the watchful officer on the bridge as he trod his beat steadily and faithfully. We walked slowly towards the smokestack, when we unintentionally overheard voices, and heard the following suggestive and interesting conversation, being drawn out in true blue Yankee style:

Mrs. Minister was saying "She did not know what love was;" to which came the reply: "Ah! dear; can it be possible you have not felt the tender touch upon the heart's sensitive chords—that you do not know what *love* is? Two souls with but a single thought two hearts that beat as one. Ah! my! could n't you love me, and teach your little D—— to love me?" (referring to the little daughter of Mrs. Minister.) She said "She could not quite comprehend the full import of his tender words;" and then, giving her a very warm embrace, he said: "Never mind, dear; have faith in God and all will come out right." Yes, and then through the day might have been seen this gentleman and lady, sitting side by side, bibles in hand, reading chapter after chapter aloud. And then the Professor spoiled the whole job by saying, "What a good cigar that was!" and of course the whole jig was up, and the Romeo and Juliet scene was knocked into "pi;" and as the curtain fell we had passed over Sunday and our fifth day out.

Monday, July 8th, the rolling had ceased considerably, nothing but a good swell being on the sea; pleasant, and aside from the pastimes engaged in, nothing occurred of much interest, save one little item, and which, by the way, was the cause of the formation of the "Quartette." At the head of our table sat a gentleman whose name we have already mentioned, very sedate and reserved in his manners, always by himself, seemed to have no particular company, was always prim and spruce, as though he spent the major portion of his life on shipboard in the dressing-room. This afternoon we observed him leave the deck, and an hour or so later we happened to look over the railing to the quarter-deck, and observed this stately and erect personage smoking a cigar, clean shaven, a tender cane in his gloved hand, come sauntering down from the saloon stairway; the vessel was rolling considerably, when suddenly along came a great heavy swell, struck the side of the ship, careened her a little, when over came a ton or so of water, and doused who?—why it was our friend the Colonel—through from head to foot, leaving him almost a total wreck; his collar hung about his neck as a piece of twine, his cigar had gone to fool some of the little fishes, while water oozed from the tops of his gaiters with every motion of his foot. He was, as usual, cool as a cucumber, to use an aged expression; made a calm and deliberate retreat to his quarters, and reappeared soon after in his former dress. We had the laugh on him; he bore it all good-naturedly and soldierly, and from that moment the "Quartette" was formed.

We have one other person to whom we wish to pay our respects, and he gets completely away with anything we have yet met in our travels, far or near. Our party has still many on its sick list, "Carlisle" being the only representative of the "Quartette" appearing at the table, the remainder taking their provender on deck. This gentleman to whom we refer, is sick; yes, very sick. He wears a heavy double shawl, is suffering severely from a disorganized liver, a stomach which refuses to perform its usual functions, and a bad dose of dyspepsia, (so *he* says, but do the facts bear him out?)

The deck steward comes around and takes the orders of those eating on deck; this gentleman with the others gives his order; the dinner bell rings; he goes down to the saloon and punishes a fair dinner there, commencing, say with soup, and winding up with plum pudding. On arriving on deck, the steward is about delivering the orders, and this poor, ill being makes away with this dinner also, and then it is a daily and usual occurrence to hear him say " Doctor, do you wish that piece of beef on your plate?" or, " Major, can I have that piece of tart, if you are through with it?" Well, we profess to be something on appetite, but we have never been answered in our prayer to have just such a liver and stomach and case of dyspepsia as has this gentleman with the shawl.

Tuesday, Wednesday and Thursday the ocean had again become as an inland river. Schools of porpoises played about the bow of the steamer, and no item of interest occurred to vary the dull monotony of ship-board life, other than the more frequent sighting of steamers and sailing vessels.

Friday morning. July 12th, we are up bright and early; it is raining very hard, and we are hugging the smoke-stack closely, endeavoring to keep warm, and waiting patiently to sight land. A heavy fog is down and around us; we go down and have our breakfast, and, coming up, we find the fog lifting, and suddenly our hearts are gratified by the cry from the look-out, "Land ahead, on the port bow, sir!" We look, and away in the distance we see the breakers. The rain is now ceasing, the misty curtain is lifting, and lo! there is the beautiful and green "Emerald Isle," and happy are we to see it; all the sick are as a miracle made well and whole, and we are all pleased that we are to plant foot first on the sod of good, grand and beautiful "Old Ireland." We are now passing at no great distance the "Skeillig Rocks."

Letter No. 2.

The Pilgrims landed at Queenstown.—Their First Trouble on Ireland's Green Sod.—Attempts at Smuggling.—Reception in Cork.—In Trouble again in a Barber Shop.—A Row with a Hotel Proprietor.—Blarney Castle.—Shandon Church.—Incidents by the Way.

AS stated in the preceding letter, we were passing the "Skeillig Rocks." Some of our party had not yet had their morning meal, when some one would come up, and, smacking his lips, say, " Porridge; go down and have some porridge!" to which would come the unanimous and echoing reply from the aforesaid watchers, in a tone of voice pitched to high E flat, "No! Get thee to a *Nunnery*, thou base serf; we will have no porridge, give us land, that's what we want, and lots of it."

So far as the writer was concerned, he knew his duty to the pantry, and to himself, had been faithfully performed, as also on the part of the Colonel—in short, on the eating line they had worked out their passages—but we exceedingly regretted that he of "Absolom's locks," and he of the " dentistry profession," had not carried out their parts of the programme so well.

Slowly and cautiously we are now steaming along, as the fog has thickened again, being now quite dense, and we obtain but a glimpse of Fastnet Rock and Light House, and then we see no more of land until 10 A. M. Old Sol, who evidently is our friend, has been earnestly endeavoring to come through and show us the " Emerald Isle,". suddenly breaks through, his bright rays penetrating and scattering the mist and fog, which lifts as a drop curtain, and there away on our left are the beautiful green fields of Old Ireland, all divided and subdivided by the neat, pretty, green hedges that prevail throughout all the British kingdom.

Away up some charming miniature valley we see the little villages dotted here and there, while, as we approach some projecting point, we see a pretty little " thatched cottage by the sea." It is a truly beautiful approach to land along the southern coast of Ireland, where you have more of the mild scenery, in striking contrast to that of the north coast of that island, which is very rough, rugged and formidable, being high rockbound all the way in to Moville or the Giants' Causeway. It has turned out one of the loveliest of days, to which we could conscientiously make but one little exception, and that, a little too warm for true comfort; the decks are piled high with portmanteaus, small trunks, large trunks, young trunks, old trunks, boxes, Saratogas, chests, hand satchels, traveling-bags, valises, and dear only knows what all; while everything around us is bustle and activity, friend chatting with newly-made friend, hopings to meet again, exchanging cards, and general invitations to "be sure to come and see us," &c., are heard all around; but we do not believe one solitary individual looking down at the deck of the ship that had carried us safely over, and wiping away the feeling of dampness from the eyes, said: "Oh, deck, must we from thee part?" "Shall I ne'er more tread thee again?" No! but "Get thee behind me or below me, deck; go down to stateroom 167 and remain there, oh, deck! and as quick as possible, too."

About 1:30 P. M. we were almost at the entrance to the beautiful harbor of Cork, when we saw approaching us rapidly, a little tug, which soon came alongside, and on her we embarked; and as we left the side of the steamer three cheers were given her, three loud and lusty cheers and a "tiger" for the beautiful and pure flag, the American stars and stripes, floating gracefully and beautifully from the foremast of the "Russia,".and a genuine hearty "sky-rocket" for our fellow voyagers remaining on the steamer to disembark at Liverpool, which was given with such a hearty good-will from thirty-eight pairs of sound and solid lungs, that caused the "red coats" in the forts at the entrance to the harbor, to imagine the Spanish fleet was chasing Sir Admiral Drake's ghost into to where his body some years before had gone—at least we saw them mount their guns and prepare at once for action.

As we parted company with the steamer, we found on board Dr. E. T. Bricknell and a committee of Free

Masons in waiting to welcome us to the hospitalities and courtesies of the fraternity, as well as to Ireland's charming shores; and anyone can imagine the feelings of each and every one of us, going ashore, where but one or two of the party had ever been before, and not knowing a solitary soul, perhaps, anywhere on that island, yet by the strong and binding chain of universal brotherhood, we were given a warm grasp of the hand, which betokened us as being at once among true and dear friends.

The Inman steamer "City of Richmond," was laying at anchor, receiving mails and passengers, preparatory to sailing for the United States, and through the courtesy and kindness of custom house officials, we were allowed to jump ashore and run to the post office with a ton or so of mail for home, and by this means of getting it on board the "Richmond," we saved some three or four days' time.

The custom house officials, sworn to do their duty, commenced operations on our arrival at the pier, and of course are not so strict in their searches as on our side of the water. The first examined was the luggage of one holding the highest office in the gift of Allegheny Commandery, and who with "Carlisle," was booked for the identical trip and room-mate on our tour. "Any firearms, tobacco, spirits, or books?" was the question put to our Eminent Commander, and in his usual emphatic manner, came the honest reply, "No, sir." The man from some reason or other, we presume being a poor judge of human nature, took his word and chalked it "passed;" but, oh! if he had known what we knew, if he had gone through that baggage, that contained some contraband stuff of an unmentionable nature, and opened a package tied up in a manner to deceive, in fact it strikingly resembled a large pair of United States signal corps field-glasses, and he could not be suspected of duplicity in saying it was such a described article, in his carrying two pair, for he had given "Carlisle," innocent as he was of this piece of fraud, the pair to carry he was presented with in New York, so that he could the better carry out his scheme of smuggling. We fear we would have been short an Eminent Commander, had we told all we knew; and despite the great wrong that was being done Her Britannic Majesty and her government, it was the policy for us to be "mum," for as stated I was his room-mate, he six feet nine, I five feet five. Oh, no; it was strictly our business to keep quiet, and we always like to leave other people's business entirely to themselves, and attend to our own, and in this instance particularly did we do it. We will say this, that the package whatever it contained, remained unopened from the date of leaving to that of our returning home, so that perhaps my own imaginations may have probably led me adrift in my conclusions, the only thing was the fact of how carefully that satchel was always handled. We got along all right, however, until the officers came to a chapeau box and some satchels, marked in bold letters, "G. S. H.," which may stand for "Great San Hedrim," but at any rate these satchels were opened, and the officer in charge again put the direct question, "Any firearms, spirits, tobacco, or books in your possession?" To which came, I have no question of doubt, the truthful answer, "No, sir; I have not." The officer looked searchingly and curiously at the proprietor of the baggage marked "G. S. H.," and the proprietor of the baggage marked "G. S. H.," looked as searchingly and curiously at him, when we all became highly interested in this somewhat novel and unexplained "go-as-you-please" staring match, and the question was again put directly and pointedly, "Any firearms, spirits, tobacco, or books in your possession, particularly tobacco?" "No, sir; I have not," came the still more decided and emphatic reply. All gathered around our nonplussed Sir Knight and fellow frater, looks of determination settling down upon every face—hands were being clinched, and motions made towards that pocket in which some gentlemen carry their handkerchiefs, and where others carry something else, not strictly speaking handkerchiefs—in all of which could be read the stern avowal, that if the worst came to the worst, that we would just topple that and all other custom house officials overboard, capture the steamer, and especially the chalk, and pass any and all baggage we saw fit. Before, however, resorting to such violent and extreme measures, we inquired of the officer what was the cause of all this looking, and staring, and gaping between he and our friend. He replied that this man, pointing to the sole proprietor of the baggage marked "G. S. H.," has said "he had no dutiable goods in his possession, and he feared he was endeavoring to smuggle, from the fact of his having two cigars in his mouth at one and the same time." After much exertion we finally convinced this scrutinous and watchful officer that he was laboring under a very vague and serious mistake, that he was totally in error, that what he supposed to be two cigars, were only and really the two ends of our friend's waxed moustache, which by some peculiar and mysterious method, have been taught to project outwardly instead of along the lip and cheek like other Christian moustaches, and so with this narrow escape from detention, which was our first trouble or annoyance of any kind we were permitted to depart in peace.

We neglected to mention a very gratifying little incident that occurred prior to our leaving the steamer "Russia." About a dozen or so of us were standing up about the foremast, chatting pleasantly over the ocean trip, when Rev. Dr. Milligan, one of Allegheny's most honored and respected clergymen, came forward. We had drifted into a warm discussion on the subject of liquors for medicinal purposes, for the stomach's sake, &c., when Dr. Milligan paid the party a very great and appreciated compliment, when he said, " Gentlemen, I have crossed the Atlantic quite a number of times, and have been away from home with quite a number of parties on excursions, but it gives me the utmost pleasure to say here, as I shall take frequent occasion to say on my return home, that I have never seen *any* party where less liquor was drank, and where everyone in the party was so uniformly gentlemanly." Such a remark was thoroughly appreciated, and though the writer was a member of that party, we trust his evidence will also be admitted when he bears testimony to the remarks of our friend Dr. Milligan.

At 2:30 P. M. we were ashore in Queenstown, a pretty little town on the south side of Ireland, originally called Cove, but receiving its present appellation, from the visit of Her Majesty Queen Victoria, in 1849. It is situated on the side of a hill commanding a charming view of the harbor we have just entered, and is frequented much by invalids, owing to its salubrious climate. There is a very handsome Protestant church and Catholic cathedral here, also a very fine hotel, the *Queen's*, but as our guide, C. P. Cooper, Esq., of Dundalk, Ireland, now has us in charge, and as we are due in Cork that evening we cannot remain long here, so we move in a body to the station near at hand; and this was attended with its little incidents too.

Immediately on landing, we were literally besieged with the inevitable " Shamrock " women, these being dressed in short petticoats or gowns, wearing " mutches " or white muslin and lace caps, in bare feet, with shoulder shawls strapped crosswise on their bodies, and they mean business " first, last and all the time." "Arrah, now, buy a wee bit o' the shamrock, dear." " Take a wee bit o' it wid yez, now." " God bless yez, me darlints, and its to Ireland yez are come." "Arrah, now, as yez are just fresh over, take a wee bit o' Ireland's green emblem wid yez;" or " Have some o' the nice fresh gooseberries," and so on, and they are like hungry leeches for holding on to you ;

there is no shaking them off, and you can, if you wish
draw down upon your head the richest blessings of heaven,
according to the manner in which you draw upon your
exchequer for the purchase " o' the shamrock," or you
can have your " sowl " cheerfully wished, with expressive
and strongly qualifying adjectives, to places in which it is
said there is no use for linen suits, and where water is at
a heavy premium, by refusing to invest in any of their
wares.

But, having run the gauntlet through this mob, we
finally arrived at the depot, and taking the 3 P. M. train,
are on our way to Cork, passing through a most beautiful
country, following the river from the Harbor of Cork to
the city of the same name. The Harbor of Cork is one
of the largest and most commodious in the United Kingdom, and capable of affording shelter to the entire British
Navy. Of the scenery on the river, Arthur Young says,
that "the country on the harbor he thought preferable in
many respects to anything in Ireland;" and Sir John
Forbes thinks " it would be difficult to over-praise the
beauty of the river from Queenstown to Cork, or the
magnificent harbor or inland bay in which it terminates,
more especially when these are seen under the influence
of a bright sun and a brilliant sky. * * * * Indeed,
every element of beauty that can mingle in such a scene
seems to be here comprised; * * * * Water of a
color and purity of the sea, lofty barriers on either side,
covered with rich woods, and intermingled with green,
park-like fields and shining villas * * * And the whole
animated and, as it were, humanized, by the peopled

steamers sweeping up and down, the boats and yachts pulling about, and a ship or two at anchor in every little bay that opened out upon our course."

Dr. Scott, of Queenstown, writes, that "the salubrity of the climate is such that it has been chosen as a residence by many invalids who would otherwise have sought the far-off scenes of Montpelier or Madeira, with their vehement Junes, and less temperate vicissitudes of climate."

It is also an interesting fact to note, that the Rev. Charles Wolfe, author of the incomparable lines on the "Burial of Sir John Moore," beginning:

"Not a drum was heard, nor a funeral note,"

who died in 1823, of consumption, lies interred on Great Island.

We arrived in Cork at 4.10 P. M., and were driven at once to the Imperial Hotel, and at this time we stumbled across some of the most amusing incidents of our trip, amusing for the time being, but one proved almost a little annoying, as we shall see later.

As already shown, the steamer "Russia" was not prolific of bath rooms, and we were by this time feeling badly the need of free bath houses, or a tub of any description, and fearing to shave on board ship, our beards had become somewhat similar to a prophet's, for a warning to us was in the case of the Major, who was always busy at the primping process, gave a steward a shilling for cutting him quite a gash 'neath the chin; a man may know all about waiting on a table, but know nothing of shaving, as was the case in this instance.

The "Doctor" and "Carlisle" boldly sallied forth in search of a "House of Tubs," and a barber shop, feeling somewhat as a Federal street jeweler, of Teutonic origin, and a friend of ours, felt, when walking over one of the bridges which form the connecting links between the two cities, in company with another friend of us both. Our friend incidentally remarked, "What a good institution these free bath houses were," pointing to one laying on the wharf on the Pittsburgh side, "that they were so good for the poor and working man, coming home from his hard toil, besmeared with dirt and smoke, to step in and take a bath in the evening," which brought from our jeweler the somewhat astonishing and amusing reply, "Path! Path! I not path me for seventeen years!" and we felt a little that way ourselves, though not quite so bad in years of lack of ablutions.

Passing along one of the principal streets, we could see no red and white and variegated barber poles or boxes, but finally observed a sign "Thomas Moriarty, Hair Dresser and Perfumer to His Royal Highness the Prince of Wales." Now in democratic America, we are not prone to run after and knuckle at the shrine of "blue blood," &c., still, when we read that sign, its length, its breadth, its meaning, our hearts fluttered a little, and we said, "Ah! has it come to this? Are we poor American Sovereigns to sit in a chair where, perhaps, has been seated the heir apparent to the British throne, (may be?)" and, gladdened by this thought, led away by vanity, thinking we had stolen a long march on the remainder of the party, we wandered into this man Moriarty's, to sit in this seat, if only that, and have our faces lathered by the same brush, our faces shaved by the same razor, our moustaches pomaded with the same stick, our hair pasted and brushed *a la* H. R. H. P. of W., and with fear and trembling we ventured in, fearing that august personage, H. R. H. P. of W., might be there then, and we, by no means, in full court dress.

We found a room about four feet by nine, a long bench, at the side of which was a table with a very large and elegant mirror three inches by five ; on the table lay a piece of kitchen soap about the size and thickness of a silver half dollar, an old strop, and a tin cup for lather ; on a little bench on the other side of the room were a shoemaker's hammer, a brad-awl, a chisel, a watchmaker's implement, a blacksmith's tools, and I don't know what else. In this room sat a little old woman, a "mutch" on her head, and puffing away at a "cutty" pipe. We inquired for the barber and were informed "he had just stepped over the way to get a drink." We ventured forth much more boldly than we ventured in, with our minds fully made up that H. R. H. P. of W. could monopolize the whole of that hair dressing and perfuming establishment, so far as we were concerned. We did not care of partaking in any of it ; we would rather go back to Pittsburgh with beards trailing on the ground as they were now almost doing, than have a man go at us with a brad-awl, a chisel, a mallet, and watchmaker's pinchers.

"If at first you don't succeed, then try, try again." Remembering this school-boy motto, we tried again, and finally succeeded in finding a shop at last, where they backed our heads up against the wall, and gave us in the language of the "*Post*," our good Democratic newspaper friend of Pittsburgh, an "*alleged*" shave. "*Alleged*" is good, it has let us out many times for a libel suit.

Here again our friend, he of the curious moustache, was in a serious squabble with the barber, each doubting the other's veracity, for we arrived there just in time to hear the tonsorial artist requesting the proprietor of the baggage marked G. S. H. to remove those toothpicks, as he possibly could not shave a man having a mouthful of toothpicks, and it was again necessary for us to pledge our words that he was telling the truth, the whole truth, and nothing but the truth, when insisting they were not toothpicks but were only the ends of his unchristianlike moustache.

After being scraped, for we could call it nothing else, we went in quest of a printer's office, having a little work to be done, and, stepping into one—a Mr. Acheson's, on George street—showed a sample of what we wanted; he politely informed us he could not do it, that he had not the facilities, but, putting on his hat, leaving a customer, his business and his store in charge of his little daughter, eight to ten years of age, said he could show us where we could and did have our work done. From the copy we had shown him, he discovered we belonged to the party of visiting Sir Knights to Ireland,

and on our way to the printer's, in true, genuine Irishman style, not, as in this country, from the love of drink, but out of kindly feeling, and a kind heart, he insisted on our going in and "taking something," but owing to our being absolutely and strictly temperate, we were obliged to decline with thanks.

We found the printer, gave him our order, asked him when it would be done, and he said in about a week. We told him we left the city on the following day at 2:30, and would want it by 12 o'clock. We told him in America the circuses, theatres, combinations, &c., when traveling, just gave their orders for several thousand posters and programmes, and by the time the troupe had finished their dinners the printer had his work in the cars, his bill receipted, and looking for another job. We take the credit of stirring up those good people of Cork, and having had done the quickest piece of "comp." ever performed in that good city.

Returning to the hotel, it was now a little late—6:45 P. M., and Table d'Hote was at 6:15 sharp—but owing to our delays we were unable to reach the hotel sooner, and here we had a funny experience. Feeling fresh from our bath and "wash-up," we walked lightly and briskly up to the Coffee Room, as they call their dining rooms, and were about to enter the door, seeing all our party comfortably seated there, our teeth watered for some of the good things borne by the table; and having had nothing to eat since leaving the "Russia," we do not put it too strongly when we say we were *desperately* hungry, but just as we were about to enter, a portly "Chief Butler" with a pair of indispensable black trouserloons, low cut black vest with coral buttons, spike-tail coat, moustache and goatee black as crows, and faultlessly waxed, hair curled up, excelling in that regard, we fear, even our own Absalom, the Major's raven hair, the admiration of all our party. This "Chief Butler," who is always a better man than the proprietor, came at us with, we are not sure whether it was a fly-brush or a young table cloth, and endeavored to "shoo" us out of the door; and there he stood, to our amazement, his arms extended and flapping like a victorious barnyard fowl, crying, "Shoo! Shoo!! Shoo!!!" "Can't get dinner here now, Shoo! Shoo!! Shoo!!!" But we struck an attitude, knowing full well the eyes of the multitude were upon us, as they sat around the richly laden table, enjoying, we may very vulgarly say, piggishly, the good things of this life and our misfortune and predicament, while the Colonel deliberately and tauntingly held aloft the "walker" of a fowl, which goaded us to despair. When we struck the afore-mentioned attitude, the "Chief Butler" sobered down a little, but was still somewhat excited, crying "Three causes over—soup, fish and chops all done!" "You will have to go down stairs and get your dinner." We looked him defiantly in the face, told him not to whisper, not to say another word; we wanted to know if he knew what our stomachs wanted before he had seen us; that neither of us so far had asked him for any soup, fish or chops, and that if anyone had told him we did, he had informed him of what was a base fabrication and perversion of the truth; that we would not eat soup if it was put down before us in vats, that we never ate chops under any consideration, and as for fish, we simply abhorred it; that for others, we cared not what they might do, but as for us, give us just a good piece of beef and potatoes, or give us death just at that time. All this, we will now state, was a deliberate falsehood to His Royal Highness, the " Chief Butler," for inwardly we felt we would have given half our wealth for a good dish of each of the above-mentioned articles of food, but we could not possibly allow H. R. H., C. B. to make away with us in that manner, especially on the last thirty or forty courses of dinner, to sacrifice three at the first. Oh! but he was mad; blood was on the face, not of the moon, but of H. R. H., the C. B. But we made our point, and were soon as busily engaged as those who had simply gone before, and we were permitted to finish our repast in peace.

At 8 P. M. this Friday evening, a committee called and escorted us to their Masonic rooms, where we visited Lodge of Ireland No. 1, the oldest Free Mason Lodge in Ireland, their Masonic charter being given them in 1731, making them at the time of our visit almost one hundred and fifty years old. They have some intensely interesting relics and antiquities; for instance, they have a bible on their table printed in the year 1526, and many ancient letters, demits and documents, coming down from age after age of ancestry to their present membership. They have also a very handsome portrait, done in oil, of

Lady Aldsworth, the only woman Mason the world ever knew, and it might be interesting to know how she came to be made a member of the craft, which we take from a little pamphlet entitled, "Memoirs of the Life of the Hon. Mrs. Aldsworth, the only female who ever obtained the honor of initiation in the sublime mysteries of Freemasonry;" a little work which was printed and prepared for our fellow Crusaders of '71.

"The Hon. Mrs. Aldsworth was second daughter of Arthur St. Leger, Lord V. Doneraile and Baron Kilmeaden, by Eliza Hayes, daughter of John Hayes of Winchelsea, in the county of Sussex, Esq., * * * The family is very ancient and honorable. Her ancestor, Sir Anthony St. Leger, of the county of Kent, Knight of the Garter, '*unus nobilium secretiorist Camaræ Regis,*' succeeded Sir William Brereton as Lord Deputy of Ireland, in the reign of Henry VIII, and was sworn July 25th, 1540, at Christ Church, Dublin, in the form following, and was five times Lord Deputy or Lieutenant during that and the succeeding reigns, and died in the reign of Queen Mary, March 12th, 1559, at Ulcomb, in Kent, the ancient seat of the family:

"You shall swear that you shall faithfully and truly to your power, serve our Sovereign Lord, the King's Majestie, in the room and authority of Lord Deputy and Chief Governor of this his realm of Ireland, you shall maintain and defend the laws of God and the Christian faith. You shall to your power, not only keep his Majestie's peace amongst his people, but also maintain his officers and ministers in the execution and administration of justice. You shall defend his Majestie's castles, garrisons, dominions, people and subjects of this realm, and repress his rebels and enemies. You shall not consent to the damage and disherizen of his Majesty, his heirs or successors; neither shall you suffer the right of the crown to be destroyed in any way, but shall let it to your power; and if you cannot let the same, you shall certifie his Majesty clearly and expressly thereof. You shall give your true and faithful council for the King's Majestie's profit, and his Highness' council you shall conceal and keep; all other things for the preservation of his Majestie's realm of Ireland, the peace amongst his people, the execution of his justice, according to his Majestie's laws, usages and customs, of this his Highness' realm, you shall perform and do your power * * *

"*Council of Trent, Folio* 392.   ‡ BORLACE."

Eliza Hayes, the subject of this sketch, was married to Richard Aldsworth, of Newmarket, in the county of Cork, of a highly respected and ancient family, long celebrated for their hospitalities and other virtues, and now deriving additional honor from this lady's having been the only female who was ever initiated in the ancient and honorable mysteries of Free Masonry. * * She was a woman of model virtue, sweetened and adorned by all the amiable qualities that grace and dignify the female character.

Lord Doneraile, Mrs. Aldsworth's father, who was a very zealous Mason, held a warrant in his own hands, and occasionally opened Lodge at Doneraile House, his sons and some intimate friends in the neighborhood assisting; and, it is said, never were the Masonic duties more rigidly performed, or the business of the Craft more sincerely pursued, than by the brethren of No. 150, the number of their warrant.

It appears that previous to the initiation of a gentleman to the first steps in Freemasonry, Mrs. Aldsworth, who was then a young girl, happened to be in an apartment adjoining the room usually used as a lodge room, this room at the time undergoing some repair and alteration; amongst other things, the wall was considerably reduced in one part for the purpose of making a saloon. The young lady having distinctly heard voices, and prompted by the curiosity natural to all to see somewhat of this mystery, so long and so secretly locked up from public view, she had the courage, with her scissors, to pick a brick from the wall, and actually witnessed the awful and mysterious ceremony through the two first steps. Curiosity gratified, fear at once took possession of her mind, and those who understand this passage well know what the feelings must be of any person who could have the same opportunity of unlawfully beholding that ceremony. Let them then judge what must be the feelings of a young girl. She saw no mode of escape, but through the very room where the concluding part of the second step was still performing, and that being at the far end, and the room a very large one. She had again resolution sufficient to attempt her escape that way, and with light but trembling step, and almost suspended breath, she glided along unobserved by the lodge, laid her hand on the handle, and softly opening the door, before her stood a grim and surly Tyler, with his long rusty sword. Her shriek alarmed the lodge, who all rushed to the door, and on finding out from the Tyler that she had been in the room during all the ceremony, in the first paroxysm of rage, it is said, her death was resolved on, but that from the moving and earnest supplications of her youngest brother her life was spared, on condition of her going through the two steps she had already seen. This was agreed to, and they conducted the young, beautiful and terrified creature through those trials which are sometimes more than enough for masculine resolution, little thinking they were taking into the bosom of their Craft a member that would afterwards reflect a lustre on the annals of Masonry.

Mrs. Aldsworth is said not to have possessed that construction of countenance which may claim the appellation of very beautiful, but a certain air of dignity to which the benevolence of her heart and sweetness of her natural disposition, more than compensated the deficiency.

It was a countenance that gave encouragement to the unfortunate to put in their petitions, and assurances that their distress would be alleviated. Having, however, obtained the foregoing particulars from persons who only knew this lady in the last years of her life, what she might have been in her youth we can only obtain from her portrait, which, though taken at an advanced period, still retains, if not the semblance of beauty, the traits and lineaments of a fine countenance, only a little shaken and defaced by time. Though the memory of Mrs. Aldsworth's beauty may have passed away, which, in a long life of eighty years is no improbable conjecture, and though the bloom and charms of the young St. Leger may be sought for in the countenance of our benevolent sister, the almost divine character which it pleased heaven to stamp upon her uncommon mind, has left so many memorials behind, that to doubt this part of her history must be blind incredulity. The truth is, her heart and hand, ever open to the sufferings and to the claims of sorrow and distress, almost prevented supplication by their promptitude to relieve, nor let it be supposed this spirit of beneficence circumscribed a circle around its action, or confined its influence; no, for though her brethren in distress had the first claims on her liberality, it was not the less open or less bountiful to the unenlightened. Best of women; mother to the motherless, friend to the friendless, benignant and generous soul, who from the bosom of affluence did'st hear the wretches' cry, and would fly from the table of comfort to bear comfort to the hovel of wretchedness, and wipe the unobtrusive tear from the eye of retired misery.

In the active gratification of her hospitable and benevolent heart, she did not, however, neglect altogether the duties of the Craft. She was, (as far as she went,) a most exemplary member and Mason, and has presided as Master of her lodge, which she headed frequently in Masonic order of procession, and it was her custom on those occasions to precede the lodge in an open phæton. * * * * One circumstance, before we conclude, deserves notice, as it is a handsome lesson to those who boast the superiority of manly discretion and understanding, and yet err in this particular. Mrs. A. had such a veneration for Masonry that she would never suffer it to be lightly spoken of in her hearing, nor would she touch on the subject but with the greatest caution in company even with her most intimate friends whom she did not know to be Masons, and when she did it was under evident embarrassment, and a trembling apprehension lest she may in a moment of inadvertence commit a breach of Masonic duty. Thus lived this pattern of female excellence, we had almost said human perfection, dispensing like a principle of good, comfort and happiness to all around her, till He that gave thought proper to call her away to participate in the joys of His eternal kingdom. Her death, it is said, was occasioned by the imprudent use of laudanum in a slight indisposition. We cannot conclude this sketch better than by giving a paragraph which appeared in a print of the day, on occasion of her death:

"On Monday last, died at Newmarket, in this county, the Hon. Mrs. Aldsworth, the wife of Richard Aldsworth, Esq., M. P. She lived to the age of eighty, and such were the effects of her early education under the good Lord Doneraile, her father, and her own happy disposition, that from her infancy there passed not a day which might not have been distinguished by some one act of her benevolence or charity. She lived for the most part of her time in the country in the midst of her tenants, to whom her house afforded the most cheerful hospitality. The meanest of them when their wants required it, had access to her, and when the indigent or sick called upon her she never failed to dispense her favors with that bounty and humanity which a large fortune enabled her, and a still larger soul induced her to bestow. Indeed, heaven seemed to have appointed her guardian of the poor, whom she relieved without ostentation. She possessed the fairest sentiments of religion, and as if the manner of her death was meant as an anticipation of that happiness which awaited her, she spent in slumber her last hours, those hours so very dreadful in the general, without the least pain or opposition, her mind quite disengaged from the world in which she did her own duty, whilst the tears and lamentations of thousands about her expressed their feelings for their kind benefactress." * * * * * *

Having spent considerable time in examination of the relics and antiquities which were carefully explained to us by our brethren of No. 1, T. C. Cooper, the Provincial Deputy Grand Master, was called to the chair, and the evening was spent in song, speeches, &c., indulged in by Major William C. Moreland, Col. McConihe, Lee S. Smith, and others, and thus was another evening happily and pleasantly passed with those who to us now are friends, while but a few hours before were perfect and entire strangers.

About 10:30 P. M. we returned to our hotel and enjoyed the witnessing of the sleeping scenes of Lady

Macbeth carried out in simon-pure theatrical style. It certainly recalled that scene most vividly to see the stately Mrs. M—— and Mrs. F——, of Philadelphia, wending their way heavenward per stairway, Mr. S—— and his bride turning the corner of a hall, and our patriarchal prelate Professor S—— of Allegheny, his good wife leaning tenderly on his stout arm, while the less happy single gentlemen, and for the time being widowers, climbing stairs, wandering around corridors, each with a brazen candlestick and sperm candle, looking for No. 68 or No. 70, etc. Oh! how sweet our first sleep on *terra firma* again; our first impression, however, on entering our rooms was that perhaps the genial and jovial friends from whom we had just parted, had not only treated us hospitably but convivially, for the bed, dressing-case, washstand, seemed to be on a general spiritualistic move, while the floor had every appearance of being movable, for we had not yet accustomed ourselves to the steadiness of things built on the substantial after passing through the nine days of rolling we had just endured. In the morning the "Quartette" was awake with the lark and into a jaunting car, and "doing" the far-famed city of Cork.

Cork is a city of some eighty thousand inhabitants, and is generally termed the capital of the south ; is a corporate city, governed by a mayor, sixteen aldermen and forty-eight counsellors, and a staff of paid officials. It is the third city in Ireland in importance and population, Dublin and Belfast alone ranking it. We visited Patrick's Bridge, Parliament Bridge, and in St. Patrick's street is a handsome statue of Father Matthew, the Apostle of Temperance. The Custom House, which is a handsome building, occupies a tongue of land where the two streams of the city meet at a somewhat acute angle on the eastern side of the city.

A tract of 240 acres of land has been recovered from the river, and laid out as a park, where are held annual races which are largely attended. The most important literary and scientific institutions are: The Queen's College, opened in 1849, which occupies a picturesque site on a rock rising fully forty feet above the level of the southern branch of the River Lee. The College is open to all religious sects; it has eighteen professors teaching languages, sciences, including Greek, Latin and the modern tongues, medicine, surgery, natural history, botany, geology, mathematics and chemistry; besides classes for engineering, political economy and law. The Royal Cork Institution, incorporated in 1807, with a view mainly to the advancement of agriculture. The Mechanics Institute, agricultural, horticultural and an art union. There are two theatres, and barracks for cavalry and infantry. Substantial quays of cut stone for the shipping, are worthy a visit, when it is known that over £300,000 have been expended upon improvements connected with the river; and when this amount of £300,000 is mentioned, or *one million and a half* of American dollars, just contemplate how miserly and niggardly they all are over there in that poor country, when we think of all of $10,000 appropriated by our supremely wise American Congress for the improvement of our beautiful stream—the Allegheny. Just think of it! Such enormous and reckless extravagance on the part of our all-wise law makers will ruin any weak or strong government ever conceived of.

A very flourishing trade is carried on in Cork, the imports consisting of timber chiefly, and the exporting of grain, live stock, provisions and linen. The registered shipping of this city is about 40,000 tons, sailing vessels and steamers. The walls of Cork were built by the Danes, in the ninth century, and it derived its name from the Irish *corroch* or *corcagh*, a swamp, was given to it in allusion to the original character of its site.

The Union Workhouse, the largest in the country, was opened for paupers in 1840; the inmates work at tailoring, weaving and other trades, and a large cornmill is attached which is worked by the paupers.

After a drive through the Grand Parade, South Mall, Great George's street, Mardyke, and the famous "Broad Lane," not a dozen feet wide, we returned to the hotel for breakfast.

At 10 A. M., the entire party were seated in large wagonettes and jaunting cars, prepared for the drive to Blarney Castle, famous the world over. It is a lovely drive of some eight miles, along a most beautiful road, and passing through a most charming country, while at many points *en route* some unusually fine landscape views are to be had. On our arrival at the Castle, the first procedure was the climbing of the seemingly interminable steps, up one hundred and twenty feet high, in search of the stone, to which old Father Prout alludes thusly:

> "There is a stone there,
> That whoever kisses,
> Oh! he never misses,
>   To grow eloquent.
> 'Tis he may clamber
> To a lady's chamber,
> Or become a member
>   Of Parliament.

Or, as he puts it again:

> "A clever spouter,
> He'll sure turn out, or
> An out and outer
>   To be let alone!
> Don't hope to hinder him,
> Or to bewilder him,
> Sure he's a pilgrim
>   From the Blarney Stone."

The Castle was built in the fifteenth century, built by Cormick MacCarty, in 1449. It stands on the side of a precipitous ledge of limestone rock, rising from a deep valley, and part of its base is washed by a small river called the Aw-Martin. There remains now of the original fortress only a square, massive tower, with a parapet breast high, and, of course, in the most dangerous looking place in the whole business. On the summit is this stone, which is said to confer on the persons kissing it the peculiar property of saying anything coaxing or complimentary or praise most agreeable to the hearer. Only for our being the head of a family, we would mildly suggest that this is our early marriage. Every one going to Blarney Castle always kisses the "real stone," and, of course, we want it distinctly understood we kissed the "*real* stone," the " rale stone " sure. The Major and Colonel would not attempt it, in fact we believe the Doctor and "Carlisle" were the only two who ventured the feat. Emptying our pockets of our "Bank of Englands," we were solemnly held over by the heels, and performed the nonsensical operation, and as we looked down through the aperture, one hundred and twenty feet high, to kiss this stone to which is ascribed the power of giving you all the "blarney" you can. very comfortably carry, we thought of our illustrious predecessors of '71, and of the portly figures the pilgrim party of that year had with them, and we wondered and pondered how they ever, and how many of them, held out our friend Sir Edward M. Jenkins, or how they ever escaped permitting another friend, Sir James A. Sholes, from slipping through their fingers, and I know it must have been an effort of no mean order to hold even our genial friend A. M. Rambo, Esq., from measuring the distance to the ground below, by as many times the length of his body multiplied by the time taken in falling, deducting the pressure on the air as he compressed it in his momentum. We all knew our venerable prelate had been at it before, and he did not try it again. Blarney Lake is a sweet little piece of water, distant about a quarter of a mile from the Castle. A tradition remains that at certain seasons a herd of white cows rises from the bosom of the Lake to graze among the rich pasture which clothes its banks. Another story is, " that the Earl of Clancarty, who forfeited the Castle at the Revolution, cast all his plate into a certain part; that *three* of the McCarthy's inherit the secret of the place where they are deposited, any one of whom dying communicates it to another member of the family, and thus perpetuates the secret, which is never to be revealed until a McCarthy be again Lord of Blarney." For traditions, for stories, for tales and yarns, before which far western snake and Indian stories would pale, and are the frozen truth in comparison, commend us to these good people in Ireland.

Then here are the beautiful " Groves of Blarney," to which is ascribed the following quotation of a song found in Mr. Crofton Croker's " Popular Songs of Ireland : "

> " The Groves of Blarney,
> They look so charming,
> Down by the purling
> Of sweet silent streams,
> Being banked with posies
> That spontaneous grow there,
> Planted in order
> By the sweet rock close."
>
> " 'Tis there's the daisy,
> And the sweet carnation,
> The blooming pink,
> And the rose so fair;
> The daffodowndilly,
> Likewise the lily,
> All flowers that scent
> The sweet fragrant air."

Having spent a few hours thus at the Castle, buying armload after armload of the genuine bogwood, sold at the Castle gate, we take our conveyances and return to the city, and here again our Masonic friends had a treat in store for us. Notwithstanding the fact the famous Shandon Church was closed for repairs, they had it opened for our inspection. The Church is a plain grotesque looking edifice, with a steeple resembling a number of stories. It was begun in 1722, and Crofton Croker informs us "that its steeple was constructed of hewn stone from the Franciscan Abbey, where James II. heard mass, and from the ruins of Lord Barry's Castle, which had been the official residence of the lords president of Munster, and from whence this quarter of the city takes its name Shandon or Seandun, signifying, in Irish, the old fort or castle." Its height is one hundred and twenty feet, and in this steeple are those Shandon Bells, of which Rev. Father Mahoney says this, in two stanzas from his song:

> " With deep affection
> And recollection,
> I often think on
>   Those Shandon Bells,
> Whose sound so mild would
> In the days of childhood,
> Fling round my cradle
>   Their magic spells."
>
> " I have heard bells chiming
> Full many a clime in,
> Tolling sublime in
>   Cathedral shrine;

> While at a glib rate
> Brass tongues would vibrate,
> But all their music
> Spoke nought like thine."

We heard those sweet Shandon Bells, and never will, we forget the emotions with which we were filled, as on that day they rang out " Caller Herrin," "America," " The Last Rose of Summer," " The Old Folks at Home," " Home, Sweet Home," and how, as they sang out with their iron tongues in sweet melody. those old and dear familiar airs, we were carried away thousands of miles across land and water to the " Smoky City," nestling amidst her bleak and barren hills.

But our time is growing short, we cannot remain longer here, much as were wont to do, so we returned to the Imperial, where our Royal Highness, the Chief Butler, has a nice lunch in waiting for us, of which we partake heartily, and are again seated in our coaches, ready again for the road. At the moment of our departure, our newly made friend of the day preceding, Mr. Acheson, came round to the hotel with a large paper containing the most beautiful and fragrant rosebuds of all varieties and colors, and a package of sweet smelling verbena, for a button-hole bouquet for each of the party, which were duly appreciated. And here the thought struck us forcibly; here we were, strangers in a strange land, not one of us knowing a single, solitary soul, yet even before putting a foot ashore we were among firm, fast friends, whose every shake of the hand betokened friendship, kindness and brotherly love; and there is one thing of which can be said of Americans, as of Scotchmen and Irishmen, for our good friends' benefit on the other side of the water, and that is, they never *forget*, and we but await the opportunity of carrying out literally the golden rule of " doing unto them as they did unto us."

A little fact, or rather incident, we neglected to mention earlier in this letter, illustrative of how stories carry and are perverted and twisted until the original becomes unrecognizable, was, we were informed of the terrible Fourth of July disaster, which happened to the Sunday School pic-nic being held in one of the groves adjacent to Allegheny City, when that fatal storm of wind, lightning and blew down trees, &c., killing a number of persons, but the version we heard was that the entire lower portion of Allegheny City was consumed by fire, that houses had been blown down, and persons numbering hundreds had been killed and wounded, hundreds of thousands of dollars worth of property destroyed; and we can assure the reader, being so far away from home, with intelligence such as that, the " Crusade," until more definite intelligence from home would arrive, would be a very tame and mild affair.

Through the kindness of the *Cork Constitution*, the live newspaper of that city, we were permitted to go over its file, but could find nothing concerning it. The Colonel, whose home was in the vicinity of that honorable gentleman, Mr. Brigham Young, and the

Major, whose residence was safe in the region of Nicholson block and locust post pavements in the City of Pittsburgh, were selfishly asleep in their rooms, while the poor Doctor and "Carlisle" spent a large portion of the night examining newspapers, and we conscientiously believe the two former mentioned gentlemen were laughing at us for doing so, and would have been pleased had the Doctor and "Carlisle" been burned out of house and home, and been to-day starring the country out of the states enforcing the Tramp Act, as the "Two Orphans."

At 2:30 P. M., we take the train for Killarney, passing through Bandon, Enniskean, Dunmanway, Bantry, Glengariff and Kenmare, and arriving at Killarney at 5:30 P. M.

Letter No. 3.

The Pilgrims at Killarney.—One of the Gems of Irish Scenery.—Amusing Scenes in Genuine Irish Life.—A Pleasant Ride Through the Gap of Dunloe and on the Lakes.—Incidents by the Way.

NO conception can be formed of the appetites we "poor and weary pilgrims traveling from afar" had on our arrival at Killarney, for we were hourly being benefited by our ocean trip, and with the crisp, bracing air of Ireland, as with a fast growing child, we could almost in the same manner see each other growing fat, and it would have been a very immaterial matter to us whether we met a man with one "shillelah" or a dozen at that moment, for we had been informed that Killarney was the place to have a glimpse of real Irish life, in all of its original phases. Shortly after our arrival, however, we filed into the large and handsome dining room of the Railway Hotel, where we seated ourselves and fared sumptuously of a magnificent dinner, composed of all the good things of this life, and they even had many delicacies and luxuries in the shape of fruits, &c., many of which are foreign to Britain, and a rarity.

After dinner, on one of the loveliest of lovely evenings, we took a stroll down through this famous

Irish town of Killarney, and, situated as this little town is, surrounded by towering hills, we were privileged in seeing one of the most gorgeous sunsets we had ever beheld. The sun had almost run his course for that day, and was just going down behind the "Purple Mountain," his golden rays spreading and shedding the beautiful light all over the heavens, and tinging the light and fleecy clouds with a richness such as is seldom seen. Now and then, as we were walking onward, a little opening in the foliage of the trees revealed to us the pretty, calm, and still Lakes we had come to see; but we are now out to see simply the town, and, if possible, to observe the quality and character of its inhabitants, and, as we have already said, for a sight of real Irish life, commend us unhesitatingly to Killarney.

As the "Quartette" passed down and along the narrow and winding streets, each of us enjoying a fragrant Havana, (the *Post's* word again—*alleged* Havana,) we were followed and literally besieged by every little urchin in the place. We are prone to believe, and we certainly would have been taken for a walking side-show had we been seen in our own country, surrounded as we were by anywhere from forty to one hundred dirty-faced, barefooted gamins, who seeing us smoking, yelled like a band of Ute Indians, "Say, misther; give's the stump?" "Jump the ditch for the stump, misther!" The crowd represented children and youth of all ages from the little bits of tads four or five years of age, to full-fledged boys of twelve, fourteen and sixteen; and no sooner had the exhausted end of our cigars left our hands, no matter where falling in the street, than would be seen one of the following, howling mob, puffing and drawing for dear life at the very small remainder of our original smoke.

As is the custom in the smaller and even the larger, but particularly the smaller towns throughout the kingdom, the work of the week being ended, the whole town turns out on Saturday nights; consequently may be seen at almost every step little knots of people, men and women, and as a general rule the " whuskey " flies. We see among the groups an old gray-haired man whose hairs attest the frosts of seventy years, wearing the half-high silk hat, a dark check shirt, black silk cravat tied in a big heavy knot, the swallow-tailed coat with gilt or brass buttons, from the pocket of the coat hangs the indispensable red Bandana handkerchief, a black low-cut waistcoat, corduroy knee pants, blue ribbed stockings—home made, and hob-nail boots or shoes; and we see this old man, diving his head into the person to whom he is talking, or "steadying up" as he inclines backwards, sideways or forward.

Again, and very probably in the same group, we see the younger man of the more modern period, having on the Christian cut of pantaloons, swaggering backwards and forward, and apparently most fearfully weak at the knees. Again we see the beardless youth, with a "cutty" pipe in his mouth, probably the pipe turned upside down, and the smoker, in short, as drunk as a loon; and even in all these motley assemblages may be seen the "gentler" sex, (still we had no desire of tackling any of the female gender, for they looked more powerful than the men,) as hot in conversation, as good at swearing, and as loud in gestures as any of their male companions, and a great proportion of them under the "influence."

Of course we could not go through all this and not see a first class "hand-to-hand," not strictly in accordance with the imperative rules of the prize ring, but more in the nature of our American lunacy walking matches, that is to say, "go-as-you-please." Two stalwarts had met and fully agreed to disagree, and after one boldly giving the other "the lie, be jabers!" with a "shillalah" in one hand, he danced around like an automaton, with a "Whoop! Who'll thread on me coat tails;" which, of course, no true man of Erin can stand for a moment. So this man's opponent was no exception to this rule, and becoming exceedingly forcible in his remarks, he gave his adversary a terrible "sockdolager" on the nasal appendage and right eye, which caused the "claret" certainly, if not the "potheen" to fly; and this had been done but a moment when about three or four "bobbies" of the constabulary force swooped down upon the combatants, and to jail they went with them in a "jiffy," but requiring an extra policeman to keep back a couple of women who, by entreaties and even by force, were earnestly endeavoring to have one of them, the man who received "the bash on the nose," as they termed it, released. But once into the hands of one of the constabulary, there is no release until you have been presented to, and had the honor and pleasure of an interview with his honor the justice.

Returning to our hotel, as it was now almost eleven o'clock, and sitting out on the piazza on that beautiful moonlit night, our thoughts were wafted homeward; in fact, we were forcibly reminded of Allegheny City at least, from the fact, as we sat there, our good, kindhearted German friend, Sir Knight Fred Beilstein, came in the gateway muttering and mumbling to himself in inaudible sounds, and when he reached us he broke out on a certain "highly respected gentleman," formerly the head of a prominent institution in Allegheny, and he went for him pretty severely, too. In fact it would not have been healthy for that "highly respected gentleman" by any means, to have turned up around the "Railway Hotel" on that evening. Whatever started Fred on that subject at that time and place is something we have still to find out.

Sunday morning, like a good pious four, the "Quartette" arose and proceeded to the Roman Catholic Cathedral and attended "early church," and at 10:30 we attended divine service in St. Franciscan Church, and at both these services we recognized one and all of our friends of the evening before, excepting perhaps the poor individual who received the afore-mentioned "sockdolager" on the nose, and the person presenting it to him. Not much can be said as regards the architectural beauty of either of these churches, but the cathedral is more than ordinarily large, and as with nearly all buildings on that side of the water, is built completely and entirely of stone. The most striking feature in common with all such public places, and even private mansions, is in the solidity and substantiability of their appearance. The interior is fitted up as is usual in churches of that denomination, the alters and pulpits all being of exquisitely carved stone, no gaudiness of any kind existing, while the beautiful work of the mallet and chisel, displayed in carving out of the rude stone the twelve Apostles, the two Marys and Jesus Christ our Saviour, while the magnificent stained-glass windows attaining the height of sixty feet, are emblematical of various portions of Scripture, and the very elaborately embroidered robes which the good father wears during the service, all tend with harmony to please the eye of the beautiful and chaste.

But there is in great contrast to this another side to this picture. In looking forward, we see only that which proves attractive, and extracts words of commendation and admiration; but turning back and looking around over a congregation of two to three thousand persons, 'tis then we see the squalor and poverty prevailing in poor old Ireland, particularly in the southern country; 'tis there we see a sight never to be forgotten, the faces of Irish men and Irish women, bearing the inevitable mark of their nationality as unmistakably as do God's chosen people, which for thousands of years, time nor change have ever been able to eradicate; we see there men, women, children, in rags, with unshaven faces and unkempt hair, in poverty, hunger and dirt, misery stamped upon each of their unhappy countenances.

Oh! how our heart goes out in sympathy towards this people, to think, that no matter how laborious, how steady, how industrious, how hard working a man may be for years, or how many generations may succeed him, earnestly working and studiously saving and economizing, they never rise above tenants, for the cursed and outrageously barbarous law of entailment, resting upon poor Ireland and her people; they are born into the world in poverty, and depart from it in poverty as they came, and although the people we are now amongst are to a certain extent benighted, yet they are a noble race of people, and the best people in their own homes in God's whole world. We express no Fenian words, nor advance no socialistic, communistic nor rebellious ideas, when we say with all our heart, we hope to see the day when Ireland will be as free as any nation on the earth; when by the enlightenment of civilization, the power of the pen, and the cultivation of that grand and noble feeling—humanity—England will take the hand of her protege—Ireland—and clasped in bonds of peace and fraternal love, with each of Erin's thrifty sons living on his own little spot of ground, in his own little home, all shall dwell together in happiness and unity.

About noon we partook of a good lunch, and having previously ordered a jaunting car, the irrepressible "Quartette' got aboard for a drive. For the benefit of any who have never seen a jaunting car, we will attempt the description of one. They are a neat little single-horse vehicle, somewhat of a box shape, the driver sitting, as it were, on the top and centre of the box, while on either side of the box are two seats, the two hold two persons each, so that the occupants face the sidewalks, instead of the road proper, and are back to back to each other; when but one person takes a car, the driver comes down from his box and seats himself with his back to you on the opposite side, which balances the thing nicely, particularly if one should have a heavy dose of dyspepsia and weigh but ninety pounds or so, and the driver with a proper digestion weighing, say, the mild weight of two hundred and forty.

We drive through the town first, and are quickly impressed with the idea that Killarney is certainly not the cleanest place in the world by a large majority. The population is about 5,000, and the principal business of the people appears to be begging, touting, acting as guides, and similar annoyances. We again quote from Mr. Croker, that "In an evening ramble through the town, the first thing that will strike a stranger, is the number of idle people lounging about the streets, or standing with their backs against the door-posts of the houses." And there is no doubt but much of this consummate laziness is due to the indiscriminate benevolence of unsophisticated tourists.

There is a dispensary, a fever hospital, and an alms-house, as well as a workhouse, in which are four hundred paupers; there is also a 'nunnery, to which is attached a school where four hundred girls are educated. Lord Kenmare, the large land-owner in this section, besides providing clothing for thirty of the girls, annually contributes £100 for the maintenance of the school, and this said, all is said worth saying of Killarney for the town itself. We drive out to Muckross Abbey, around the Lower and Middle Lakes, ascend the Torc Mountain, and see the Torc Waterfall, and from the side of this mountain the finest view is to be had of one of the prettiest pieces of Irish scenery, for such the Lakes and surrounding country of Killarney really are.

We had, aside from the beauties of nature which we were enjoying and permitted to visit, a most amusing time with the driver provided us, which was well worth all the cost alone. He was a young fellow, a genuine Irishman, and whilst we were for the greater portion of the time convulsed in laughter, yet from him we obtained much valuable information as to the means of support of the inhabitants, the wages usually paid, and in every respect he was witty, quick and bright. We made one terrible mistake, however, with him, which came near proving fatal,

H

and from which we have scarcely yet recovered. In an unguarded, thoughtless and unfortunate moment, we asked Mr. O'Flaherty, (the driver's name,) if he could sing? Oh! fatal conundrum. "Oh! yes, he could that, be jabers." And without further suggestion or solicitation upon our part, he started up, and notwithstanding the fact we have held several meetings open and private since, and carefully gone over all the Irish, Scotch, English, French, German, Italian and other composers, we can arrive at no reasonable or definite conclusion as to what that man sang for us on that day, and we still remain in the darkness and bliss of ignorance. He sang and pitched his voice in a beautiful minor key, similar to the sound of a circular saw striking an old and rusty nail, and the " Doctor " looked at " Carlisle " and " Carlisle " looked at the " Doctor ; " we turned and saw the " Colonel " looking at the " Majah " and the " Majah " looking at the " Colonel ; " and then we all turned and gazed on the driver.

The Colonel thought to break the excruciating sound by asking, "Will you be so kind as to tell us the name of that mountain?" The singing goes on, heedless of the question put. The Major asks, "What ruin is that in the distance, on our left?" The singing continues. The Doctor asks, "Who owns this estate?" Always a safe question to ask. No cessation to the croaking on the driver's box. " Carlisle " taps him on the shoulder, tells him " If he was in Pittsburgh he would be in jail in twenty minutes from date, for violating the Sunday laws for sawing wood on Sunday." But still the abominable squeaking goes on, from flats to sharps and majors to minors in horrible style, and we will never believe anything else than that man was wound up just to run a stated length of time, and nothing under heaven could stop him unless you smashed in the works. All four of the "Quartette" then lend their "infloocnce" to endeavor to stop the agony. We entreated him, we begged and plead with him in the name of all that was good, and for the sake of our dear wives and families so many thousand miles away, for the sake of humanity, to please stop; but our entreaties were of no more avail than had we remained dumb. Then we tried the custom of dealing with Pennsylvania legislatures by endeavoring to bribe him with money, pearls, precious stones, U. S. bonds, or even offered to stop somewhere and make him a present of a whole barrel of "Jersey Lightning," if he would only do as the wicked, "cease from troubling," and allow the weary to rest; but there was the difference between Pennsylvania State legislatures and that poor jaunting car driver: they accept, while he simply laughed us to scorn. Now we were *positive* he was wound up, and our next fear was that he was an "eight day" one, too.

There was but one final resort for us, to save ourselves from dying a lingering and miserable death away from home, and we regretted the necessity that compelled us to use it, though it was in reality a simple question of life or death; and as we felt we had not quite finished our mission here below, in true American style, in the twinkling of an eye, we covered him with four "Colts' Navy six-shooters" and four seven inch "Bowie knives," which made the hair on that Irishman's head raise his hat and forever squelched his excruciating, painful and sickening singing propensities, for he immediately and vociferously yelled, "Och! Mister; do n't shoot! Be all the powers that was, is, or is to come, put away your cannons and bloody weapons o'war! and I'll do anything in the world for yez." We put away our young Fortress Monroe, and we had a most docile driver all the afternoon.

During our conversation with him we asked if he would not like to go out to America? He said, as do nearly all over there, that he would if he could only raise the "necessary." We asked him "If he had any relatives in America?" "Divil a one," says he, "but I've got two *brothers* about Boston," and that struck us as a little singular, for we asked very few in Ireland if they had any relatives in America, but who had a father, mother, sister, brother, cousin or an aunt, and all "about Boston," which leads us to the conclusion that the "Hub," with all its "culchah" is but a southern extremity of Ireland itself, its Yankee notions and professions to the contrary notwithstanding.

A LITTLE TOO MUCH POLITENESS.

We entered the beautiful grounds of Captain H. A. Herbert, M. P. for Kerry, and one of the largest proprietors in the South of Ireland; and as we rode along upon the elegant and smooth roads, we saw posted at frequent intervals the following notices: "Drivers stopping or allowing visitors to pull flowers or leaves, or cut trees, etc., will be expelled from the grounds," "Flowers taken from visitors," or "Prosecuted according to law," etc., etc. But the desire to obtain little mementos of places visited is inherent in everyone, so that so far as we were concerned the notices became as many of our laws, strictly a dead letter; so we worked away, the driver now being completely under our control, pulling an ivy leaf here, a sprig of heather there, a "bit o' the shamrock," occasionally a pretty little flower, until our pockets were overflowing, and resorted to filling our hats; knowing full well that we were American Sovereigns, and compelled by no law save that of etiquette to lift our hats to any foreign potentate, landed proprietor or aristocracy of any kind, so we kept placing the little souvenirs in our *chapeaux* until the space between the crown of our heads and the crown of our hats was actually jammed, when we came to the pretty little shaded resting cottage, placed there by Mr. Herbert for the accommodation of visitors.

We entered quite unconcernedly, to find the keeper of the grounds with his little family comfortably seated at dinner. The "Colonel" kept nudging us with his elbow and gently whispering, "Keep on your hats," "Keep on your hats;" but we did not understand him, and having forgotten all about the hat being full of "forbidden fruit," our American politeness, in slang parlance, "gave us most emphatically and completely away," for off went our hats as we entered the door, and down fell a quart of leaves, flowers, &c., and lay scattered at our feet. To say it was a predicament but mildly expresses the feelings we then endured; the sagacity of the "Colonel" saving him nicely, while "Carlisle," seeing the predicament we were in, as well as our liability to see the inside of the "Bastile," considered discretion much the better part of valor in this instance, and so made a hasty exit, followed rapidly by six feet more of discretion, namely, the Doctor, amid roars of laughter; and so we were compelled to again fill all our receptacles the second time with aforesaid mementos, but we shook hands on our resolution never again to lift our hats to any one under any circumstances while traveling in foreign lands. It was late in the evening when we returned to our hotel, after having had a most delightful drive. We had three young ladies in our party, (not Knights Templar though,) and by a singular coincidence we might call it, three young gentlemen—susceptible young gentlemen, too. One from Allegheny City, a son of one of our most respected citizens, and who for many years graced the bench of Allegheny county, (so Edward M. Jenkins says,) though we have none of his able opinions nor decisions before us; another from West Virginia, and another from New Jersey; and although so far on our tour we have not frequented any "Missionary Society," "Sewing Society" or "Church Social," we cannot expect to be posted in *everything* going on about other people's business, still at this point matters looked mighty interesting, and we certainly hoped to see our venerable Sir Knight Prelate obtain something to do, for he, the Em. Commander and Captain-General, and even our very stately Generalissimo, were actually becoming rusty for want of use. We simply mention this little coincidence, for having traveled that road, we know whereof we speak, that moonlight drives, and seeing old abbeys, &c., by candlelight, are conducive towards the end to which we allude.

Knowing we had a big day before us the following day, Monday, we all went through the "Lady Macbeth" scene again, and retired early; and we thought of all the poor plebeians at home; of how, about that time they would also be retiring, tossing and rolling around, sweltering in hot rooms with a fan in one hand trying to keep cool, and a towel in the other, striking recklessly at pestersome and troublesome flies, longing and praying for daylight and the morning, and remarking then what a horrible night you had passed, and sighing for the primitive days of light-wearing apparel, such as is worn in the lower tropics, and that, say a pair of "sox" and a paper collar might be the full dress for July and August; and we wealthy, traveling, sojourning nabobs, ensconced snugly in our little beds, beneath blankets and comforts, rather too cool if anything for comfort; but as our wealth was exhausted on this pilgrimage, we presume we will have to put in some horrible nights ourselves for some summers to come.

Monday morning at 9 A. M. we were all seated in

jaunting cars and wagonettes, ready for our trip through the celebrated Gap of Dunloe, and down the lakes by boats, and at 9:10 the procession of forty persons in nine vehicles, were on our way thither; down through the pretty roads of Killarney, and as all their roads are macadamized, they are perfectly smooth, and covered over with a beautiful arch of green, the boughs of the large trees growing on either side of the road intertwining and interlacing, forming a beautiful shelter from a sun that would have rendered our ride at least a little uncomfortable, and made it to us so cool and pleasant.

Leaving the streets of Killarney, we passed the Union Workhouse and County Lunatic Asylum on our right, and the handsome Roman Catholic Cathedral on our left. On our way we are given a magnificent view of the picturesque scenery surrounding Killarney and her lakes; on our right, in front and behind us lies a rich and fertile landscape, every inch of which that can possibly be utilized, under careful cultivation, which we are also happy to say is being done by all the latest improved American agricultural machines. A little to our left is the broad lower lake or Lough Leane as it is called a very pretty sheet of water; while on the extreme left as a handsome background to the beautiful valley below, is the chain of mountains all along on that side. On our right, as we pass out from the town, perched on a piece of rising ground are the venerable ruins of Aghadoe, one of the most delightfully situated assemblages of ruins in the kingdom. The castle is but a fragment of a tower about thirty feet in height; the church, a low oblong building, consisting of two distinct chapels, built in 1158, and dedicated to the Holy Trinity. The Round Tower is in no better condition than the Castle; the greater part of the facing stone having been carried away for the erection of tombs in the adjacent burying-ground. About a mile farther along we pass Aghadoe House, the pleasant mansion of the dowager Lady Headley. To our left on the lake side is the *Lake View House*, the residence of James O'Connell, Esq., brother of the late agitator in Ireland. On the same side is seen *Killalee House* and *Beaufort House*, having an extensive and beautiful demesne, and crossing the river Laune, which conveys the surplus water from the upper lake, at Beaufort bridge, and here we are immediately beseiged by a cavalcade of seemingly Mosby guerillas; some one-legged, one-eyed, one-toothed, one-eared, and altogether about as hard a looking "gang" as it was ever our misfortune to meet. These fellows ride along, and blather away about taking their horses or ponies at the entrance to the gap. Finally we arrive at the famous cottage of Kate Kearney; when out comes little old Kate, (not the original Kate to be sure,) with a jug of the "potheen" under one arm, and a bottle of pure "goats' milk" under the other, but we can say Kate will not speedily become a landowner through the means of such parties as that day visited her.

Here after a little delay we were provided with ponies —ladies having side-saddles to be sure—and we must say all did nobly, including Mrs. M———— of the city of Brotherly Love, who was with us on the tour solely and wholly for her health, she being extremely delicate, and we all sincerely trust that she derived much benefit since from her trip, and was enabled to return to her friends hale, hearty and stout; for, having fallen away as she had done before leaving home, she must certainly have been very ill; and she being a most agreeable and pleasant traveling companion not to speak of her charming daughter Mrs. F————, we should only be too gratified to hear of her complete recovery to her wonted health. Mrs. M———— was the only one of whom we had any fear, thinking it might probably be too rough a ride for her, but she managed through it appearing none the worse. (But, oh, heavens, how we did pity that pony!)

We proceeded on our way through the gap, and everything was going on all right until our friend from St. Louis was giving us a few circus feats and performances. He had been riding successfully for some time with his face to the tail of the pony until tiring of that position, he concluded to turn round without going to the trouble of dismounting, and of course not being used to such "ring tricks," it was like two trains attemping to pass on the same track, it could not be done, for down came our poor friend at the pony's feet, and it was truly a comical sight to see our St. Louis friend alight on his head, his neck, his back, his limbs, his feet in rapid succession, and the poor little innocent pony gazing intently at Robert, and Robert gazing intently at the pony.

The Gap of Dunloe is a wild and narrow mountain pass between the range of hills known as Macgillicuddy's Reeks and the Purple Mountains. It is four miles in length. Sterling Coyne thus writes of it: "On either hand the craggy cliffs, composed of huge masses of projecting rocks suspend fearfully over the narrow pathway, and at every step threaten with destruction the adventurous explorer of this desolate scene. In the interstices of these immense fragments a few shrubs and trees shoot out in fantastic shapes, which, with the dark ivy and luxuriant heather, contribute to the picturesque effect of the landscape." We pass the *Black Lough* where it is related Saint Patrick banished the last snake. A small stream called the *Loe* traverses the whole length of the Gap, expanding itself at different points into five small lakes, each having its proper name, but which are known in the aggregate as the *Cummeen Thomeen* lakes.

We come to Echo Rock, where our guide took his cornet and played several familiar airs, such as "Home, Sweet, Home," "The Old Folks at Home," &c., and the rock echoing back those sweet airs in eight separate and distinct keys, apparently, commencing loud and close to hand, until growing sweeter and fainter as it climbed the mountain side. it was lost in the ninth echo, yet in the eighth each trill or flat or grace note sounded, came back as perfectly and as sweetly as though there had been eight different cornets playing the same bar in different keys. Touters along the road fire off cannon to awaken the magnificent echo which passes from hill to hill, and at every little step are to be found deaf, dumb, lame, decrepit, deformed, maimed persons begging for a six pence. Emerging from the gap we come within sight of the Black Valley, which stretches away to our right and seems lost in its own profundity. The Irish name for this Valley is *Cummeenduff*, *Commenduff*, *Com-a-Dhuv*, *Com-Dhuv* and *Coom-Dhuvh*, and of either of these unpronounceable words the reader may take his or her choice. Mr. Inglis in writing up Irish scenery, says, "this vale is much more striking than that which we have just left, for few could look into its wild recess without a feeling akin to horror." The darkness of the valley is not caused by any excess of vegetation, what exists being, on the contrary, very stunted and sparingly scattered. The effect is produced by the height of the hills surrounding the valley, and the immense quantity of dissolved peaty matter in the water. Mr. Wuidele describes the valley much more concisely and truly than we could attempt to do, and he gives this as his description: "On our right lies the deep, broad desolate glen of Coom Dhuv, an amphitheatre, buried at the base and hemmed in by vast mountains, whose rugged sides are marked by the course of the descending streams. At the western extremity of the valley gloomily reposes, amid silence and shadows one of the lakes or rather circular basins of dark still water, *Loch-au-bric-dearg*, 'the lake of chav, or red trout.' Other lesser lakes dot the surface of the moor, and uniting, form at the side opposite the termination of the gap. A waterfall of considerable height enjoying the advantage not common to other falls in Ireland, of being plentifully supplied with water at every season of the year."

The whole valley is a black, scarcely defined prison, and the water throws back the light, which it receives by reflection from the clouds, giving the idea of being lighted from below. We now proceed down the pathway leading through the valley, and speaking a moment ago of begging, we will give one example which for notorious and unmitigated cheek surpasses anything we have ever met in our little experience. We were passing down this little narrow path when we were tackled by one of the most frightful looking women we had ever beheld, in her bare feet, with her hair dirty and tousy, and her face accustomed to long exposure in the burning sun, one solid mass of freckles the size of three cent silver pieces, and she styled herself the "Colleen Bawn." Heaven preserve us from the Colleen Bawn! Eileen was her name, and as we rode along, Eileen importuned us one by one to invest in one of her "picturs," asking a sixpence therefor, and there is nothing we regret so much now, that we did not invest in a "sample copy" of the same, that through the aid of woodcuts or steel plate, we might be able to produce the image of "Eileen" in this work for the inspection of the reader, and our fortune would have been an assured fact. However, to resume, "Carlisle" happened to be riding in company with the "Major," who was carrying an awful look of disdain upon his usually pleasant countenance, and muttering some camp meeting revival sentences on begging in general, when to rid himself of "Eileen, the pest," he dived his hand deep down into his pants pocket and pulled forth an American five and one cent piece. Holding the five cent piece towards "Eileen," he inquired of her "if she knew what it was?" "Of course," says she, "its a five cint piece." "Well," says the Major, "take that and go away from me forever;" at the same time replacing the one cent piece in his pocket, when "Eileen" coolly said, "but, Misther, couldn't yez give me the other cint, too." It is scarcely necessary to add that the look of disgust on the Major's face did not change to a pleasant smile by any means, at this further show of consummate impudence. A certain gentleman from Allegheny City, who enjoys a wide reputation of supplying juicy pieces of tender meat to the families of said city, became quite infatuated with the "Colleen Bawn," and invested in one of her pictures, saying "he just wanted to show it to his wife;" but none of us believed a word of it, and we do not think he has shown it to this moment to her.

It was also rumored at headquarters, as well as in the camp, that the Doctor, and even our gallant Colonel, were very much taken with "Eileen." Of course they were very careful, but the Major and "Carlisle" can at any moment testify to the sweet glances cast by them to she of the tousy hair and little "barefoot." All along this path we are met by women, children strapped to their backs, *a la* Indian squaw style, and they knitting at stockings thick enough for horse blankets, and the prices asked for a pair would keep a horse comfortable under a covering during the winter.

Arriving at the head of the Upper Lake, we seat ourselves on the grass, and are served with a fine luncheon of cold chicken and sandwiches, brought us by the boatmen, and, having finished the same, we enter the boats with four rowers to each boat, dressed in pretty white sailor suits, the grand old "Stars and Stripes" at the bow of each of the little boats, and three rousing cheers are given for the flag of our country as we sight it.

We now proceed down the Upper Lake, near which is situated Lord Brandon's cottage, from which the tourist, if he is so disposed, can ascend the Purple Mountain; this we failed to do, owing to lack of time. The Upper Lake is in length two and a half miles, and three-quarters of a mile in breadth, covering an area of 430 acres, containing twelve islands, ranging from a rood to an acre in size. It is generally admitted to be the finest of the three lakes, not for the lake itself, as the Lower Lake far surpasses it for grandeur, combining, as it does, many of the softer beauties of wood and water with the grand mountain scenery, and the wild rocky shores, which hem it in on all sides.

Arbutus Island is one of the largest in the lake, and takes its name from the fact of its being completely covered with the beautiful plant whose name it bears. The leaves of this plant, even in winter, are of a rich, glossy green, and so clustered at the termination of the branches, that the waxen, fresh-like flowers which hang in graceful racemes, or the rich crimson, strawberry-like fruit, seem cradled in a nest of verdure. Mr. Coyne, who, we think, rather exaggerates in his writings of Irish scenery, leading the tourist to expectations even greater than in reality are to be gratified, and in speaking of Macgillicuddy's Reeks, in connection with this lake, puts his description in these lines:

> "On the left, the Reeks
> Lift to the clouds their craggy heads on high,
> Crowned with tiaras fashioned in the sky,
> In vesture clad of soft ethereal hue,
> The Purple Mountains rise to distant view
> With Dunloe's Gap."

And Weed, in his work, says "The Upper Lake displays much greater variety than the others, but that variety arises from different combinations of the same wild and uncultivated features; in picturesque scenery, indeed, it far surpasses all the other lakes, and it is only by a patient examination of its shores, and particularly of the deep inlets along it, that ts full beauties can be discovered. As we near the eastern end of the Lake, it becomes but a narrow strip of water, more than half a mile long, called Newfoundland Bay, and every little island has a yarn about it which the boatmen will spin out; indeed, from the time you enter Ireland until the time you leave it, you become literally jammed full of lies, so that there would scarcely be room enough for another square meal.

One huge mass of rock, called the "Man of War," resembles an upturned hulk of a vessel, exactly, and of course there is a lie in connection with it; and there is another with the resemblance of a foot-print in it, and that is where some ancient giant stepped in crossing the lake, once upon a time; and from its appearance, not only "were there giants in those days," but those giants must certainly have been troubled with corns. We then come to the Eagle's Nest, a precipitous rock, rearing its head seven hundred feet above the river, and is eleven hundred feet above the level of the sea, and in its chasms the American Bird of Paradise makes itself comfortably at home. The echo from this huge rock, as well as those surrounding it, is remarkable; a call from the cornet or bugle is repeated nearly a dozen times, and answered from mountain to mountain, sometimes loud and without interval, and then fainter and fainter, and after a sudden pause again arising as if from some distant glen, and then dying insensibly away. As we approach the "Meeting of Waters," the entrance to the Middle Lake, we pass through below the Old Weir Bridge, through the arch of which the water rushes, so that the boatmen stop rowing and simply guiding the boat, and we dash through into Muck Ross, or

Middle Lake, containing an area of about six hundred and eighty acres. All will remember Thackeray's description of the Middle Lake, in his "Irish Sketch Book," when, in answer to the question, "What is to be said about Torc Lake?" replies: "When there, we agreed that it was more beautiful than the large lake, of which it is not one-fourth the size; then when we came back, we said, 'No, the large lake is the most beautiful,' and so at every point we stopped at we determined that that particular spot was the prettiest in the whole lake. The fact is, and I don't care to own it, they are too handsome. As for a man coming from his desk in London or Dublin, and seeing the 'whole lakes in a day,' he is an ass for his pains. A child doing a sum in addition might as well read the whole multiplication table and fancy he had it by heart."

Thus saith Mr. Thackeray, and we do not know whether that gentleman was aware when he wrote the "Sketch Book," that Allegheny Commandery was going to see "the whole lakes in a day," or not, but we agree with Mr. Thackeray fully, that we did make asses of *ourselves* in spending but one day on the lakes, and if the admired author will forgive us this time, though he has been dead some sixteen years, we would never give him another chance, were he living, to fore-ordain our coming to the "Lakes of Killarney."

We now enter upon Lough Leane, or the Lower Lake, by passing below Brickeen Bridge. This Lake is five miles long by three in width, and covers an area of some five thousand acres. There are some thirty islands in this lake, none over an acre in area. The names of the islands are derived from the supposition of their being the resort of different animals, or from some fancied resemblance to some inanimate objects, such as Lamb Island, Elephant Island, Heron Island, Rabbit Island, Stag Island, Otter Island, Gun Rocks, O'Donoghue's Horse, Crow Island, Gannet Rocks, &c.

One legend, of which every inch of ground has a dozen, concerns the O'Donoghues of the Lakes, whose castle on Ross Island lies in ruins, but the fame of whose deeds still lives in the memories of the people, and that legend may be worth giving: " Once every seven years, on a fine morning before the first rays of the sun have begun to disperse the mists from the bosom of the Lake, the O'Donoghue comes riding over it on a beautiful snow white horse, intent upon household affairs, fairies hovering over him and strewing his path with flowers. As he approaches his ancient residence, everything returns to its former state of magnificence; his castle, his library, his prison, and his pigeon-house, are reproduced as in olden time. Those who have courage to follow him over the lake may cross even the deepest parts dry footed, and ride with him into the opposite mountains, where his treasures lie concealed, and the daring visitor will receive a liberal gift in return for his company; but before the sun is risen, the O'Donoghue re-crosses the water and vanishes amidst the ruins of his castle." Now, when the seventh year comes round, Mr. O'Donoghue can count us in for his company on the trip to his hidden treasures, and he can re-cross as much water as ever he has a mind to, or vanish all he pleases, we will take the risk of finding our way home.

Glena Bay is the part of the Lower Lakes first entered, and the quiet beauty which surrounds it, coupled with the sheet of water beyond, which seems to melt into the horizon, gives a favorable impression of the Lake. Then O'Sullivan's Cascade is worthy of a visit, and then we row to Innisfallen Island, which is about half way between the east and west shores of the Lake, and is interesting on account of the historical associations in connection with it, and the charm thrown around it by the poetry of Moore. The island is about 21 acres in extent, and commands the most varied and lovely views of the Lower Lake, its shores, and the mountain scenery. On the island are the ruins of Innisfallen Abbey, which are scattered over the island, and were supposed to have been founded by St. Finian, in A. D. 600, to whom the Cathedral of Aghadoe was dedicated. In this Abbey the celebrated "Annals of Innisfallen" were composed, which work contains scraps from the Old Testament, a compendious, though not by any means valuable, universal history, down to the period of Saint Patrick, with a more perfect continuation of Irish history to the beginning of the fourteenth century. The Annals record that, in 1180, the Abbey of Innisfallen, which had at that time all the gold and silver and richest goods of the whole country deposited in it, as the place of greatest security, was plundered by Mildurie, son of Daniel O'Donoghue, as was also the church of Ardfert, and many persons were slain in the very cemetery by the McCarthys.

There is on the island a curious freak of nature in the shape of a tree which spreads at the ground like two separate and distinct trees, and some distance up meets and grows together again, which gives it the appearance, as it is called, of "The eye of the Needle," in connection with which there is the customary yarn, that any unmarried person passing through the space, (about six inches), they will be married within a year; and it was wonderful to see how agile, and particularly, through how small a space the unmarried portion of our party could pass. And after all, it may be necessary for us to take back our assertions of all being yarns and falsehoods in Ireland, for in one instance the legend proved true since our return home, in the case of one of our number.

With the lines of Moore, we say farewell to Innisfallen Island:

> "Sweet Innisfallen, fare thee well,
> May calm and sunshine long be thine,
> How fair thou art, let others tell,
> While but to feel how fair be mine."

> "Sweet Innisfallen, long shall dwell,
> In memory's dream that sunny smile,
> Which o'er thee on that evening fell,
> When first I saw that fairy isle."

We then rowed across the lake to Ross Island, on the eastern shore, on which is a copper mine, opened in 1804. Crofton Croker asserts that "during the four years that Ross mine was worked, nearly £80,000, or four hundred thousand dollars' worth of ore was disposed of at Swansea, some cargoes producing £40 per ton." He adds "that this very richness was the ultimate cause of its destruction, as several small veins of pure oxide of copper split off from the main lode and ran towards the surface. The ore of these veins was much more valuable than the other, consequently, the miners, who were paid by the quality as well as the quantity, pursued the smaller veins so near the surface that the water broke through into the mine in such an overwhelming degree, that an engine of thirty-horse power could make no sensible impression on the inundation.

The Ross Castle is the next object of our visit, which is a conspicuous object from many positions on the lake, and from the summit is obtained a most delightful view; and from its top we waved the little "Star Spangled Banner" our colors, kindly presented to us on our departure by Mrs. E. C. Rafferty, and which was carried with us all round on our "Crusade." The Castle is, of course, in ruins, being the last to surrender in Munster. It was on the 26th day of July, 1652. Lord Muskerry had been defeated in the County Cork, and many of his followers slain; and retreating to Ross Castle, he held out against the repeated attacks of General Ludlow, and not until "Ships of War" were seen upon the lake did the garrison surrender.

In his memoirs, Ludlow thus narrates the incicident: "When we had received our boats, each of which was capable of containing one hundred and twenty men, I ordered one of them to be rowed about the water, in order to find out the most convenient place for landing upon the enemy; which, they perceiving, thought fit, by a timely submission, to prevent the danger that threatened them. After the surrender, five thousand of the Munster men laid down their arms. Lord Broghill, who accompanied Ludlow, had granted to him " £1,000 yearly out of the estates of Lord Muskerry."

We then visit Muckross Abbey, which is very interesting for its wonderful state of preservation, its age, and beauty of construction, with its pleasant and happy location, standing, as it does, on a beautiful plateau of ground hidden from sight amidst magnificent shade trees of various kinds, while around almost as far as eye can see, what a lovely landscape view, and how strikingly beautiful the fields and grounds are at present, in their bright and pretty green, owing to their season being much later than ours, and they not yet having garnered their harvests, while occasional glimpses may be had of the Lower Lake, from which we have just come.

The Abbey is on the demesne of Mr. Herbert, M.

P. It was founded in 1440, and consists of the Abbey and a church. The cloisters belonging to the Abbey are in the form of a sombre piazza, surrounding a dark court yard, made still more gloomy by the presence of a magnificent yew tree growing immediately in its centre. In the grounds, and within the ruin itself, are the tombs of those who have been and passed away to sleep the long, last sleep, to awake when "the last trump shall sound." One, we deciphered on a tomb-stone as being dated August 12th, 1213, and several more from that date up to 1700; and on one stone, we saw that one man had died in 1799, at the age of one hundred and fourteen years.

Here our jaunting cars are in waiting for our return, to convey us to the hotel, and, driving along the beautiful drive, with constant and ever varying scenery, clumps of trees, elegant and rare ferns, and blooming heather, with occasionally small open places to spacious grounds, we see growing many fine species of sub-tropical plants; sometimes in the shade of trees, at others full and enchanting views of the lake and scenery opening out to us; all around on our left are the mountains, all covered with heather, and the "Myrtle of Killarney,"—the Arbutus wood. Not a speck of cultivation is to be seen on the side of any of the hills which range from 1,100 to 3,000 feet in height, and the more mild and picturesque scenery on the right, makes them grander and nobler than were the country continually mountainous, and relieves what would be a monotony of beauty in the valley below. On the summit of one of these mountains is one of the *alleged* deepest lakes in the world, called the "Devil's Punch Bowl," so deep, in fact, that one day some foolish, venturesome man, (we will wager some Yankee to plant a "Bitters" or "Cuticura" sign) climbed to the top of this mountain and tumbled in, going all the way through to Australia, landing at some lady's feet, and men were so scarce in those days, that she gobbled him up and took him unto herself. *Fact !*

We can truthfully say, this day, a glorious day spent amid glorious scenery, is one that will ever be remembered as one of the brightest, sparkling gems in all our bouquet of sight-seeing, as well as the many pleasantries interspersed and experienced throughout the day, and which will never be forgotten.

As we neared our hotel, the coach of another hotel passed us, filled with newly arrived tourists, and happening to have our flag floating in the breeze, it was greeted with cheers loud and strong, and clapping of hands, and we were satisfied America was to be represented on the following day on the same ground we were just leaving.

We should liked to have made the ascent of Mangerton, until lately considered the highest mountain in Ireland, and also Macgillicuddy's Reeks, but our time being short, we were for the time being compelled to forego that privilege; so after satisfying our appetites after our hard day's sight-seeing, we retired to our rooms, and at nine o'clock Tuesday, the following morning, bade farewell to Killarney and take train for Dublin.

Letter No. 4.

Killarney to Dublin.—Knights Templar transposed into Knights of Submission.—Full Account of the Impressive Ceremonies of Initiation, as well as the Grand Ennobling Principles of the Order.— In Dublin.—Incidents by the Way.

IS with sincere regret we leave Killarney. We would feign have remained and rested a few days longer, for it seems to us we could never tire of its scenery, or of talking of it; and we have been wonderfully favored as to weather, not having had since our day of landing, one drop of rain, nor even a mist, though we had been lead to believe it rained about three hundred and twenty-five days in the year in Ireland. It is a feast for the eye here —all that beautiful, rich and fertile valley round and about us seems to lift itself, and smilingly say: " Pilgrim, I greet thee." We would tarry, if we could, much longer to feast our eyes on such a banquet as Dame Nature has prepared for those who will only come and partake.

And just here the beautiful thought struck us,

expressed by one of the brightest, shrewdest and most astute criminal lawyers at our county bar, if he has his equal in this great Commonwealth, who, in a murder trial on one occasion in pleading the defendant's cause, brought forth this thought: " That although the poor prisoner at the bar had no friend, no relative in this wide world to plead his cause, save a paid advocate, yet to some one that face had been as sweet and dear as were any of those he was then addressing to their friends;" and we thought it aptly applied here in this little town where we were, that no matter how bloated, how scared, how besotted, how haggard, how ugly a face was, yet to some one in this wide world, thousands of miles off in America, Australia, or to some one now filling a narrow grave, that face had been as dear, sweet and beloved as the most beautiful face and complexion of any fair Cleopatra. Some one living, or that has lived, loves or loved that face—though now with sunken eyes or bleared countenance—as dearly as they loved their own. And so it struck us, continuing the thought in the National face of Ireland. Cursed by the corruption of her notorious land-owners, the finger of scorn and ridicule pointed towards her, for her people, their darkness superstition and ignorance, yet an Almighty Being has given her in nature a face that every Irishman justly loves, and loves so much they would die for her. And no wonder they love that face; no wonder they love to call it the Green, the Emerald, and Erin's Isle. 'Tis here nature shows her beauty. Covering her face at many points on the approach to her rock-bound coast, yet as you advance to her Killarney Lakes, she boldly removes her hands and exposes to the tourist a profile, rich in beauty and handsome in features; and as the great galaxy of beauties are presented in the famed mountains of Switzerland; the gardens of France and Italy; the stern expression of Scotland; Ireland can modestly and conscientiously thrust herself in upon the claimants for praise, and though perhaps not to receive the prize, will at least be furnished the highest commendation.

But we are traveling on schedule time and our timetable says: "Leave Killarney 9:10 A. M., Tuesday, July 16th," and at that hour we bid farewell to Killarney, and are on our way to Dublin, the capital city of Ireland; the distance thither being one hundred and sixty-five miles, and time to run it, eight hours and twenty minutes. These facts and figures we know only because the time-table said so, for we will be honest and make an open confession here, and we will venture to say in every particular we are correct, that with the exception of one short glimpse at the great bogs between Mallow and Dublin, not one person in our compartment in the railway carriage, saw any of the country we passed through, know any of its features or anything else concerning it. For our own part, the 16th day of July, 1878, so far as scenery, distance traveled, or time consumed in traveling it, is in our mind a perfect blank—a page in memory vacant, save the aforesaid compartment, the scenes enacted therein, and *they* are ineffaceably written on the tablet of our mind; and this leads us to the famed " C." K. of S., or one hundredth degree or Knights of Submission.

Our compartment held, as did all the others, eight persons. In it were the irrepressible " Quartette "—the Doctor, the Colonel, the Major, and " Carlisle "—and our venerable, handsome friend John Amsden, Esq., Robert Baxter, Esq., (the renowned and celebrated equestrian, *a la Gap of Dunloe*,) and our friend from Womelsdorf, Pa., one of the noisiest, funniest fellows and loudest talkers we ever had the pleasure of meeting. To our knowledge the poor fellow, who was really very delicate, had never open his mouth from the day of leaving New York up to the time of our parting in London, save to eat his meals and occasionally to yawn. These were the occupants of an Irish railway carriage, and seating themselves the " Quartette " were soon deeply engaged in the usually quiet yet fascinating game of eucher. Now eucher is an innocent little game as a rule, even the rector of the parish may consistently sit down with his wife and children, and " order up and go it alone " with none of his parishioners to "molest or make him afraid," but eucher as all other things can be fearfully abused, and it was on this occasion. We do not desire to be personal in this instance, though duty in writing up the history of this " Crusade " would almost lead us to tell all the truth and nothing but the truth, but we will spare the two who debased the pasteboards. Millions were staked on each game, two of the party, (two well versed in army tactics,) betting their wealth profusely, while the other two looked sadly upon the demoralized pair and meditating upon the fearful consequences, a high official of Allegheny Commandery and an epauletted officer of the United States army were setting to the youthful Amsden, the guileless Baxter, and the noisy Laucks, not to speak of the "innocents abroad" the Major and "Carlisle." On the peril of our lives and the cheerful assurance of a terrible threat of instant death, we were commanded not to tell on them upon our arrival home, not even to ever whisper anything concerning their gambling propensities, but acting under the advice of eminent counsel and a reminder by conscience of our duty in the premises, we cannot afford to be derelict; and there we were, covered by a Colt's five-shooter in the hands of one, and a full grown stiletto in the hands of the other, and patiently compelled to sit and hold the sovereigns those two money-making plebeians were playing for. The eucher playing went rapidly on; both were euchered out of all they had, for we had been gradually coaxing up our courage, and having nursed it to the proper pitch, the Major suddenly rushed his hands up through his raven and beautifully curled locks; "Carlisle" loosened his cravat and by a strategic movement captured the money, pocketed the bank, dared either to lay hands upon us, and from that date the playing proceeded in a manner becoming people hailing from a land of freedom, an enlightened nation and a Christian country. (All fact!)

As the day advanced it became very warm, a hot sun was pouring down its rays upon the roof of the carriage, and having worn out a couple packs of pasteboards, we were left in a state of " unfixedness," nothing to do, time hanging wearily upon our hands, in short, Micawber like, we were simply waiting for something to " turn up."

Active minds such as those could not long remain idle, and knowing full well humanity was suffering very greatly from the evil of never knowing how to patiently submit to misfortune, evils, drawbacks, adversity, &c., it dawned upon the minds of the " Quartette," and, singular coincidence, almost simultaneously, proving again the oft-used expression, "that great minds run in the same channel," to take up the mantle of philanthropy, in favor and hope of benefiting mankind ; so, following the thought, and girding our loins with these noble principles, we founded then and there the one hundredth degree or Knights of Submission. We trust the time draws nearer and nearer when we shall see this order—founded, as it was, by noble men, and for a noble purpose—spread rapidly from quarter to quarter of this great and magnificent world of ours, until the American, the European, the Asiatic, and the African shall be brought within the fold of its well founded principles and teachings ; and then, and not until then, shall this world—not as in parts, but as in one vast whole—move forward in the steady tread of progress, making the ball of advancement, elevation and education roll as though regulated by a faultless machinery.

Oh, yes! ye nations; nations yet in darkness, and yet unborn, away in the unseen and unknown future, the generations now rising and still to come will turn back the pages of history and sing loud songs of praise to the Doctor, the Major, the Colonel, and "Carlisle." Parents and grand-parents will sit around the cheerful fire of midwinter, in the happy family circle, with children upon their knees, and tell of the heroic deeds and humanitarian thoughts of the aforementioned personages, and their names shall be lauded in the mouths of the nations, and, more than that, to those four will be given the honor, by all the sterner sex, who, from excess of work in the club room of the evening before, unselfishly sleep their sweet sleep, while their wives, who never have anything to do, no sick children to attend to, arise early to see that the household duties are proceeding in a manner that will prove satisfactory to their weary liege lords; we say, to those four will be given the honor due them, of having instituted an order, whose first fundamental principle is Submission, so that with the thermometer twenty degrees lower than nothing, he may with due propriety, at 5 A. M., awaken and gently remark, "Arline or Rosalba, get thee down and start the fires," and Arline or Rosalba patiently, beautifully and cheerfully submits to this noble Sir Knight, and many other such cheerful examples we could set forth.

The "Quartette" formed the charter members, and constituted themselves at once the Subordinate and Grand Lodge of the World, and, as is supposed by many, that all secret societies love darkness rather than light, we could not depart from the customary usages and so constituted this a very dark-lantern society, and at once proceeded to the election of officers, the Doctor being *unanimously* elected Grand Mogul—we say *unanimously* for very simple reasons, these were the stubborn facts, that the Major had too much of his otherwise symmetrical frame turned under for pedals, the Colonel had grown too much broadways, and "Carlisle" had not yet reached the height of a giant, and, of course the Doctor usurped the position, none of us, in fact all combined, scarcely felt the ability to compel him to submit to a decorous nomination and parliamentary election, so we simply had the pleasure of teaching ourselves the first cardinal point our order—we submitted. We then went into secret council, " pulled down the blinds," that the curious and outside world might have no knowledge of our secrets, formed the obligations to our degree, which ran about in this wise: " That if any of the secrets were ever revealed by the candidate, they would, upon their arrival in London, be taken to London Bridge, at the dread hour of midnight, and there chucked over to become food for the little fishes in the Thames, or converted into oleomargarine mud, which is prolific in the river of that name," &c. Then we formed our pass-words and our signs, but fearing to leave weeping and mourning friends we dare not give them; we leave them to the charitable and thoroughly posted people who make up the Anti-Secret Society. We were then declared constituted, open and ready for business, and, without further ado, proceeded to the initiation of the remaining occupants of our compartments, the first being our venerable and worthy and social friend Mr. Amsden, then Robert Baxter, but for fear our friend Laucks would make more noise than ever, we made him an honorary member, declining to put him through.

We needed a solicitor for our order, and employed our friend Mr. C. P. Cooper, our gentlemanly conductor, for that responsible position, and made him an honorary member also, and he did his work nobly, as he can do all he takes in hand, and at each station he furnished us a fresh candidate, and between each station the degree was conferred, so that the order flourished beyond our most sanguine expectations, and we can assure you it was healthy. The ceremonies were very solemn, impressive and interesting, particularly impressive, and varied to suit the various candidates. For instance, our two jolly good friends, Clinton and Fullerton, (very healthy gentlemen too, by the way,) were our first victims. They were poked into our compartment beaming with smiles. All within was quiet; calm and death-like stillness prevailed; but no sooner had the train pulled away from the station than Grand Mogul—the Doctor—vociferously yelled in his deep basso voice we have heretofore alluded to, "for the two villains to take off their hats." All sat looking on solemnly, and the poor fellows looked around in blank astonishment at this stern command, and, we presume, during their thoughts forgot to carry it out, at least the hats did not come off as briskly as should have been done, so in an instant the hands of the " Quartette " swept off the head coverings as though by magic, portions of their natural capillary substance with them. " Sit down," yelled the Grand Mogul in a still louder and deeper voice, and, of course, there were no places for the poor fellows to rest their weary, trembling bodies, when immediately four hands placed them in a horizontal position. This latter part of the imposing ceremonies they attempted to resent, it was getting pretty warm in there, so off went coats and hats; and handling the candidates thusly until we reached the next station, we inculcated into them, practically and thoroughly, the beauties of Submission, and on the stoppage of the train we were all serenely settled for another unsubmissive victim. Along came our hard working Solicitor with poor Dr. Wm. M. Herron. We felt sorry for the Doctor, as he was suffering considerably from an attack of rheumatism, but he, with all other fellow mortals, must be taught the principles of our order. Yet he did look like a lamb led to the slaughter. We dealt with him as gently as possible, however—put him on the broad of his back, and six or seven sat down on him.

We got fearfully weak in the back when we tackled

our venerable prelate, Sir Wm. H. Slack. He wore his usual serene countenance, a merry twinkle was in his eye as he surmised some job was afloat, and was smoking the inevitable "tobie." With all our combined force it was as much as we could do to plant the professor on the back of his "Prince Albert," but having him once there, his stately person made an excellent cushion for the valiant Knights of Submission, while the combined whoops in the victim's ears would have done credit to the noble Sioux warriors. Poor Stackhouse! will any ever forget him? he wasn't well at all. He was a lover of our favorite American garden vegetable, the cucumber; he didn't feel good nohow; we put him through in haste, and as tenderly as possible. Then there was Eyster and Levis, always prim, neat and just so; of course they suffered fearfully. Levis bought two new pairs of eye-glasses in Dublin, and Eyster—well, George didn't wear any, else he would have been necessarily compelled to go and do likewise. Then there was our friend who had had the trouble with the custom house officers at Queenstown, and with the barber at Cork; we refer to the gentleman of the peculiar moustache, and it was a much meditated upon question whether to run the risk of having our eyes put out in initiating him or not, but we accepted the danger, and he—well he went with our two last friends and bought himself a new moustache.

Our good friend, Fred Beilstein, was commanded to take off his coat in the presence of the Grand Mogul. No, he wouldn't do it; the result was, he was but as an infant in there, strong and all as he is; and we'll guarantee Mrs. B. has every reason to be thankful, for if her husband will not carry up the coal, cut the kindling wood and start the fire on cold mornings—we simply hint—several members of the order live in the city in which her husband resides, and can most effectually put him through again if necessary and in the shortest kind of metre.

Seeing that we have so frequently committed ourselves in exposing the forms and ceremonies of initiation, we cannot see that much more harm can befall us by giving the "passwords." They were "Sit down!" given in a loud tone of voice, and in a manner only members could recognize, and the answer to that was, "Come down and we'll make it pleasant for you." Yes, *pleasant*. Exceedingly so. Thus the day passed, and it was a terrible one, equaled only by one other to which we are to come, and no one could adequately describe the doings of that day.

At 5:30 P. M. we arrived in the famous Irish capital, and were driven to Morrison's Hotel, where we had supper, then the "Quartette" made for a shaving saloon. We struck one, and even in so large a place as Dublin it was not much better than our experience in Cork. We got scraped, returned to the hotel and retired early. In the morning some ill-disposed wretches stuffed the toes of the "Majah's" and Colonel's shoes with wads of newspapers, and only the ever-ready corkscrew of the Colonel relieved the necessity of their staying indoors that day, or buying a new pair of "brogans."

After breakfast the "Quartette" procured a jaunting car and were soon down to work at sight-seeing in the Irish capital. We had a hard day's work of it, for Dublin being a very old city, full of interesting objects and points of interest for strangers, and our visit to this ancient city being confined to one day, every moment of our limited time was fully occupied, and to advantage.

Dublin is situated on the river Liffey, which, running from east to west, divides the city into nearly two equal parts, and upon a noble bay bearing the same name as the city.

This famous old Irish city contains about 300,000 inhabitants, represented in religion by about these figures: Catholics, 240,000; Episcopalians, 40,000; Presbyterians, 5,000, and of various other denominations, 5,000. It contains many fine buildings and is the seat of the famed Trinity College, and has beautiful parks, botanical gardens, museums, a picture gallery, and theatres. We visited first the Bank of Ireland, which building was formerly used by the Irish House of Lords, which was begun in the seventeenth century and cost £4,000. Originally intended for a hospital it became successively the seat of justice and a mansion. The present building, however, was commenced in 1729 and completed in 1787, costing altogether £95,000. The company of the Bank of Ireland purchased it in 1802, for the sum of £40,000 and an annual rental of £240. There is nothing particularly striking about the building itself, it being like all others over there, evidently erected to stay. It is somewhat semi-circular in shape, with a beautiful colonnade of Ionic columns facing College Green, and a portico in the centre, in the tympanum of which is placed the Royal Arms, appropriately surmounted by emblematical figures of Hibernia, Commerce and Fidelity. The entrance to the former House of Lords was by a portico on the eastern side, the columns presenting the anomaly of the Corinthian order. The figures here are Fortitude, Liberty and Justice. The House of Lords to which visitors are admitted remains unaltered, save that the site of the throne is occupied by a statue of King George III.—America's sincere and great friend. (?) The chairs as used by the lords, are still in their places, the long table in the centre and the old tapestry hangs upon the walls. This has on the left a representation of King William crossing the Boyne, with poor Schomberg expiring almost under his horse's feet; and on the right the siege of Derry. Both these pieces of fine needle work, which eclipse all efforts of our American ladies with their fancy work, are in most excellent state of preservation.

The mantle-piece in this room is very deserving of notice, being formed of dark Kilkenny marble, beautifully sculptured. We were kindly shown, by an attendant clad in livery that for gorgeousness would make a United States Major General's handsome uniform actually appear shabby, the interesting operation of printing bank notes.

Directly opposite the Bank stands Trinity College,

a handsome Corinthian structure. It was founded under authority of Pope John XXII, closed in the time of Henry VIII, and re-opened in the reign of his daughter, Queen Elizabeth, who incorporated it in 1592, as the College of the Holy and Undivided Trinity.

James I. and Charles II. befriended the College, for it had fallen to a very low ebb after the civil wars of the protectorate, endowing it with lands in Ulster and other parts. Private individuals also made liberal bequests, among others those of Erasmus Smith are deservedly esteemed, seeing that no less than five professorships have been endowed by him alone.

For a thorough good education, practical in its results, it exceeds, perhaps, Yale, Oxford or Cambridge, although not bearing the same name for entering young men into society as either of the last named, which should be the best recommendation it could have. It is built of Portland stone, and measures 300 feet in length, the color of the stone is black, and though plain, is very beautiful in appearance. At the entrance are very handsome statues of Burke, Foley and Goldsmith, cast in bronze.

The Museum of the College, though small, contains a very fine collection of birds, the specimens being in the best of condition, and in fact all but complete. Among the antiquities are the old charter-horn of King O'Kavanagh, and an ancient Irish harp, said to have belonged to Brien Boroimhe. The examination hall is hung with portraits of illustrious characters, some of them originally students of the College, such as Dean Swift, Bishop Berkely, Archbishop King, Lord O'Neil, and others. In this hall is Hewitson's noble monument to the memory of the Provost Baldwin, a liberal benefactor to the College, who died in 1758. This monument, which is placed on the west side of the room, is composed of black and white marble, with the addition of Egyptian porphyry. It is emblemmatical, and represents the Provost in a reclining position, with an angel at his feet holding a palm branch, while the genius of the university bends over him. Then there is the dining room, containing portraits of Grattan, Lord Avonmore, Lord Chief Justice Downs, Frederick, Prince of Wales, the father of George III., and others. A handsome granite bell tower, ornamented by four statues typifying Divinity, Medicine, Law and Science, was erected at the sole cost of the late Primate Beresford.

The Library is perhaps the most interesting portion of the College, is 270 feet in length. It is entitled by law to a copy of every work published in Great Britain, and contains at present about 250,000 volumes. There is one single collection in one portion which belonged to one person, Baron Fagel, and contains about 22,000 volumes, most of which are very rare, there being one copy of the Gospels, a Latin copy, known as the Book of Kells, and attributed to Saint Columbo, who lived in the sixth century.

In College Green is an equestrian statue, in lead,

of William III., erected in 1701. The figures are bronzed and gilt, presenting rather an imposing appearance.

Dublin, like every other town, has a castle, but not so imposing a one by any means as many others, as it was not intended in its day for defense against invaders from foreign countries, but simply for the protection of its peaceful citizens against the attacks of unruly neighbors.

The Royal Chapel is worth a visit, it being one of the handsomest wood-carved churches in the kingdom, the gallery around the pulpit being surrounded by the elegantly carved coats-of-arms of all the Lieutenant-Governors of Ireland, from 1173 to 1874; and it is now the place of worship of the present Lieutenant-Governor, his family and household. A new handsome pulpit, the gift of the late Lord Carlisle, has lately been erected at the northeast side, and is entered from one of the pilasters, no stair-case being visible from the Chapel. Over the altar window, which is of painted glass representing the Passion, are figures of Faith, Hope and Charity. The Chapel was opened in 1814.

St. Patrick's Hall, or the Grand Ball Room, is a spacious apartment, appropriately ornamented; the empannelled ceiling bears in its centre a large allegorical painting of George III., supported by Justice and Liberty. In it are also chairs for the Queen and the Prince and Princess of Wales, which they all sat in when here in 1861. Of course, we all "obsquatulated" ourselves into each of the three chairs. Then the Royal Palace is to be seen, where Queen Victoria also sat in 1861, and, of course, we "sitted" therein too.

An Act of Parliament was passed August 10, 1854, to provide for the establishment of a "National Gallery of Paintings, Sculpture and the Fine Arts," for the care of a public library, and the erection of a public museum, and the building was begun in 1859, and opened in 1864, and cost £29,000. We next visited the Cathedral of St. Patrick. This venerable saint erected a place of worship near the well in which he baptized his converts. The present building was begun by Archbishop Comyn, in 1190, though the original building was founded in 890. In 1362, the Cathedral was accidentally destroyed by fire, but was re-built and decorated in 1370, by Archbishop Minot. The building is cruciform, consisting of nave, transepts, choir and lady chapel. Many monuments decorate the interior; in the chapel is a tablet to the memory of the Duke of Schomberg, with an inscription by Dean Swift, at one time Dean of the Cathedral. Then there is a monument to the Earl of Cork, consisting of black marble, decorated with wood carving, gilding and painting, and represents the Earl and his lady in recumbent positions, surrounded by their children, sixteen in number. In close proximity are two marble slabs, which mark the resting place of Dean Swift, and Mrs. Hester Johnston, the "Stella" of his poetry. The Cathedral has been entirely restored since 1860, at the sole cost of the late Sir B. L. Guinness, the celebrated brewer, who expended upwards of £140,000 upon it.

The General Post Office is a building of considerable beauty, surmounted by figures of Hibernia, Mercury and Fidelity. Nelson's Monument, a tall, fluted column 121 feet high, exclusive of the statue, stands beside the post office, and cost £6,856, raised by subscription.

The Four Courts we visited with Judge Moreland, but no courts were in session save the Court of Chancery, and we were deprived of the pleasure of hearing a good Irish speech from one or more of their learned barristers.

The Four Courts is termed that, from the courts of the Queen's Bench, Chancery, Exchequer, and Common Pleas, being situated within one building. The present structure was commenced on the site of a decayed Dominican monastery, in 1776, and it was finished in 1800, and cost £200,000. (It will be observed they know how to spend money in Ireland quite as well as in Pittsburgh, Allegheny, &c.) A handsome Corinthian portico occupies the centre and over it rises a finely proportioned pediment, bearing on its upper angle a colossal statue of Moses; the other angles bear like statues of Mercy and Justice; and on the corners are statues of Wisdom and Authority. The great hall is circular, and sixty-four feet in diameter; and serves as a common hall, with exits to the different special courts. It is illuminated by jets of gas issuing from a torch borne in the hands of a colossal statue of Truth.

Another statue, that of Sir M. O'Loghlen, by McDowell, is worthy of notice.

We then visited Christ's Church Cathedral, sometimes styled the "Church of the Holy Trinity." This building was commenced in 1038, and has quite an interesting history in connection with its age. It was made the repository for various relics, and among others the shrine of St. Cubie, stolen by the people of Dublin from the Welsh. It was in this Cathedral that the church liturgy was first read in Ireland in the English tongue. In 1553, Queen Mary ordered mass performed in the Cathedral, which was done for six years, when the reformed style of worship was restored. This place of worship is a great attraction to those fond of display of a cathedral service, which is performed every Sunday at eleven o'clock by a full choir. Henry Roe, distiller, expended £200,000 in the restoration of the building to its present beauty.

From the centre of Carlisle Bridge, so called in honor of Lord Carlisle, who was viceroy at the time when the bridge was commenced in 1782; is obtained one of the most interesting views within the city.

In front of City Hall is Hogan's statue of O'Connell; the Hall contains a celebrated statue of Grattan, with the appropriate inscription—

FILIO
OPTIMO CARISSIMO
HENRICO GRATTAN
PATRIA
NON INGRATA
1829.

In Aungier street, we find at No. 12, a queer looking old house, the birth-place of Moore. In this house the Bard of Erin was born on May 28th, 1780.

Surrounding Stephen's Green are the finest houses in the city. Fronting upon it are the Royal College of Surgeons, and the Royal College of Science, the Catholic University, the Shelbourne Hotel, and St. Vincent's Hospital. In the centre of the Green is a statue of George II.

We then drive to Phœnix Park, the Hyde Park of Dublin and the Central Park of New York. It covers an area of 1750 statute acres, and is well planted with timber. Deer are plentiful, and as in other extensive grounds where they are frequently caressed by visitors, are very tame and docile. The park is beautifully laid out in walks and drives, and handsome flower beds. The first object noticeable is the obelisk—the Wellington Testimonial—erected in 1817, by his fellow townsmen of Dublin, to testify their great esteem for him as a military commander. It cost £20,000.

The Carlisle memorial statue which is placed in the "People's Park" is a successful work of art by Foley. It commemorates the Lord Lieutenancy of the late Lord Carlisle, who for six years acted in that capacity. To the right, near the entrance of the park, is the military hospital, with a fine granite front, ornamented with a clock tower and cupola, also the constabulary barrack, where each member of the corps spends a portion of his time in training in the use of arms and other military exercises, subsequent to enlistment, and the zoological garden, and the summer residence of the Lord Lieutenant, and we are through with the park.

Returning to the city we proceed to the exhibition palace, a very elegant building, composed of iron and glass, with a large concert hall to accommodate 3,000 persons and one to accommodate 1,500 persons, a lecture room to hold 500 persons, a practice room for a large orchestra, and a dining room one hundred and seven feet in length and thirty feet wide, and there are also extensive picture galleries, constructed on the most improved principles. The hall, which has its floor laid with encaustic tiles, forms a permanent sculpture court. On entering, the cascade at the end of the pleasure garden is seen in the distance from the hall, which with its Caen stone columns with carved capitals, and those of the picture gallery, form a very effective design.

In the centre of the building is an elegant fountain with groups of figures representing Leinster, Munster, Ulster and Connaught. At the southern end is a picturesque grotto fountain, surmounted by a figure of Erin, and most natural in its construction, beautifully covered with plants of various descriptions.

During our visit to Dublin, the annual rose show was in exhibition at the palace, and such a display of those beautiful flowers we have never seen; every possible variety and family, and had we not seen the size of some and been told of them, we could not possibly have been led to believe it; oh! how rich and beautiful they were; and such a collection of pansies; while the fragrance filled the air so sweetly, we should have loved to have remained forever in that approach to the dwellings of the fairies.

But we cannot stop to describe minutely all the buildings of prominence with which Dublin abounds, for our time is limited and we must hurry on. There is the Custom House, in the centre of the front of which is a fine allegorical composition, representing Britannia and Hibernia in a marine shell, a group of merchantmen approaching, and Neptune driving away famine and despair. An attic story rises behind the pediment and on this are placed right above the doric columns of the portico, colossal statues of navigation, wealth, commerce and industry. On the north side it is decorated with well designed figures representative of Europe, Asia, America and Africa. Then there is the Mechanics Institution and the Royal Hibernian Academy, erected in 1824, for the promotion of the fine arts.

In Britain street is the gloomy building named Newgate, the scene of poor Lord Fitzgerald's death in 1798, where in the same year the barristers, Henry and John Sheares, with John McCann, Secretary to the Leinster Committee of United Irishmen, were all executed for high treason. We then come to King's Inns, a beautiful and imposing building. The Library is a new building erected in 1827, and cost £20,000. But we must hastily pass over Stephen's Hospital, the Royal Hospital, the Corn Exchange, Linen Hall, Conciliation Hall, the

K

scene of the great O'Connell triumphs; St. Mary's Church, St. Michael's Church, St. Andrew's Church, one of the oldest chapels in Dublin; St. Nicholas' Church, and many other interesting points. And feeling that we had done a hard day's work, we returned to our hotel about 6 P. M., for dinner, and to prepare for the reception to be tendered us on that evening by Lodge No. 33 of Ireland, and presided over by the Grand Officers of the Provincial Grand Lodge of Ireland.

At 8 o'clock a committee called and escorted us in a body to the Masonic Temple, where the Grand Officers of the Grand Lodge of Ireland were in special session to receive us. Here we saw the Masonic work of Great Britain exemplified, and about 10 o'clock we were conducted through the building, which was illuminated throughout for our benefit, and they have a very handsome building indeed. A strange but beautiful feature in their commandery room is the reflection upon the windows (stained glass,) which has the appearance of the lights being on the opposite or outside of the windows. The Prince of Wales, his brother the Duke of Connaught, and several other dukes and earls, have their own chairs here, with their coats-of-arms engraved thereon. We were then conducted to the large and spacious banquet hall, where an elegant repast was spread, consisting of meats, vegetables, etc., in many courses, as well as all the delicacies of the season in fruits, not only of their own, but also of our own and other countries, common with us, but rare there. We spent with our brethren of Dublin an evening that shall never be forgotten; the social and fraternal kindness shown us by each and every individual was truly great and beyond any anticipation. Speeches and songs were indulged in, and loud were the shouts of applause and cheers that rang through that hall upon Deputy Grand Master Shekleton concluding his address of welcome, which was cheerfully responded to by our Em. Commander, Lee S. Smith. But the palm of the evening, notwithstanding the fact that most of the presiding officers there were Dublin's pick of barristers, was our little Captain-General's reply to the toasts of "Our American brethren" and the "President of the United States," when our modest and unassuming friend, Sir William C. Moreland, arose, and in his slow, quiet manner commenced his remarks, every word and sentence measured, weighed and counted. He spoke for three-quarters of an hour, and seemed in such excellent trim for it, the words seemingly rolling from him as pouring water from a bucket. His language, eloquence and oratory, of which he is the most gifted person in our knowledge, were simply grand, and with what wonderful beauty his periods were rounded, equaled only on one occasion, viz: on his address at Library Hall, New Year's Eve, 1876, when his vivid and eloquent description of Samson being brought forth from his dreary prison, to bring, in a few moments, death to so many of his enemies, none will ever forget who heard him. It took some time to settle down after the cheers and applause of the Major's address, and no more speechifying for that evening.

Several songs were given by one or two of their members, and by Mr. Slack and one or two others of our party; by the way, one by Col. McConihe, who has a very sweet tenor voice—no, we were mistaken, it wasn't the Colonel either. The meeting was closed by prayer by Sir Knight Dr. Robinson, of Dublin, chaplain of the body we visited. The doctor is one of the finest scholars and linguists in the world, being a good grammatical teacher of thirteen languages. Thus we were received in Dublin, and to one and all of our Dublin friends we can truthfully say, for all our party, it was an evening spent that will ever be remembered as one of the brightest of our Crusade.

We said the Colonel didn't sing there that evening; no, that's so, he didn't. We remember now, the "Quartette" was broken on that evening; Smith, Moreland and "Carlisle" attended the banquet, and we appointed the Colonel a committee of one from the "Quartette" to prepare an "*itinerary*," at which he was an admirable adept. We just left it all to the Colonel, and he did his work nobly, having it ahead as far as London when we were in Dublin; but on our coming back to the hotel after the reception, we were surprised not to see the Colonel busily engaged at his allotted duty, he had concluded to go the theatre. The Colonel was a wonderfully self-denial man.

Morrison's Hotel, at which we stopped, we are sorry to say, was not quite "A 1," and up to the mark, meals being very poor, attendance worse, and house accommodation not much better. We are perfectly willing, however, to make all due allowances for the latter, as the house was undergoing improvements; but we must repeat that the bill of fare, and particularly the attendance, was very poor. It was, however, the only place at which we stopped on our whole tour that was not strictly first-class, and up to the letter of the contract. We will never forget poor Baker at this hotel, the morning we left, and didn't get his breakfast—the look of disgust on Baker's face, to any incoming travelers, would have killed any hotel dead.

The next portion of our letter brings us to one of the most pleasant portions of our tour anywhere, viz: a day with our brethren of Enniskillen; and we are almost afraid to tell how those, noble, big-hearted, grand Irishmen—we cannot use better words than call them genuine Irishmen—received and treated us, for fear of a whole batch of American Masonic bodies packing up and going over there and taking those good people completely by storm; but even with that risk, we cannot refrain from relating one of the most glorious days of the Pilgrimage, so that our good friends of Enniskillen must not hold us accountable if we are the cause of a wholesale imposition upon their kindness and good nature.

Letter No. 5.

Dublin to Enniskillen, Londonderry, Giants' Causeway and Belfast.—Riding on an Irish Locomotive.—A Grand Day Spent with a Glorious People.—A Gala Day with True Friends and the Ladies of Enniskillen.—Incidents by the Way.

ON Thursday morning, July 17th, at 9 A. M., we took train for Londonderry, as prescribed upon our schedule, but through the kindness of our agent, Mr. E. M. Jenkins, subsequent to the arrangement of the tour, and being earnestly solicited to spend a short time at Enniskillen, and from the pressing manner of the invitation we were induced to break our route, to accept the invitation so warmly and cordially tendered, our warm friends of that old city contracting to make up all lost time, and place us again on schedule time table, and had we not done so, had we missed that day, we should never have forgiven ourselves, and knowing what we do now, we should rather have omitted half a dozen other places and sights, than the pleasure of one shake of the hand with those good people. We, never having been there, presumed it would be rather an informal affair in that little inland town; but on our arrival there at 1 P. M., the hearty social welcome tendered to each and every one of our party, made us feel so much at home, that we have many times regretted our visit was not lengthened there to as many days or weeks, as we were there hours. On our way to Enniskillen, passing through a beautiful country, we were kindly permitted to ride upon the engine drawing our train, and there to see how the engineer handles the " throttle" on one of those " blarsted British engines," and it may not prove uninteresting to know how they railroad in that country.

The road on which we are traveling is single track, the engine is not so fine looking as are our American locomotives, not so handsomely finished, nor so symmetrical looking in its entirety; the engineer has no " cab," and consequently is continually exposed to the inclemencies of the weather, and while on duty is not permitted to sit down under any circumstances. They have, however, a method for running trains on single line tracks, that is assuredly a preventative to railroad collisions, instead of by telegraphic and written orders as we do; it is done in this wise: To use an illustration:—Say for instance we use our Union Depot in Pittsburgh as a starting point, and the city of Philadelphia the next nearest stopping station, just before a train would leave the Union Depot, the train dispatcher hands the engineer of the train a wooden block, say six or eight inches long, on which would be a brass plate engraved " Pittsburgh to Philadelphia;" this he places in a socket for the purpose in his cab, or where the-cab should be, then he starts with his train, having the right of way on that stretch to Philadelphia, he then hands the block to the depot master or train dispatcher at Philadelphia, and is again given one stamped say, "Philadelphia to New York" and so on according to distance or schedule time consumed in running his distance.

Now there being but one of these blocks for use between any of these points named, the engineer, and he only, holding the same has the right of way between the two points for which he carries the block; so it will be perceived the chances of collision or colliding are an impossibility, for on a train reaching Philadelphia coming west the engineer could not, and dare not enter the next block until the train bound east on that block reaches Philadelphia, and they exchange their " wooden orders" at that point. Such a system is much slower, of course, than ours, but it is entirely and absolutely safe and secure against accidents, such as telescoping, &c.

As stated, at 1 P. M. we arrived at Enniskillen, which is the chief town of the county Fermanagh and contains about six thousand inhabitants. It is built on an island in the river connecting the Upper and Lower Lough Erne. The principal manufacture is cutlery; a considerable quantity of straw-plait is made in the neighborhood, and the butter market is one of the best in the kingdom. The town is quite an important military station, containing large barracks, and two forts to command the pass across the river. But we prefer to speak more of the people of Enniskillen, their generosity and goodness, than of the town itself, for though on every hand while on our tour kindness was only known to us from the people we had the pleasure of meeting and visiting, yet going there, to every one of them being entire strangers, and they to us the same, the magnanimous reception accorded us on that day will ever remain one of the brightest and greenest spots in our memory of our European Crusade.

Through the kindness of railway officials our effects were permitted to remain in our cars, and during our stop in Enniskillen were sent by special train to the lower end of the Lough to await our coming by steamer.

Arriving at Enniskillen, as stated, we were impressed with the idea that "Barnum" was exhibiting in the neighborhood of the depot, for we are prone to believe not one single person of the six thousand inhabitants was missing, from the crowd that greeted us on our arrival there.

We were received by Dr. O. Ternan, Past Provincial Senior Grand Warden ; Pro. W. Jones, W. M., of 891 of Ireland, and Dep. Provincial Grand Master Col. J. G. Irvine, D. L., High Sheriff of County Fermanagh, and after a hearty handshaking and welcome by these brethren, we were conducted down to the Royal Victoria Hotel. The streets were crowded with the good people of Enniskillen, they coming up indiscriminately to our side, engaging us in conversation, and exchanging many pleasant words with us; while it was a most amusing sight to see the "wee Irishmen" and "wee Irish

lasses," to the number of four or five gross, perched on
the fences like chickens at roost, getting a good square
look at the " Yankees," with loud cheers of pleasure from
their good hearty lungs. Reaching the hotel, we were
immediately taken into the dining-hall, where, if such a
thing were possible, a banquet exceeding even that of
Dublin was prepared and in waiting for us, the table
being profusely covered with beautiful baskets, pillars
and columns of exquisite cut flowers, the air filled with
their sweet perfume, while on every napkin was pin and
button-hole bouquets, all prepared by the young ladies
of the town. Even in that little place the table was
laden with all the delicacies of the season, and with the
notorious appetites each had, and was obtaining. we can
vouch for the fact that Allegheny Commandery did not
have a black mark on that occasion, for any remissness
in duty. Each Sir Knight stood by his post nobly, determined to die ere having the stigma of traitor or traitor
attached to his name, and for " A 1 " staying qualities,
commend us to our worthy friends the Doctor, Major and
the Colonel on such occasions.

We spoke of the young ladies of Enniskillen a moment
ago—ah! there's the point; such a collection of beauty,
rare opportunities are ever proffered for such a sight,
and we venture the very broad assertion, that the daughters, the young ladies of Enniskillen, are not excelled,
if equaled, in their bright, rosy-red cheeks, their every
evidence of robust health, laughing, sparkling eyes, and
teeth of pearl; and there is where we married men who

had left our wives at home, unwilling sacrifices to mosquitoes and "sich," in vulgar *parlance*, had the inside track on our venerable prelate, Professor Slack, and our good friend Schroeder, who, by the way, was on his bridal tour, and it was just about at this point that that fact leaked out, though it was fearful to hear the Doctor, vowing and declaring to some fair young lady of Enniskillen that such a thing as being married had never been thought of by him; and the Major, smiling sweetly, captivating his fair hearer with some beautifully-worded sentences, declaring it had ever been his desire to meet some fair young lady of the Emerald Isle who could love him for himself, and curl his beautiful locks preparatory to wending his way to the four courts of Grant, Fifth avenue, Ross and Diamond streets; while it was even worse to hear the Colonel avowing himself to be a widower living on a full pay pension of the retired list of Uncle Samuel's brave men; and Professor S., telling all around that his wife, who accompanied him, was "Carlisle's" mother, and she his own sister; and Schroeder—well, we won't say anything about him, we'll let him off easy; and Dr. H., too, for we occasionally require the latter gentleman to come and visit us; but the Recorder of the Commandery, feeling it to be his duty, gave each young lady a roster of the Commandery, with a check mark opposite the name of each, which fully explained the bachelor or benedictine state of all.

After our banquet at the hotel, from which floated the beautiful, grand old flag, the "Stars and Stripes," alongside the British Union Jack, the lines were formed and we proceeded to the Militia Barrack Quay, on Lough Erne, but our proceeding there may be better described than we could do it ourselves, by giving an extract from the *Fermanagh Mail*, the live paper of Enniskillen. It says:

"About two o'clock the party proceeded to the steamer " Ross Clare," which lay off the Militia Barrack Quay, where the following awaited the excursionists: Col. Irwin, D. L., High Sheriff of Tyrone, Deputy Grand Master of Tyrone and Fermanagh; Bro. Ternan, Past Prov. Senior Grand Warden, and Mrs. and the Misses Ternan, (3); Brother Price, Prov. G. S. B.; Mrs. Innes, Dunbar, and her sister; Miss Patterson, Clenross; Miss Molyneux; Brother W. C. Trimble, P. M. 891; Miss Trimble; Brother Sinclair Trimble, 891; Brother C. J. Jones, 891; Brother William Jones, W. M., 891; Brother Edward Athill, P. M., 891; Miss Athill; Brother W. H. Morrison; Miss Morrison; Brother J. McCausland, the Lusties; Brother S. Armstrong, W. M., 473; Mrs. Armstrong; Bro. Gunning; Brother B. Gamble; Brother R. C. Donnell, Newtonstewart; Mrs. Scott, O'Magh, and her sister; Brother Dr. Todd; Brother Captain Irvine; Bro. R. Fawcett, Derripin; Brother Dr. Fawcett; Brother G. Duggan; Mrs. O'Leary: Miss James; Brother G. Elliott; Miss Elliott; Brother J. Elliott and Mrs. Elliott; Brother G. Bradshaw; Brother G. Pratt; Brother W. Teele; Brother Ryan, Mrs. Ryan, Miss Ryan, &c., &c."

We would say here, by way of parenthesis, to the *Mail*, who modestly refrains to tell all the story, that we were immediately taken round and introduced, and soon were made to feel, from their general warm-heartedness and sincere kindness, perfectly at home, and were soon well acquainted—no half-way meeting and greeting, but real, true whole-souled welcome.

To resume, the *Mail* says: "About half-past two, the steamer was under weigh, that fact being signified by the discharge of two guns from her stern. On past Portora and Derrygore, the old castle and devenish hoary with age, and rich in the memories of the past and present, past Rossfad and Ross Clare, where the hotel looks down on one of the fairy scenes of Ireland—looks down on a hundred islands clothed in the ripe foliage of summer, rising gracefully as swans from the water—looks down on projecting headland and receding bay, far stretching hills and mountains that distend themselves to the horizon till sky and mountain merge as one in a dim azure blue. The various objects of attention *en route* were pointed out, and as well as the intervals of refreshment and conversation would allow, the legendary stories in connection were told. From Killalea's noble tower a flag betokened a hearty greeting from the owner, who so graciously made it convenient to be present with us, when passing the Lusties, seven small cannon thundered out with a salute, which was answered by lusty cheers from the *voyageurs* on board; and thus with a bright sky overhead, and below the blue lake, and away in the distance the green fields and the blue hills, did the few hours pass—alas! too quickly—while Americans and Irishmen exchanged ideas and related adventures, and perhaps indulged in a little sentiment, for there were many fair ladies on board. Dr. Robert Armstrong, of Belleek factory, presented each of his American brethren with one of his Masonic plates, on which various symbols of the craft are described in order and in artistic style, as a *souvenir* of our visit, the whole illustrating the lectures of the three degrees as is shown by an accompanying circular written by Mr. Armstrong, and which alone would indicate that he is what is popularly known as a "bright Mason."

As the boat approached the wooded shores of Castle Caldwell Point, the Eminent Commander, Sir Lee S. Smith, called our party together and said they had just passed through scenes of singular beauty, and been the recipients of great kindness and cordiality, and that the beauty of Lough Erne and the kindness of Enniskillen friends could not be excelled. Ireland was

"The gem of the ocean,"

and Enniskillen the gem of the tour.

Therefore he called them to order for the purpose of giving them an opportunity of presenting their thanks to the Enniskillen brethren as a testimonial of how they appreciated what had been done for them—(applause) and to Brother Ternan.—(Cheers.)

Sir William C. Moreland, Captain-General, moved that a committee of three be appointed to draw up suitable resolutions expressive of the feelings of the party. The motion was warmly adopted. The Commander then proposed three rousing cheers, American cheers, for the brethren who had done them such honor that day. The cheers, and rousing ones at that, were immediately given, and followed by three "sky-rockets" a peculiar American style of showing approval, in which the "hiss"— "boom" and "ah" are made to resemble the noise of the pyrotechnic article from which it takes its name.

Brother Ternan was then called on, and in reply to loud cries of "speech," then said that Irish Freemasons were always delighted to meet their American brethren. It had afforded the Enniskilleners the greatest pride and pleasure to bring so distinguished a company down the lake, and he hoped they had enjoyed themselves. Their "best" in Enniskillen was small, but they had done their best to give their visitors a cordial Irish welcome, and had they had more time, perhaps more would have been done. But there was a lesson here for outsiders. Years had proved that brotherhood was not merely in name; and he was satisfied that if he went to America he would be received in the same spirit. (Just come out and try, Brother Ternan. In the motto of our noble Order, the Knights of Submission, "We'll make it pleasant for you.") Brother Ternan continued to say, that it was his pride to be not only an Irish Mason, but an American Mason by adoption, for they had adopted him into two of their encampments; and if ever he crossed the Atlantic he would find himself as a brother amongst brethren. The Enniskillen brethren had entered into this matter heartily, and none more so than Brother Armstrong, of Belleek, whom he was glad to see they were about to thank for his plate. Brother Ternan concluded by giving a hearty welcome from the brethren of Fermanagh and Tyrone, and wishing the American visitors a safe and pleasant journey. (Cheers.)

Brother R. W. Armstrong having been called upon amidst loud cheering, arose, and having a satchel in his hand, and said that Brother Ternan's exhaustive speech had left him nothing to say. But he was there as a bag man (laughter,) and though he was bankrupt in words, he was solvent in gratitude. It had been his honor to be a member of this distinguished Order in Fermanagh for twenty-five years, and he could state without fear of contradiction, that no man would be as good and not being a Freemason, as he would be if he were a Freemason. (Cheers.) From his knowledge of the world as a Christian and as a Freemason, he held that religion was a chain that binds man to God, and Freemasonry the silver cord that binds man to his fellow man.

Sir Knight, Major W. C. Moreland, was then called on to "speech," and in reply said that if he remained long in Ireland he would be an Irishman. We had had so many acts of kindness crowded upon them that one place seemed to vie with another in showering its favors upon them; but he thought the handsomest Irish Masons were to be found amongst the Enniskillen party. (A voice: What about the ladies? The Major replied he would come to that.) The Enniskillen Masons were all handsome men, and their remarkably intelligent appearance was only equaled by the modesty with which they had shown their good nature and hospitality. But there was a star that outshone them all. Not only had these Enniskillen brethren brought their hospitality with them, but they had also brought their wives and daughters, their sisters and sweethearts, who were the crowning glory of the Masonic fraternity. There was a young lady in the party he had the good fortune to meet (you see we told you so earlier in this letter, he was happy,) who had the good taste to say she would not marry a man who was not a Freemason. (Must have gotten down to "business" right quick; don't you think so, reader?) He would never forget that sentiment so long as he remembered the emerald green of old Ireland itself. And as long as they had the attachment of their wives and daughters for their brotherhood, all that could be said against Freemasonry would not prevail; no, it would remain as long as the glorious sun kissed their glorious hills and fertile valleys. The feeling of the ladies will make you better and truer men, and more constant lovers. Brother Moreland then proceeded in a flowery strain of oratory suitable to the "silver-tongued orator of Allegheny," to speak of the beauty of Ireland, and concluded with thanks to his host.

Brother Slack, who had been round the excursion in 1871, and was warmly recognized by Dr. Ternan, Price, and others, then sang in truly good style, and with well trained and cultivated voice the Masonic song, "We meet upon the level and part on the square."

All this time we must not forget the scenery of the lake on which we are sailing. Lower Lough Erne is styled the Windermere of Ireland, although wanting the varied picturesqueness of Killarney, it is undoubtedly a charming lake, and abounds with interest to the artist, the antiquary and the naturalist. It is studded with little islets, which dip their luxuriant foliage into the water, adding the beauties of a sylvan stream to the placid sternness of a majestic lake.

To quote again from the *Fermanagh Mail* and reporter; "As we approached the landing, having sailed the entire length of the Lake, some twenty miles, two guns were fired, and the party disembarked at Castle-Caldwell, walking through the demesne to the railway station. Here Brother Calhoun, of Enniskillen, sang a few verses of a "Warrior Bold," and "Carlisle" of Allegheny Commandery, whom it appears they always hold back to the last, made a beautiful flowery speech, which brought forth tears from host and visitors. When we heard those remarks, delivered in his own inimitable style, it was then we wished the party were only arriving instead of leaving." (The reader is asked to please pardon this little piece of Washington or Cocoanut or Lemon thrown in by ourselves, for the *Mail* didn't say anything of the kind.) " Here we took the special train of first-class carriages, which was courteously sent by Mr. Henry Plews, in order that the American party might make up any lost time, and the excursionists took their seats, and amidst hearty farewells and waving of handkerchiefs, the train started for the junction, the writer of this article having consented to a cordial invitation to accompany the party to Derry.

The day spent at Enniskillen, so bright in its memory of things pleasant, will ever be to us an oasis in the desert to the weary and thirsty traveler—one full of delightful remembrances, happy thoughts and pleasant meetings. The warm shake of our right hand will ever feel the tingle of fraternal greeting and brotherly love as given us in the hearty grasp by our Enniskillen friends, and that day the happiest spent by this Commandery on her second crusade.

The *Fermanagh Reporter* thus speaks of the ride to Derry. " What followed in one of the compartments of the down train it is outside my duty to chronicle. The inventive American genius had invented a special degree for the occasion, and in one of the compartments of our carriage sat the head of the Order of Submission, the Grand Mogul. The reader may smile, but perhaps his face would have turned ashy pale if he had been summoned to the august presence. Some gentlemen held back, but the order could not be gainsayed. I was summoned, like the rest, but pleaded that a paper collar and paper cuffs were not fitting attire in which to enter his highness' presence, and the Grand Mogul's Emissary did not take time to examine into the truthfulness of my statement, but subsequently informed me that the G. M. had taken the facts into consideration, seeing that I was away from home and the washerwoman, and in the com- the company of ladies, and that he would postpone the conferring of the 100th degree upon me until I had furnished my wardrobe in Derry with such apparel as would bear the strain. "We will make it pleasant for you," said the valiant, submissive Knights near me; but I escaped the pleasure, and thus my hair remained unruffled and my collar whole.

Let it not be imagined for one moment the gentlemen had all the fun to themselves, for in the next compartment, we heard the cries of ladies as if in distress, and as looking out at the window, I espied two novices as if endeavoring to escape from some tormentor within. They were undergoing initiation in some other degree confined to the gentler sex."

'Twas here the Knights revolted against their head, for we all made one sudden break, and laying Grand Mogul Smith on the broad of his back, using his six-feet eleven for a seat or foot-stool, made Col. McConihe Regent; but soon tiring of his outrageous sway of the sceptre and his villainous decisions, we deposed him as quickly and suddenly as we did Dr. Smith, and the Hon. Judge Moreland was unanimously—not elected, but "boosted" into his place. It was a fearful sight to see the Major sitting on top of a pile of bags, coats, hats, newspapers, sandwiches, canes, dusters, &c., for a throne—collar "busted," necktie flapping in the wind, and face red with laughter. The Major may be very good at running a law office, or conducting a fine case in our Common Pleas or Criminal Courts, may cover himself all over with glory in his addresses to jury and judges, but he is a most complete failure in running a Knights of Submission shop. He occupied the chair for about ten seconds by the watch, and that was the winding up of his bobbin—he soon occupied the horizontal position as did our first-self elected G. M., when "Carlisle" accepted the crown and sceptre and ruled with legal sway—for about two minutes.

A committee received our party at Londonderry on arrival there, but owing to our remaining so long at Enniskillen, we were compelled to forego the pleasure of a banquet and reception which our brethren of Londonderry had prepared for us. It was ten o'clock at night when we reached Derry.

The *Reporter* and *Mail* again says: "Breakfast at eight; was the order that night; it might not have been given but for sake of formality. At ten minutes past one the last gentleman left the coffee-room, and at a quarter past four they were down stairs again. 'They hardly ever sleep,' was observed to me concerning some gentlemen of the party. One thing was clear. They had come to Ireland for sight-seeing and determined to make the most of the time."

In the morning the time-honored walls that witnessed the defeat of the Jacobites and the heroism of its brave defenders were traversed; the Cathedral, with its bomb of 1690, its colors taken from the French, and its organ from the Spanish Armada, was visited; also the Walker column, the great enduring monument of a great leader.

From the tower of the Cathedral could be traced the winding banks of the Foyle, and the spot observed where the boom was placed across the river, and which gave to the shock of the "Mountjoy," and the Heights of Clooney, where the army of King James lay encamped; and we saw "Roaring Meg," that often hurled defiance at the foe, and other guns of similar date.

. Londonderry is situated on the magnificent river Foyle, just before it flows into the Lough of the same name, and which more than half surrounds the hill on which the city stands.

An abbey for regular canons of the Augustine order was founded in Londonderry, in 546, by St. Columbkille, which will give some idea as to the youthful age of the good old city of Derry. The town was fortified by walls, which are still preserved as a promenade, and there were six gates.

The four original gates were called the Bishop's Gate, the Ship Quay Gate, the New Gate, and the Ferry Port Gate. Between 1805 and 1808 the three first were built. The Bishop's Gate and Ship Quay's Gate are are alone embellished. The former is a triumphal arch, and was erected to the memory of William III, in 789, by the corporation, with the concurrence of the Irish Society, at the centenary of the opening of the Gates.

From the tower of the Cathedral, a plain gothic building, erected in 1633, may be had a magnificent view of the neighborhood which it commands, but the most interesting object in the town is the monument raised in 1828, to the memory of the Rev. George Walker, which consists of a handsome doric column surmounted by a statue.

From *Gordon's History of Ireland*, we find the following account of the siege of Derry, which may here prove an interesting item to those who have not read it, and will serve to freshen the memories of those who have. " A letter was dropped at Cumber, in the County Down, where the Earl of Mount Alexander resided, dated December 3, 1688, informing that nobleman that on Sunday, December 9th, of that year, the Irish throughout the whole island, in pursuance of an oath which they had taken, were to rise and massacre the Protestants, men, women and children; and warning him to take particular care of himself, as a captain's commission would be the reward of the man who would murder him. The Protestants were terrified; several of them assembled in groups about the streets. The apprentice boys, with a mob of the lower orders muttered something about closing the gates. They got some private encouragement to do so at first, but that was soon retracted and the minds of all the men fluctuated in a miserable doubt of the most prudent course to take. Two companies of the Irish appeared on the opposite side of the stream and were ferried over to make proposals for entering the town, which was nearly betrayed into their hands by the treachery of the deputy mayor, who was inclined to favor James. The soldiers getting impatient for the return of their officers, crossed the river and were within three hundred yards of the Ferry Gate. The young men of the city observing this, about eight or nine of them, whose names deserve to be preserved in letters of gold, viz: Henry Campsie, William Crookshanks, Robert Sherrard, Alexander Irwin, James Steward, Robert Morrison, Alexander Connigham, Samuel Hunt, with James Spike, John Connigham, William Carns, Samuel Harvey, and some others who soon joined them, ran to the main guard, seized the keys after a slight opposition, came to the Ferry Gate, drew up the bridge and locked the gate. Lord Antrim's soldiers had advanced within sixty yards of it. The siege lasted one hundred and five days, during which time the citizens were reduced to the direst extremities. Reduced to the extremity of distress, and endeavoring to support the remains of life by such miserable food as the flesh of dogs and vermin, even tallow and hides, nor able to find more than two day's provision of such substance, the garrison was still assured by the harangues of Walker, that God would relieve them; and men reduced almost to shadows made desperate sallies, but were unable to pursue their advantage. The besiegers had thrown a boom across the river to prevent navigation, and Kirk, the Orange admiral, had already been deterred by it from attempting the relief of the town. At length two provision ships and a frigate drew near to the city and one ship dashed with giant strength against the barrier and broke it in two, but, from the violence of the shock, rebounded and ran upon the river's bank. The satisfaction of the enemy was displayed by an instantaneous burst of tumultuous joy. They ran with disorder to the shore, prepared to board her, when the vessel firing a broadside was extricated by the shock, and floated out nobly into the deep again. It was calculated that twenty-three hundred persons died of famine or by violence during the siege."

About a mile from the city is the Magee Protestant College, a very handsome building which cost £20,000, left by Mrs. Magee, of Dublin, for the purpose of training young men for the Presbyterian ministry in Ireland.

Time was fleeting and at 10 A. M. we were ready for the road again. The railway company kindly placed at our disposal the large saloon carriage of the Lord-Lieutenant, with its glass sides and two mirrors. The ride along the coast was charming. On the one side lay well tilled fields and proud mountains, on the other the blue sea, which burst on the shore in foaming waves. Coleraine was reached, and to prevent the ordinary delay of three-quarters of an hour, an engine was attached to our carriages and took us on " special " to Portrush, where we put up at the fine hotel, the Antrim Arms, with our rooms fronting on the broad blue Atlantic.

Portrush has a charming situation. "The Skerries" line of rocks, at one time joined to the mainland, form a breakwater to ward off the force of the Atlantic waves that tumble on the shelving rock or shell-strewn strand. From the green in front of the hotel the line of coast is discernible as far as the Giant's Causeway, eight miles off, and coasting craft and huge Transatlantic steamers are ever to be seen gliding along the deep. Having dispatched lunch in American double-quick time, some vans and cars seated the party, and the procession was formed for the Giant's Causeway.

On, then, along the winding road that takes you along the coast. The "Lion's Paw" and the "Giant's Head" arrest our attention, and as our driver points out the rock fashioned by the water so as to resemble the human countenance, he reminds us of Lot's wife. The The Castle of Dunluce, grand in its silent solitariness and awe-inspiring, historical memories, invites us from the highway, though a few decline to cross the narrow causeway that at one time was a great defense to this formidable stronghold. The date and founder are unknown, but we told of the M'Quillans who owned it in 1580, from whom it passed to the M'Donnells of the the Isles—the ancestors of the Antrim family—in whose possession it still continues.

We run through the village of Bushmills, arrive at the Causeway Hotel, and are forthwith besieged with boatmen desirous of conveying us by water to the Causeway; but we defer the use of boats till our return journey, and wrongly, as we subsequently ascertain.

The guides of the Causeway connect everything notable about it with the Irish giant, Fin McCoul, and it is not many years since an enterprising Yankee pretended to find to find the body of the giant, and exhibited a stone man thirteen feet long to people credulous enough to believe the "find" was genuine. We are pointed out "The Little Causeway" and "The Middle Causeway." We get to "Lord Antrim's Parlor" where names and dates are inscribed, the oldest date being 1717, and take a drink out of the "Giant's Well." Then we are ushered to the "Wishing Chair," and each one of the party, young and old, quietly sits on the single pillar, so depressed below the other as to form a comfortable seat, and wish. But the injunction is given that to reveal the wish is to vitiate the mystic power which grants it, and so we hold our peace on that subject. We linger round the Honeycombs, and the Great Causeway, at times quizzing the guide about the meaning of the terrible words he has used descriptive of the stones. Pentagon, hexagon, octagon, flow freely from his lips, with a display of learning wondrous to unlearned ears, and we ask him again and again to point out those pillars which are "fiveagon" and "eightagon" till he suspects our chaff and becomes wary. Very few of the pillars of the Causeway are nearly square; one pillar is seven-sided. There are several octagon, and three stones have been discovered with nine sides. It is computed that there are about 40,000 pillars comprising the Causeway. They sink to an unknown depth, and if a pillar have a split, that split runs down as far as has ever been discovered. The tall pillars of the "Giant's Loom" are thirty-three feet high. The "Giant's Organ" bears a wonderful resemblance to that instrument. "The Chimney," as some stones are so called, deceived some vessels of the Spanish Armada into the belief that they were part of Dunluce Castle, and received a cannonading in consequence. But the guide tells you one of the vessels was wrecked, which gives the name to " Port-na-Spania." Boats take our party to Portcoon and Dunkerry caves, and we are well rewarded for our venture.

Having received a tongue thrashing from a female for not employing her boats at the time she chose, and because they were hers, with an injunction to the driver to mark all those specially out who did not put their money in her pocket, he promising faithfully to tell Mr. Linden, we started in fear and dread of the consequences till the "go" of the horses and bracing breezes revived us. We discovered we were in a free country, and that " women's rights " were not paramount, and that neither the lady in question nor that worthy gentleman whose name she took in vain had any claim on our bodies or purses. We escaped being locked up for the night in a police cell, and that night fervently prayed for a quieter tongue and a patient husband for that woman. But let us not too hastily over the points we are visiting, for they are well worthy of note. The White Rocks on the way to Dunluce, are among the most interesting objects on this extraordinary coast. It is said that within a distance of two miles and a half there are not fewer than twenty-seven caverns, all natural excavations, worn by the action of the waves on the white limestone of which they are composed, into the most fantastic shapes.

Dunluce Castle, of which we have a moment since spoken, has a fame almost as wide as the Giant's Causeway itself. The Castle stands about one hundred feet above the sea, on a perpendicular and insulated rock, the entire surface of which is so completely occupied by the edifice that the external walls are in continuation with the perpendicular sides of the rock. The rock, though insulated, is not completely water bound, being united to the mainland, at the bottom of a deep chasm, by a single wall not more than eighteen inches broad. Owing to the perpendicular nature of the rock it must have been impossible to take the Castle, or to enter it all, except by the bridge across the yawning chasm. In the autumn of 1814, a visit was made to the ruins of Dunluce, by Sir Walter Scott, who observed a great resemblance in to Dunottar Castle, in Kincardineshire, a detailed description of which is given in the great poet and author's diary.

The Giant's Causeway was first called to public attention about 1693, since which time it has been visited by thousands upon thousands of tourists, and many scientific men. It is a wonderful formation of perpendicular stones, fitting so close together as to exclude, in some places, even a sheet of paper. Nor are the pillars continuous, but composed of several pieces fitted together by convex and concave surfaces. It is said there is but one triangular pillar throughout the whole extent of the three Causeways. These columns are composed chemically of about one-half flinty earth, one-quarter iron, and one-quarter clay and lime. Kohl's remarks on the Causeway are worthy of being given. He says: "With all the explanations that can be offered, however, so much is left unexplained that they answer very little purpose. On a close investigation of these wonderful formations, so many questions arise, that one scarcely ventures to utter them. With inquiries of this nature, perhaps not the least gain is the knowledge of how much lies beyond the limits of our inquiries, and how many things that lie so plainly before our eyes which we can see and handle, may yet be wrapped in unfathomable mystery. We see in the Giant's Causeway the most certain and obvious effects produced by the operation of active and powerful forces which entirely escape our scrutiny. We walk over the heads of some forty thousand columns, (for this number has been counted by some curious and leisurely persons,) all beautifully cut and polished, formed of such neat pieces, so exactly fitted to each other, and so cleverly supported, that we might fancy we had before us the work of ingenious human artificials; and yet what we behold is the result of the immutable laws of nature, acting without any apparent object, and by a process which must remain a mystery forever to our understanding. Even the simplest inquiries, it is often impossible to answer; such, for instance, as how far these colonnades run out beneath the sea, and how far into the land, which throws over them a veil as impenetrable as that of ocean."

Of course there are all kinds of traditions in connection with the Causeways, one being that "the giant, Fin McCoul, was the Champion of Ireland, and felt very much aggrieved at the insolent boasting of a certain Caledonian giant, who offered to whip every one who came before him, and even dared to tell Fin that if it were not for the wetting of himself, he would swim over and give him a good drubbing. Fin at last applied to the King, who, perhaps not daring to question the doings of such a weighty man, gave him leave to construct a causeway right to Scotland, on which the Scot walked over and fought the Irishman. Fin turned out victor, and with an amount of generosity becoming his Hibernian descent, kindly allowed his rival to marry and settle in Ireland, which the Scot was not loath to do, seeing at that time living in Scotland at that time was not the best, and every body knows that Ireland was always the richest country in the world. Since the death of the giants, the Causeways, being no longer wanted, has sank under the sea, only leaving a portion of itself visible here, a little at the island of Rathlin, and the portals at the grand gate on Staffa.

The *Pleaskin* is the finest of all the Causeway, and of this Kohl writes thus: "The natural basaltic rock here ies immediately under the surface. About twelve feet from the summit the rock begins to assume a collumnar tendency, and is formed into ranges of rudely collumnar basalt, in a vertical position, exhibiting the appearance of a grand gallery whose columns measure sixty feet in height. This basaltic colonnade rests upon a bed of coarse, black, irregular rock, sixty feet thick, abounding in air holes. Below this stratum is a second range of pillars forty-five feet high, more accurately columnar and nearly as accurately formed as the Causeway itself. The cliff appears as though it had been painted for effect in various shades of green, vermilion rock, red ochre, grey lichens, &c., its general form so beautiful, its storeyed pillars, tier after tier, so architecturally graceful, its curious and varied stratifications supporting the columnar ranges; here the dark brown amorphous basalt, there the red ochre—and below that again the slender but distinct lines of wood coal—all the edges of its different stratifications tastefully varied, by the hand of vegetable nature, with grasses, ferns and rock plants. In the various strata of which it is composed, sublimity and beauty have been blended together in the most extraordinary manner."

A few of the names given to some of the rocks, which resemble those after which they are called, may serve as a means to give the reader an idea of the curious and wonderful geological formations abounding in the Causeways, viz: The Horse Shoe Harbor, the Lion's Head, The Tunis, the Giant's Pulpit, the Giant's Granny, the Priest, the Stack, the Giant's Chimney, the Giant's Organ, the Hen and Chickens, the Nursing Child, the King and his Nobles, the Highlandman's Bonnet, &c., &c.

As we stood in the Causeway we saw the magnificent Anchor Line Steamer, "Circassia" pass by so gracefully and beautifully on her voyage to New York.

A GOOD IDEA.

As we wandered over the rocks in the Causeway, we heard a very good suggestion made by a member of our party who supplies the first families of Allegheny and Pittsburgh with juicy tenderloins, and is thoroughly posted on "fine cuts," &c., none other than our jolly good friend, Fred Beilstein.

We noticed Fred gazing abstractedly at the wonderfully formed rocks, saying nothing, but evidently turning some mighty question over in his mind. He had not made a remark for quite a while, when suddenly turning to some of us, he remarked: "Do you know boys, I have a mighty good notion to take over two or three of these pillars and have them cut down to proper lengths, to place in front of my meat stand, for the accommodation of my customers, and *would n't that draw?*

This put us in mind of one on the same gentleman, which it may not be out of place to relate here.

When the party was in the King's Palace, in Amsterdam, in which is a magnificent and very large carved marble vase, which, perhaps, no money could buy, and around this the pilgrims were gathered, and exclamations of delight and admiration were being poured forth most extravagantly, and none were louder in their praise of this beautiful piece of art than our good friend Fred. Stepping up to Prof. Slack, who was standing near by, he quietly tapped him on the shoulder and said, "Is n't that an elegant piece of work, Mr. Slack?"

"Oh! my, is n't it grand?" "Do you know what I was thinking, Mr. Slack?" "No, Fred, I do not, what was it?" "Well," says Fred, "I was just thinking if I only had that vase at my stall to keep corned beef in, would n't it make the other butchers sick?

Next morning our saloon-carriage was again in waiting, and we started for Belfast. The swelling hills and fertile valleys of Antrim—green with unripe corn and rye and barley, and yellow with newly-cut hay—could not escape the eye of the traveler, nor the white cottages embosomed amid flowers, nor the dark green hedge rows, nor the neatly kept railway stations through which we passed.

From Carrickfergus Junction we looked on the blue waters of Belfast Lough, dotted with many a sail, and the capital of Ulster at the extremity where the Lagan joins the salt sea. The terminus is reached, and and carriages and cars convey us to the Queen's Hotel.

Arriving in Belfast we took a Turkish bath-house by storm, and, enjoying the luxury of a bath therein, we returned to our hotel for dinner, and at 6:30 we went down to the wharf and saw our fraters of Mary Commandery, No. 36, of Philadelphia, who were making their "*First European Pilgrimage,*" and were to leave at 8 P. M. for Glasgow. We spent an hour pleasantly with them, and, bidding them good-by, we took a stroll through the principal streets, and must confess that Belfast was the first city in Ireland we had visited giving any appearance of enterprise, business activity and life. The shops, as they are pleased to call their stores there, had an inviting, business-like appearance, people moving more rapidly and actively as though they were doing something to give them the wherewithal that they might live, move and have their being.

As the " Quartette" were moving along the street, the noble heart of the Doctor was suddenly enlarged, for to our amazement he invited us into a " green-grocer's" to " take something" with him, so he invested half a crown (62½ cents) in five peaches, eating three himself, dividing the remaining two among the Colonel, Major and '· Carlisle," and those two were bad, of course, for they were bought with the money alluded to in our letter from Killarney to Dublin, and no good ever came from those who do not do right. Moral—" never buy peaches in a foreign country with money bagged as that was?"

As it was Saturday evening, and nothing much could be done on that evening, the committee appointed on Lough Erne, to draft resolutions expressive of the appreciation of the kindness of our Enniskillen friends and Brother R. W. Armstrong, met and prepared the following, which were unanimously adopted by the Commandery, and handsomely engrossed and forwarded respectively to those for whom they were intended:

"*Whereas*, On our pilgrimage to Europe it was our extreme good fortune to travel by the way of Enniskillen, where we were met and most elegantly and courteously received and entertained by the Masons of Enniskillen and the surrounding country. And whereas, this courtesy was as spontaneous and magnificent as it was unexpected, and came to us in such a manner as to arouse our warmest feelings of gratitude to the brethren who originated it and executed it, and is an incident in our trip as fragrant and beautiful as the bouquets with which they decked us, and will be as lasting in our memory as recollection and gratitude exist, and will be treasured as an offering to that noble fraternity of which they and we form a part, and whose 'universal chain' binds together men of all climes, nation and professions, and as an humble recognition of the kindness and hospitality thus shown to us, it is resolved—

"1st. That we hereby tender to Bro. O. Ternan and the brethren of Enniskillen our thanks for the marked kindness shown by them to us in the royal reception extended, and in the most courteous and hospitable entertainment provided."

"2d. That in the action of our Enniskillen brethren we recognize that the stranger sinks into the brother, that distance strengthens rather than weakens the 'mystic tie,' that nationalities become a brotherhood, and that in the mellowing influence of our order men of all sections and places 'meet upon the level,' and become one in feeling and sentiment, as they are one in a common purpose, understanding, and duty."

"3d. That the bright jewels accompanying the brethren, and forming a conspicuous part in the entertainment, have our warmest thanks for their presence and aid; and that to these ladies we are deeply indebted for much of the pleasure and profit derived by us. May they ever be recognized and honored by our fraternity, as forming the chief corner stone upon which must rest all that is noble, pure, and good. May they ever be made welcome in our journeys, and honored in all our councils. To them we extend the right hand of fellowship, and invoke the benediction of Almighty God upon them and theirs."

"4th. That we assure any and all our friends a warm and hearty welcome to our homes and hearts, and cordially invite them to come with us that we may show them how deeply we feel indebted, and with what willing hands we will seek to pay this debt. 'The Emerald Isle and the gem of the ocean' will mingle and harmonize, and the brethren shall know that the west has room for them, and to which they shall be made 'as welcome as the flowers of May.'"

And to Brother R. W. Armstrong the following was prepared, engrossed and forwarded:

"Among the many pleasant incidents occurring to us on our pilgrimage none is brighter than the unexpected and unselfish action of our friend and brother, Robert W. Armstrong, of Belleek, in the County Fermanagh.

Visiting his neighborhood as strangers, and having no claims upon his time or kindness, we were, nevertheless made his debtor to such a degree that we feel that we can never fully repay the debt. His finished and exquisite memento, wrought out through patient toil, and with marked originality and skill, will be kept and treasured by us so long as we keep life, and whenever seen and whithersoever we go, it shall remind us that a brother's hand made it, and a brother's heart suggested it. All that can be said by us is, that he lives in his act and has sent his name and fraternal feeling into homes and families which, though divided from him by an ocean are linked to him by an indissoluble tie, and will receive him at their fireside with all the warmth which gratitude and love can prompt. And as he travels on through life, cheering the hearts of others by his benefactions, and lightening the labor and struggle of life by his kindness, may his pathway grow brighter and brighter until it shall melt away into that supreme light and life which is the reward, as it is the home, of the just and the good. And may he and his be blessed even with the blessing of the promises. May this simple tribute of thanks, given from Allegheny Commandery, No. 35, of Allegheny City, Pennsylvania, be accepted by him in that spirit which prompts its offering, and be one flower in that chaplet which nothing but love can weave."

Retiring early to catch up our lost sleep, the following day (Sunday) found the "Quartette" all in their own room, hard at work writing, for here we had the pleasure of receiving our first letters from home, and we never saw a man work harder in our lives than the Colonel. He first sorted out all our "soiled linen," and piled it up in the centre of the room, taking an inventory of the same; then into his trunk he went, bringing out a box of elegant note paper—various flowers beautifully painted by hand on each sheet—with envelopes to match, and seating himself at the table, he spent the day with "pen in hand," and as the Colonel hailed from Salt Lake City, he had quite a novel way of doing his letter writing. He would compose a beautifully worded letter addressed to "My Dear Winona." When finished, all he had to do was to copy the same a dozen times or so, merely changing the address as many times to "My Dear Lurline," "My Dearest Adele," "My Sweet Evelina," "My Loving Amanda," "My Tender Susan," "My Own Margaret," etc. I know at any rate that "Carlisle," as banker, had a bill against the Colonel, for postage in Belfast, about two shillings and sixpence.

While engaged in writing thusly, rather an amusing thing occurred. We would hear a bell down stairs in the office ring, and the attendant call up to the servant, "No. 19!" and "One bottle of beer to No. 19!" It went on thusly for a couple of hours, about every fifteen minutes, "One beer to No. 19!" being called. At first no attention was paid to the matter, but finding it so interrupted the Colonel that he was addressing one of his telling epistles as "My Dear Number Nineteen," we could n't stand having the Colonel interrupted in this manner, and going down to the office, we found it was none of our party were in No. 19, so we begged that the hotel proprietor remove the bar up to 19, or have 19 removed down to the bung-hole. Now, it appears there was a social party of four on the floor above room 19, and they had ordered up "four beers," and the girl carrying it up had occasion to set the "four beers" down opposite No. 19's door while she went into an adjoining room to attend to some duty there. The occupant of 19 evidently scented beer in the air, and slipping out gobbled the social party's "four beers." It was truly a funny sight to see the girl looking round for the four bottles labeled "Bass' Pale Ale," and stepping into 19 and looking out into the yard see the four innocent bottles standing upright on the ground beneath the window! In the evening we took a jaunting car for a drive, to air the fevered brow of the Colonel, after his arduous labors of the day.

Belfast is a progressive city, and the only progressive city in fact in Ireland, while she is the linen market of the world. In the course of fifty years the population has increased fivefold. In 1821, the inhabitants numbered only 37,000, in 1851 they increased to 100,301, and in 1871 to 174,394.

The city stands upon the property of the Marquis of Donegal, and it is said that but for long leases granted by the former proprietor, the income of that nobleman from the town alone would amount to £300,000. The city is situated on the river Lagan and on Belfast Lough and is distant from Glasgow only one hundred and thirty miles, and from Liverpool, one hundred and fifty-six. It has one of the best harbors in the United Kingdom, though the river Lagan was formerly but a creek. It was here the far-famed White Star Steamships, the largest that cross the Atlantic, were built and launched. The estimated shipping tonnage is 1,500,000 tons, the recent improvements costing £250,000, or a million and a quarter in American money.

The buildings in Belfast are good, and the town in a a business manner has the appearance of Manchester or Glasgow, and many of the streets are regular and wide, particularly around the exterior of the town. It cannot, however, claim the same age and antiquity of Dublin, being unknown prior to the twelfth century. Edward Bruce on his way south on his raid of robbery and plunder, completely sacked the city; and very shortly after the death of Bruce, the Earl of Ulster was murdered by some of his own family, and the Irish once more held out against the English aggression, rebuilt the Castle of Belfast, and held it for two centuries.

In 1612, Belfast was presented to Sir A. Chichester, the ancestor of the present Marquis of Donegal.

Perhaps the most remarkable fact in the industrial history of Belfast, is, that no printing press was ever brought into the city before the year 1696, yet Belfast was the town where the first Bible ever printed in Ireland was published in the year 1794, and where the oldest Irish periodical, the "Weekly Magazine," was originally published. They now have some eight daily and weekly papers.

The most important features of interest in this enterprising city are the *Commercial* Buildings, built in 1820, and cost £20,000. The Presbyterian Church in Rosemary street, the handsomest structure of that denomination in Belfast, and cost £10,000. This leads us to the division of religious sects here; there are twenty-eight congregations of Presbyterians, eighteen of Episcopalians, five of Catholics, and three of Unitarians. In 1871, the Protestant population was 118,868, while the Catholics numbered only 55,052, and of the former 60,811 were Presbyterians.

Then there is the Provincial Bank, built of white Cookstown stone and cost £18,000. The Ulster Bank is one of the finest and handsomest buildings in the city; built of polished red sandstone, and which has a capital of £1,000,000.

The new Custom House is the largest building in Belfast, constructed of the finest Glasgow stone and affording ample room for the custom house, post office, inland revenue office, stamp office, and an office for the Board of Local Marine. Then there are the Northern Bank, the Artillery and Infantry Barracks, Trinity Church, Court House, Royal Academical Institution, and Government School of Art, St. Malachy's Roman

Catholic Chapel, the Music Hall, the Queen's College, Presbyterian College, Methodist College, the Hospital for the Deaf, Dumb and Blind, and the Museum, all buildings and places handsome in their architectural design, and worthy of a visit by the tourist. Then we come to the life and support of the city of Belfast, namely, her linen manufactures. We visited the York Street Spinning Company, and that some idea may be had as to the enormity of this trade, we will give a fact or two in connection with figures, which may appear astonishing to purchasers of table linen, towels, napkins, etc. For instance, the York Street Spinning Company, formerly the firm of Mulhollands, employs nearly three thousand hands, and has generally £100,000, or $500,000 worth of flax in course of manipulation.

In Ireland we find the first spinning factory was established in 1806, and consisted of two hundred and twelve spindles, adapted for canvas yarns. The linen board, by a bounty of thirty shillings per spindle, succeeded in causing the establishment of others, which in 1809 contained 6,369 spindles. In 1815 there were in Ulster five mills, the largest having 1204, and the smallest 300 spindles; in Leinster two mills, and in Munster, seven, only one of which was in operation owing to the depression of trade at that period. In 1841 there were forty-one mills, containing 280,000 spindles, and in 1852 the number had increased to seventy-three mills, and 339,000 spindles, and two years later there were eighty-one mills, and 500,000 spindles in operation, representing a capital of some three to four million pounds sterling, or fifteen to twenty million dollars ; the number of factories now being about one hundred and sixty, and giving employment to upwards of sixty thousand persons.

The quantity of flax grown in Ireland has been generally on the increase. In 1847 there were 58,132 acres sown, each acre yielding about five hundred weight of scutched fibre, altogether worth about £656,100, while in 1870, the estimated value of the crop was nearly two million pounds sterling. The product of one acre of ground under flax, requires a day's labor of sixty-four females, and fifty-three males, or one hundred seventeen persons in all, from the time it is pulled to the time that it goes to the mill.

The Linen Hall was erected in 1715, at a cost of £10,000. The linen trade being almost exclusively confined to Ulster, it was found inconvenient to have the business conducted by agents in Dublin, in consequence of which was instituted the Linen Hall. In MacCullough's Dictionary of Commerce, we find that "in 1698, both houses of English Parliament addressed His Majesty William III., representing that the progress of the woolen manufacture of Ireland was such as to prejudice the trade of this country (England,) and that it would be for the public advantage were the former discouraged, and the linen manufacture established instead;" and King William adopted one of the most illiberal pieces of policy ever practiced by England to

Ireland, when he said, " I shall do all that in me lies to discourage the woolen manufacture in Ireland, and to encourage the linen manufacture, and to promote the trade of England," and strange to say that was what gave the first decided impulse to the linen trade.

We also visited the Greenmount Spinning Company, but our friend, Mr. Houston, being absent in Paris, we were most agreeably entertained by Mr. Montgomery of that company, with whom we dined, and a good preparation made for the custom house officers of New York by the manner in which the trio of the " Quartette " dived into table cloths, napkins, handkerchiefs, etc.

We were also shown through Marcus Ward & Co's famous printing and lithographing establishment, the largest of the kind in the world.

Returning to hotel after our day's work, we had a good dinner, which they know how to set up at the " Queen's," and that being finished, the ladies of our party presented to Mr and Mrs. Cooper a handsome pair of silver napkin rings, and the Commandery passed a resolution to Mr. Cooper for his every attention, politeness and kindness. His prompt attention to all our comforts, the care taken for us all, his own genial manners and exertions, gave Mr. Cooper a warm place in our affections, and to him we owe very much for our agreeable recollections of Ireland. Not an accident occurred under his care, not a piece of baggage went missing, not a train was lost, but everything under his direction and pleasant way of going about it, moved so harmoniously and smoothly that everything added to our enjoyment, having nothing that could in any way detract or mar our pleasure. In whatever station Mr. Cooper may be placed, we wish him unbounded success, and we trust to see him in our country and city, when we will endeavor " to do unto him as he did unto us."

Bidding them " Good bye " at 9 P. M. that Monday evening, we stepped aboard the boat and were soon putting down the Lagan into Belfast Lough on our way to Glasgow.

Letter No. 3.

Up the River Clyde.—In and Around Glasgow.—The Grand Reception by St. Mungo Encampment and others.—Purchase of a Clothing House.—Trouble with Gents' Furnishing Goods.—A day Spent with Friends.—Separation of "Carlisle" from the Remainder of the "Quartette."—Arrival in Edinburgh.—Incidents by the Way.

ON the following morning might have been seen on the deck of the "Petrel," the noble and ever faithful little band, the "Quartette," up and with eager eyes, taking in the far famed scenery, of what we are pleased to call our old home river—the beautiful Clyde—and singular as it may seem, and perhaps hardly creditable, it was actually raining—well, not exactly raining, but just a good healthy Scotch mist, as many are well aware, it seldom rains in Scotland, which recalls to our mind a little incident in the Rev. Dr. Plumer's tour in Europe a year or so ago.

He had just landed from the steamer at Greenock, and was seated in the railway carriage, and though a day in May, he with his friends were clad in their heavy winter under clothing, heavy suits, overcoats, and the Doctor had even a shawl about him in addition to all these, when along came a Scotchman employed about the depot, in his shirt sleeves, and stopped in front of the Doctor's compartment. Presently another canny, warm blooded Scot approached and greeting his friend with, "Guid morning, Geordie, hoo' are ye the day, man?" to which he received the reply, "oh! I'm fine, Jock, thank ye for speirin', but its unco warm the day, man!" It is scarcely necessary to say that this made the Doctor shiver harder than ever, and express the wonder what a real cold day was like in Scotland.

We were just approaching "Ailsa Craig," a huge rocky island, which rises abruptly from the sea, is 1,103 feet in height, about two miles in circumference at its base, and its nearest distance to land about ten miles. There is an old ruin of a tower on its summit, and this queer rock is inhabited by millions and millions of birds, and is utterly devoid of life of any other kind.

Passing Rothesay, a beautiful little town in the county of Bute, a great resort for invalids and pleasure seekers, owing to its mild and genial climate, we enter the Clyde—and this is certainly an incomparable sail—with features clear and distinct from the beauties of our great American river, the Hudson, or the beautiful Rhine of Germany.

Away on our right are the hills of Ayrshire, while on our left are the pretty little towns dotting the banks at frequent intervals, while Scotland's noble mountains form a grand background to the pretty picture in the fore. We pass the delightful villas of Dunoon and

Inellan, and a little further on the river expands at Helensburg, making an admirable anchorage for sea vessels, and here at what is called the "tail of the Bank," are loaded all the sea-going vessels, as above this point, owing to the most unfortunate narrowing of the river, it is impossible to bring down from Glasgow a heavily laden sailing or steamship.

On our right is Gonrock, which is three miles distant from Greenock, but may be considered simply a continuation of the latter place, and presents a splendid appearance from the passing steamer, the town being made up of fine stone residences and handsome mansions. Between Gonrock and Greenock stands Fort Matilda Battery.

Shortly we call at Greenock, at which point we enter the narrow stream, which water-course, troublesome as it is, prevents Glasgow from being the greatest city in the world, had it the harbor and access to a harbor as have Liverpool and New York.

The situation of Greenock is a beautiful one, and most convenient for commercial interests, the principal trade being sugar refining and ship building. Close upon the fine quay stands the custom house, a very commodious building. In the burying ground of the old West Kirk of Greenock, Burns' Highland Mary is interred. Steaming away from this busy town we pass Port Glasgow and the ship building yards, but we were disappointed at not seeing all the stocks full of the newly laid keels and skeletons of vessels, and at not hearing the same pounding noises and clitter-clattering of hammers as they rounded the heads of rivets and bolts which were being driven through the plates and stanchcons of iron, as we saw and heard but a few summers before. Here we met the good old steamship "California" coming down in charge of two tugs on her way out to sea, and we sighed a deep long sigh for the days gone by as we looked on the noble boat gracefully turning the windings of the stream, for many a good day and hour we had spent in her commodious rooms and on her spacious decks.

We soon come to Dumbarton rock on which stands Dumbarton Castle, two objects as inseparable with Scottish history as would be Scotland itself. This curious rock, or rather high bluff, rising precipitously from level ground as does "Ailsa Craig" from the sea, is a mile in circumference, and rises to a height of two hundred and forty feet terminating in two peaks, the highest of which is called "Wallace's seat," and one part of the Castle bears the name of "Wallace's tower," for it was here the Scottish hero was once confined. The ascent to the Castle is by a narrow steep stair, built in a natural fissure of the rock. In the Castle is the armory, in which are exhibited a poor collection of weapons, said to have been found on the battle field of Bannockburn, but the Secretary of War of the Kingdom has ordered that the two-handed sword shown here as "Wallace's Sword," shall be no longer exhibited as such, as it has been ascertained that it is of the period of Edward IV., and consequently could never have belonged to Wallace.

In the time of the wars, which abounded in Scotland plentifully in Queen Mary's time, this Castle was taken by an ingenious strategem by Captain Crawford of Jordan hill, as is given in the history of Scotland by George Buchanan. "Taking advantage of a misty and moonless night to bring to the foot of the Castle rock the scaling ladders which he had provided, he chose for his terrible experiment the place where the rock was highest, and where, of course, less pains were taken to a regular guard. This choice was fortunate, for the first ladder broke with the weight of the men who mounted it, and the noise of the fall must have betrayed them had there been any sentinel around or within hearing. Crawford, assisted by a soldier who had deserted from the Castle, and was acting as his guide, renewed the attempt in person, and having scrambled up to a projecting ledge of rock, where there was some footing, continued to make fast the ladder by tying it to the roots of a tree which grew about midway up the rock. Here they found a small flat surface, sufficient, however, to afford footing for the whole party, which was, of course, very few in number. In scaling the second precipice, another accident took place; one of the party subject to epileptic fits, was seized with one of these attacks, brought on perhaps by terror.' * * * His illness made it impossible for him either to ascend or descend. To have slain the man would have been a cruel expedient, besides that the fall of his body from the ladder might have alarmed the garrison. Crawford caused him, therefore, to be tied to the ladder, and thus mounted with case over the body of the epileptic person. When the party gained the summit they slew the sentinel ere he had time to give the alarm, and easily surprised the slumbering garrison who had trusted too much to the vigilance of the sentinel to keep good watch." There is still in the archives of the Duke of Montrose, a juvenile letter of James VI. written in his ninth year, addressed to Captain Crawford, who performed this service.

The town of Dumbarton lies directly at the base of Dumbarton Rock, and is now a very important seat of industry, containing some 11,500 inhabitants, has large shipbuilding works and employing thousands of men in this enterprise of fitting-up and building sea craft, in which the Clyde is celebrated, as in every water on earth almost floats the handiwork of ship-builders of the Clyde. A little further on we come to Dunglas Point, and here has been erected an appropriate monument to Henry Bell, who first introduced steam navigation on the Clyde. We are now in the midst of busy shipping interests, huge sailing vessels, immense steamers are loading and unloading valuable cargoes consigned to and from all quarters of the globe; the river has narrowed down almost to a good sized American creek, until the numerous water craft, we would almost think, would be entangled in an inextricable confusion. We meet the fine river steamers loaded down with passengers on their way to the coast, to spend the day, the week or the summer; all around are signs of life and prosperity, while the noise of the hammers of hundreds of men beat and pound the driving rivet; and here we sight the busy city of Glasgow, her tall stacks pouring forth their black smoke, making us feel we were rather approaching home than otherwise, so far as soot, dirt and smoke are concerned at least.

We arrive at the pier about 7 A. M. in Glasgow, where we are met by our new conductor, and driven at once to the new and elegant Cockburn Hotel, feeling quite ready so far as appetites were concerned to most effectually "clean out the hotel" in less time than it would take to say it, and as we passed through "Argyll," "Buchanan," "Queen," "Sanchichall street," etc., those names appeared to us as familiar as the chimneys of our mills, or our Fifth avenue, or Federal street were in good old grimy, smoky Pittsburgh, and more inviting Allegheny. Here, too, we are made more at home, for we meet dear, good friends, some from across the Atlantic, also strangers in a foreign land, and some in their own homes. And here also the "Quartette" are made acquainted with their first "*grief*"; the mournful, sorrowful parting of the "Quartette," for here the "Quartette" were to be separated for a little time, and we can never extinguish from memory—though we cry with *Lady Macbeth*, "Out dark, blank spot!"—the swollen, grief-lit eyes of the Doctor, the "Majah" and the Colonel as they shook hands with poor lonely "Carlisle," when they parted from him and left him weeping over their sad departure; and to settle a little bill from a proprietress of a laundry which the trio had forgotten (intentionally) to liquidate.

At the Cockburn, was a committee from St. Mungo Encampment of Knights Templar, of Glasgow, in waiting to receive us, and informed us they would at 8 P. M. escort the Commandery to attend the banquet to be tendered by St. Mungo Encampment, and the other Masonic bodies of Glasgow, in the Queen's Rooms on that evening.

And here upon the door step of the hotel we were greeted by the cheerful smile of our very handsome, jovial and genial friend, W. Stilwell, Esq., of Philadelphia, Pa., who had been making a four months' tour of Continental countries and the British Kingdom, thereby adding vastly to his already large and accumulated stock of knowledge, who said "Hello! there, what are you doing here?" We immediately gave him the oath of allegiance, made him a Knight of Submission by borrowing a five dollar bill—or, rather, a pound note each from him—and giving him our individual checks on the Allegheny Trust Company; the Major's, however, being, I believe, a lien on some property in the East End, which he wanted to donate to the city of Pittsburgh if that corporation would relieve him from street improvement assessments.

After a good hearty breakfast, consisting of "purritch" followed by other good substantials, we repaired to our rooms, and, being refreshed by a good "wash up," we were prepared to "do" Glasgow.

From the date of our sailing from New York we had heard continually what a stock of clothing was to be laid in on our arrival in Glasgow, so the "Quartette" then started on their day's sight-seeing, first striking a merchant tailoring establishment where "Carlisle" was well acquainted, and he impressed upon the remaining trio of the "Quartette" the cheapness of wearing apparel in the British domain. The consequence was, they rushed down to the City of Glasgow Bank, and while speaking of this unfortunate bank, it might not be improper to state here an incident that goes far towards accounting for the sudden going down of this famous banking institution, which had always been considered as solid as the British throne itself, and we state it more for the benefit of the unfortunate shareholders of that bank, many of whom are now ruined, widows and orphans supposing themselves sufficiently well off to carry them nicely through this world, and who are now in a condition of penury and poverty, that while the Major was in the Bank of the City of Glasgow he meandered into a little room off to one side and had little "confab" with the general cashier, and on coming out his person seemed much stouter than usual. Of course we do not, under any circumstances, mean to insinuate that, for the financial crash that was soon after to fall upon that institution a little "Yankee" advice and counsel from an attorney to that general cashier had anything whatever to do with the Major's sudden development; we simply state the case, and would add that, at any rate, it is a very reckless way to carry money so that corners of five-pound notes may be seen sticking out of pants' pockets and peeping out from coat tails, etc. They then rushed back to the tailoring establishment and the result was: the Major, four suits and two overcoats; the Doctor, three suits and one overcoat—he also left his linen duster to be padded for fall wear; the Colonel, *five* suits and as many overcoats. A wink to proprietors from "Carlisle," and net results to that personage in that transaction was "two pound ten;" and they—the Major, Doctor and Colonel—don't know it yet.

Here also we met our kind friends, John B. Main and Alexander Main, of Glasgow, to whom also we are deeply indebted for many kindnesses and courtesies shown us during our short visit.

Through the kindness and courtesy of the Sir Knights of St. Mungo, each of the pilgrims were presented with a complete guide book to the city of Glasgow, each book having inscribed thereon the name of each individual Sir Knight of the Commandery, and "with fraternal greetings from St. Mungo Encampment of Knights Templar, of Glasgow," a work we proved of invaluable service to us while there.

We took carriage and proceeded to visit the places of interest in this fine old city, and perhaps no city in the world furnishes so much of interest to the tourist as does Glasgow. Scarcely can you turn from one street into another but some object of ancient and historical interest is arrived at, and too short time we must say, was allowed to take in all the sights with which this city abounds. Glasgow has a population of about six hun-hundred thousand, and is the third city in point of wealth in the United Kingdom.

In 1801 the entire population of Glasgow was only about 75,000, which shows the remarkable growth up to present date, of almost 700 per cent. It has always been the veriest stronghold of Presbyterianism, and therefore been constantly engaged in all the religious struggles which have in their time racked good "Auld Scotia" from one extremity to the other. It will appear a singular statement, but none the less a fact, when it is known that only one hundred years ago the entire commercial prosperity, and the entire capital of Glasgow was invested in the tobacco trade. The finest mansions and buildings in the city to-day are still the property of what the civilians are pleased to sarcastically term the "Tobacco Lords," in which connection, we might here say, that in Britain, the mercantile business is not looked upon in the light of Americans, the class of persons engaged in business, particularly a "Draper," though they may be the sovereigns of aristocracy in thought and business qualifications, are looked upon as a very common sort of people indeed. The late rebellion in our own country to a large extent broke up the tobacco business of Glasgow, and since that time her coal, iron, cotton, ship building and marine interests have been making gigantic strides towards eclipsing all other cities in the world in vastness of commercial importance, the shipbuilding of the Clyde alone, is almost as vast as all the other ports of Britain combined.

Over £5,550,000 sterling or 27,750,000 dollars have been expended in widening and deepening the Clyde, the length of quay-wall being 17,000 feet, and the river instead of admitting vessels of forty tons burthen, as it did not a century ago, now admits the largest class of vessels afloat. Few who have not visited Glasgow within late years would recognize the place now, with street railways, and the vast improvements going on by the Caledonian Railway, with a railroad bridge at the "Broomielaw," and running up through the centre of the city, magnificent stations and elegant hotels.

Glasgow Cross is passed, and the scene of the midnight adventure of Francis Osbaldistone and Rob Roy, and the old Court House, in front of which all criminals were executed, a drive through Argyle street, and Buchanan street, and we come to the Royal Exchange, a handsome building erected in 1829, costing £50,000. In front of this building is a collossal bronze statue of the Duke of Wellington, erected by private subscription, and costing £10,000. Oh! for a few Scotchmen, Irishmen or Englishmen, just to loan us poor Americans one of their thousands of fine statues, to commemorate the name of the father of our country. In George's square are several fine monuments, the finest being one to Sir Walter Scott, there are two bronze statues to Sir John Moore and Lord Clyde, two brave generals, and natives of Glasgow, also, one in bronze to James Watt, another to Sir Robert Peel, and another to Dr. Graham, an eminent chemist, also in the square equestrian statues of Queen Victoria and the late Prince Consort. Facing the square is the Andersonian University, attended by 1,700 students. The old Glasgow College on High street, is now converted into a railway station. We then drive to the Cathedral, the largest and best preserved building of the kind in Scotland. This fine old structure was founded in 1136 by John Achains, who was appointed by David I, to the Bishopric of Glasgow in 1127, and was dedicated in 1136, but restored in 1197 by Bishop Jocelyne.

The Cathedral is in length 319 feet, and sixty-three feet wide. The interior contains 147 pillars, and is lighted by 159 windows. A splendid tower surmounted by a graceful spire rises from its centre 225 feet in height. The Choir, which is locally known as the High Church, is now used by one of the city churches for their place of worship, and behind it are the lady chapel and chapter house, in the latter the bishops held their ecclesiastical courts. The Dripping Aisle, so called from the perpetual dropping of water from the roof, is the lower part of the unfinished transept. The Crypt, under the Choir, is not surpassed by any similar structure in Great Britain. It is 108 feet long, 72 feet wide, supported by sixty-five pillars, some of which are 18 feet in circumference, the height of each being 18 feet long. The building contains many rich and ancient ornamental tombs of the worthies of the old city, and of the dignitaries of church and state. Mr. Edward Blore, under direction of the government, repaired and renewed certain parts of the building which had fallen into decay. During the progress of the operations, several fragments of mouldings were found which had been used in filling up some of the walls, of a much older date than any part of the Cathedral, thus proving the existence of a previous structure on or near the same site. These mouldings are of beautiful workmanship. In the year 1856, the citizens of Glasgow projected a movement to enhance the beauty of the Cathedral, by a series of stained glass windows. In this they were assisted by the government, who placed the east window, the finest in the series. The subjects in the windows are arranged in chronological order, commencing with the expulsion of Adam and Eve from Paradise, and other Old Testament characters; subjects taken from the history of the Jews, the Prophets, and John the Baptist; illustrations of the Parables, the Apostles and the Evangelists. The Necropolis, adjoining the Cathedral, rises steeply 200 to 300 feet in height. The entire surface of the rock is divided into walks, and on every hand are every variety of columns and monumental erections, some being very beautiful in design. From the side of this resting place of those who sleep therein a very fine view of this solid city is to be had, with its countless spires and chimney stacks, intersected by the ship-laden Clyde.

A beautiful drive from here is had to and through Sanchichall street, at the western end of which are elegant modern terraces and streets which constitute the residences of the aristocracy of Glasgow. Here is Kelvin Grove, known as the West End Park, laid out at an expense of £100,000 to the corporation. A very elegant memorial fountain is in this Park, erected to the late Lord Provost Stewart, who was instrumental in introducing into Glasgow, for its use, the clear and delightful water from Loch Katrine. Facing this beautiful park is the unusually handsome structure, the University of Glasgow, and from the park the view of this building is unusually fine. The floor space of this building is 29,200 yards, or about six acres, and has a tower 300 feet high. It is the most complete and thorough institution of the kind in the world, in every respect, the heating and ventilating of the building being constructed on a method approved by the professors. For instance, the vitiated air is withdrawn from the rooms by the suction power of heated flues, and the fresh air is drawn down from the middle height of the tower, and propelled over the surface of very numerous and extensive hot water pipes, by means of a steam engine acting as fanners; about two million cubic feet of fresh air may be propelled per hour through the fanners into the building. Then there are the Botanic Gardens, beautifully laid out, with a good collection of foreign plants, and the Observatory, the famous Glasgow Green, and the Broomielaw, or harbor of Glasgow, comprising an area of seventy-six acres. The City of Glasgow is supplied with water brought all the way from Loch Katrine, a distance of forty miles, being of the purest quality, and the supply is about 28,340,000 gallons, or nearly fifty gallons per head.

Having done thus as much of the town we could, and as it was now almost 5 o'clock, we wended our way back to the Cockburn hotel, to make preparations for the reception and banquet to be tendered us in the evening.

We must state an incident, however, of those poor common plebeians, the Major and the Doctor. Passing a trunk store, the necessity of purchasing a couple of "Saratogas" flashed across the minds of the two, and they must needs hail the driver to slacken his pace, pull into the curb, and permit us to dismount. They were "Closing Out Stock at a Great Sacrifice," in the trunk shop, and it was a big bonanza to the Doctor and Major. They finally struck two that just suited them—one was seven guineas, the other "six pounds, fifteen." They opened the trunk, put down the lid, played with the buckles on the strap; the Major admired his curly locks in the gilt buttons or nail-heads in the trunk, while the Doctor examined his "amalgam" and "double uppers," or some such thing in his business, in the nail-heads of the other. In the meantime the Colonel and "Carlisle" had enjoyed several games of croquet on the floor of the store, while the other two were trying to calculate and find out what the lady who was waiting on them meant by saying she would not let them have the two trunks for a "bawbee" less, and the Colonel and "Carlisle" were only caused to look up at hearing the Doctor commence an outflow of refined German, while the Major was muttering something about "Scire facias, nolo contendre, nolle pros," etc., in reply to the lady saying something about that innocent little piece of money, the " bawbee." We righted them, however, and finally "Carlisle" was urged on to "jew" the woman down, and succeeded in spending the funds of the two—our dentist and barrister. Returning to the hotel, and relishing the good dinner in waiting for us, we were called upon by our escort, and were driven to the Queen's rooms, where was accorded us the largest largest reception we had the honor and pleasure to receive while on our crusade. It was tendered us by St. Mungo Encampment and the Masonic bodies of Glasgow in general; but the former body having charge of the affair, it was a reception in full Templar uniform. Ex-Provost Bain, of Glasgow, occupied the chair, and delivered the address of "welcome" in words of which only genuine Scotchmen are capable of giving, and Sir Knight Shaw, the Eminent Commander of St. Mungo Encampment, also gave us hearty welcome to the bounties of St. Mungo in a few kind words, and the following poem, written for the occasion of the grand reception and banquet:

Welcome.

BY R. S.

To the American Sir Knights of Allegheny Commandery, No. 35, K. T., on their visit to Glasgow, Scotland, July 23d, 1878.

Ye valiant Sir Knights from far distant shore,
As pilgrims you're welcome to Scotia once more;
Where some of your forefathers first saw the light,
Ere they sailed to the west, with the craft to unite
In that glorious work, the red and the blue,—
In your land sought a home as citizens true,
And adopted your laws, and made them your own;
They have fought for your cause, adorned your throne.

Hence naught can estrange, nor the ocean divide
These true hearts where precepts like ours doth reside;
Where charity reigneth and unity dwell,
No creed in creation can ever excel
Those tenets so bright, those principles pure—
Love God and thy fellow man, wealthy or poor.

Though submerged for a while, that great mystic chain,
At sight of Old Erin, 'twas soon linked again,
With that kind of friendship there's none can withstand,
With pure aspirations, fraternal and grand;
A cause that is holy, a cause that's sublime,
Embracing adherents of every clime.

Then here's to that band of great enterprise,
Where the Star Spangled Banner majesticly flies,
Where Washington's name is displayed on your chart,
And the name of a brother dear to the heart,
Who, if found in distress is welcomed and cheered,
For feelings of charity there are not seared,
There none but the honest and just are enrolled,

Well known to be such ere they enter the fold,
Not merely in name, but by scrutiny's lance,
Which raises you far above misguided France,
Who now are cast out like that fallen host,
Whom Milton portrays in his Paradise Lost;
Rebellious, unfaithful they've heaped on them shame,
They've purchased dishonor, they've sullied their fame.

May Omnipotent power upon you attend,
To guard you wherever your tour doth extend,
That nothing may happen to cause you regret
Is the heart wish of all who to-night here have met,
May that fire of friendship so nobly portrayed
By our sage from Kentucky in your breasts never fade;
And when to your far distant homes you return,
In your hearts may true friendship continue to burn.

Of this reception the *North British Mail* of Glasgow the following day, says: "One of the most successful and enjoyable meetings ever held in Scotland in connection with the ancient order of Freemasonry took place last evening in the Queen's Rooms. The occasion was the reception of a deputation of American Sir Knights and brethren, some of whom were on a second pilgrimage to Europe. In order to make the reception worthy of the occasion, all the arrangements which the Provincial Grand Lodge of Scotland, and St. Mungo Encampment of Glasgow could devise were concluded, and those who took an active part in the ceremony may be congratulated on its signal success. For a long series of years. ever since Masonry gained a footing in the United States, reciprocal feelings and aspirations have been breathed from both sides of the Atlantic for its welfare, and none were more willing to extend that feeling than the brethren of the United States, whose forefathers, no doubt, had first received the precepts of the order in the old country. Shortly after eight o'clock the company began to arrive at the Queen's Rooms, and there could not have been far short of five hundred Masons of all grades met to do honor to the distinguished American Masons, the most of whom are clothed in their handsome regalia as worn in America by the Knights Templar. They were received through an arch of steel formed by St. Mungo Encampment, and introduced by their Eminent Commander, W. F. Shaw, to the Provincial Grand Master, Colonel Montgomery Neilson."

After the reading of the poem we were soon seated to a royal feast, every delicacy of the season being spread upon the banquet boards, and fully five hundred Templars and Masons sat down at that table, every one of those five hundred, in their overflowing goodness of Scotch heart, caring kindly for each of us " poor, hungry, ill-fed" pilgrims in a foreign land. The tables were ladened with sweet flowers, and large and beautiful silver and crystal epergnes stood upon each table filled with the most lovely of cut flowers, the fragrance from and the appearance of the whole resembling one vast garden of the most beautiful gift of God to man. Those good people had an American garden growing somewhere in anticipation of our visit, for nothing that is plentiful with us was missing in the way of fruits. It may be considered a pardonable breach of etiquette on our part if the guests speak of the table of the host in this instance, for everything savored so of the good things of this life, on that evening, that to show our fellow brethren here in this country how our fraters of St. Mungo anticipated our American likes, we cannot refrain from mentioning a few of the delicacies spread before us at that reception. Following the more substantials were watermelons, citrons, grapes, pears, peaches greengages, bananas, pineapples, and so on ; and is it necessary to add to this vulgarity about eating, to say that every mother's son of the pilgrims of Allegheny Commandery did their duty nobly on that occasion ? Our Eminent Commander replied to the address of welcome by detailing the origin of their visit to the old country, and referred to the kind reception we had received in Ireland, before coming to Scotland. "The grand Masonic chain," he said, "which had been, so to speak, broken by the Atlantic, had been linked again when they met their brethren of Ireland and Scotland, and the present was by far the largest and grandest link they had ever seen. He and his brethren would not easily forget the kind reception they had that night received. Their Grand Master had just referred to the erection of a temple, but what better temple could they have in view, than the one referred to by our Lord Jesus Christ, in which brotherly love, charity and all the graces had their abode. He concluded by wishing every prosperity to the Freemasons of Scotland." The toast was pledged with three ringing American cheers " sent home" with an American skyrocket, a genuine " fizzer." The " Queen and Craft" were pledged and enthusiastically received.

Brother Cowper, the American Consul at Glasgow, who occupied the vice chair, in welcoming his brethren, said the Scotch were hard to become acquainted with, but when one knew them thoroughly, they found them possessed of the biggest hearts in the world." Brother Ex-Provost, Sir James Bain, responded to the toast, the "President of the United States," and cheerfully referred to the kindness he had received while acting as one of the Judges at the Centennial Exhibition in Philadelphia. Prof. Wm. H. Slack favored the company, in answer to calls for him, with one or two of his most pleasant songs, and we never recollect hearing Mr. Slack in better trim for doing so than on that evening.

Speech followed speech and song followed song, among which was a most pleasant feature. In the company were a body of Masons, composed entirely of Highlanders, all dressed in their handsome kilt costumes —and to see a handsome body of handsomely built handsome men, commend us to our good Highland fraters of St. Mungo—and we were treated to a couple of Highland songs in their Gaelic tongue; the airs were beautiful, and we are certain the words were also, and they were sung to the music of the bagpipes—a novelty to nearly all of the party. Deafening cheers ran through that hall, one thousand feet stamped the pleasure of all, and that substantial building was almost fairly made to shake as round after round of applause went forth at the words of speakers. After considerable speechifying had been done, towards the close of the evening, when the best of words were becoming a little droll, Major W. C.

Moreland arose in response to a toast, and commenced his remarks in an unusually low tone, and there sat the ex-Provost of Glasgow, the Sheriff of Glasgow, the Provincial Grand Master of Masons of Scotland and his officers, and no one was expecting much from the manner in which the speaker commenced; but as he warmed up in his eloquence, as he breathed forth his seemingly inspired thoughts, as he worked out his wonderfully exquisite and beautiful periods, with not a grammatical or rhetorical error in his remarks, we looked around and saw those five hundred heads motionless and still, those thousand eyes and hands as immovable as the walls of the building surrounding them. Assuredly on that evening he excelled himself, for, on closing his remarks, had heaven's artillery rolled its loudest battery, it would have been but as a whisper in that hall, compared with the terrible outburst of actual yells and applause from those present. Imagine if you can, dear reader, "Auld Lang Syne" sung by such an audience; it was the only "Auld Lang Syne" we ever heard. No wheedling "Auld Lang Syne," but good Scotch "Auld Lang Syne" poured forth in the broad accent of that noble people.

As the "wee sma' hours" were in upon us we parted company, assuredly with deep regret. The hearty shake of the hand to Allegheny by St. Mungo will ever be impressed with the most vivid and pleasant of recollections; the St. Mungo can ever rest assured that while Allegheny lives she will ever remember the evening spent 'neath the tents of our warm-hearted, generous and kind fraters of Glasgow.

"CARLISLE" SEPARATED FROM THE QUARTETTE.

Despite the pleasantries of the evening alluded to, through it all there was evidently in the interesting proceedings and general mirth a sigh of sadness coming at intervals from the Doctor on whose right sat "Carlisle," while on the left of the presiding officer's chair sat the Major and the Colonel, over whose faces rested a shade of melancholy; and we feign would know the reason of these sombre appearances. Towards the close of the evening these became more apparent, until reaching our rooms about one o'clock in the morning, the stout heart of the Doctor completely gave way, and bursting out into tears and howls, as we have known him to do over a "deceased purp," he exclaimed, "Oh! 'Carlisle,' must we go and leave you? Oh, I am sorely 'grieved.'" This "fetched down" the house. It was too much for the Major and the Colonel, and immediately every appearance of a funeral or a "wake" was in that room; the tender "boo-hoos" of the Colonel brought the hotel proprietor to see what poor soul was in grief; and although our separation was to be but for a day or so, yet the trio refused to be comforted or consoled. The Colonel perched on the side of the bed, his head buried deep in a pillow resting on his knee, while on a little bare spot on the summit of his cranium were nine Scotch flies, drawn up like an American base-ball field; but to these the brave warrior was oblivious. But to part we had, and "Carlisle" advised them to take it all philosophically and we would soon be re-united once more. Accepting which, they finally subdued their "overcomeness." We then proceeded to lay out our plans; and now we are satisfied the whole " boo-hooing " plan was a complete " set up " job to prey upon the feelings of poor " Carlisle," as the sequel will show.

The Doctor, if anything, the deeper villain of the three, commenced by saying, " ' Carlisle,' I had n't time to get my ' washing done ' to-day, I'll leave it here, and you bring it to me at Edinburgh, and I'll settle with you there." It evidently was a preconceived plan, for the " Majah " and the Colonel both had forgotten to attend to that duty on that day, and " Carlisle," innocently and unsuspectingly, from the goodness of his heart, proffered his ever-ready services to the distressed, and agreed to do so. All three then fell upon the neck of " Carlisle " and wept severely, the " boo-hoo-ing " was revived more than ever, good-bye was repeated over and over again, and we repaired to our room. The reason of the separation was, that having all gone over the ground the party were going over,—viz.: to Loch Lomond, Loch Katrine, Sterling, etc.—we did not care to repeat it; and as we had many kind friends to see around Glasgow, we separated, to overtake the party at Edinburgh. We will return to the " wash bill " later on.

At 5 A. M., the following morning, Mr. W. Stilwell, and " Carlisle " were called, had breakfast, and leaving our fellow-companions comfortably asleep, we took train for Hamilton. Having a " dog-cart " in waiting for us by Mr. William Wallace, of that place, we drove away up to the Hairshawhead, four miles above Straven, and twelve above Hamilton; the drive is through a beautiful country, though hilly, but the air is so pure and free, that you are at once invigorated and feel good and fresh. Arriving at the Hairshawhead, we find our old kind and good friend, Mr. James Semple, the owner of the place, and with his estimable wife, we all enter the house to enjoy a little social and pleasant chat. Perhaps no farm in Scotland, vast as it is, comprising some seven hundred acres, bears a better name for care and production than the "Auld Hairshawhead," while at every fair is carried away the first prize for stock by "Auld Hairshae." As we could remain but a short time, we enjoyed a hearty dinner, appetite for which had been given us by an early start and a long drive. We "buckled the beast," and returned to Hamilton, spending half an hour and enjoying the hospitality of our friend, Mr. Colin Spalding, whose name is well known there as being the prince of hotel keepers in his commodious and very comfortable Commercial Hotel, under whose roof many a pleasant evening has been spent by the writer.

Having done ourselves the pleasure of calling on the Misses Sommerville, of Hamilton, we took tea in the pleasant little cottage of Mrs. James Main, whose husband (now deceased) bore for many long years the honor of Baillie of Hamilton.

By the way, here, allow us to suggest to intending tourists to Scotland—by no means allow the points of interest and beauties of Hamilton and Lanarkshire and vicinity to be missed in your sight-seeing. Hamilton itself is a beautiful little town, and is noted for its fruit and flower gardens. In the old town is a spot called "Queenzie Neuk," where Queen Mary rested on her journey to Langside, and many other places of interest in Scottish history. Here also is Hamilton Palace, the seat of the Duke of Hamilton; it is a magnificent building and is shown only to well introduced visitors. The pillars of the portico, twelve in number, are twenty-five feet high and fully ten feet in span, and are each formed of a solid block of stone, quarried at Dalserf and requiring thirty horses to draw each stone to its position. Its interior is richly and fitly furnished and contains a number of costly works of art and virtu. The picture gallery is one of the finest in Scotland, and contains many famous pictures, such as the "Entombment of Christ," by Poussin; "The Ascension," by Giorgione; "The Madonna of Corregio;" "A Stag Hunt," by Snyders; Ruben's celebrated painting of "Daniel in the Lion's Den," etc., etc., and there is some £15,000 worth of rare prints. The plate, including a gold set, is valued at £50,000. Then within the grounds is the magnificent Mausoleum, and within short drives of the Palace are Cadzow Castle, Bothwell Castle, a handsome old ruin, Bothwell Bridge, the field of Drumclog, and many such places identified with the Scottish wars and history, over all of which we cannot in this work justly go. Let us not, however, forget to mention the beautiful Falls of Clyde, a short distance above the town of Lanark, and tourists will be deprived of a rich treat in not paying these pretty little Falls a visit, for these and all around this delightful section will find it more than usually attractive to readers, lovers and admirers of that grand and noble old people, the Scotch. They are a grand people in the truest sense of the word—no particular hurry and bustle, it is true; but straightforward, honest and canny—you can depend on them every time.

A noticeable feature between this people and those of the pretty Emerald Isle we have just left—and we mean no disrespect in saying so (for it would be hard to find a better people than the Irish)—and that is this: An Irishman will tell you the longest Indian and snake yarns for the honest, serious, pure God's truth; but a Scotchman will tell you the same yarns, but will add, " that it is *said* to be true," or " *said* to have occurred." While speaking of the Scotchman, we lately heard a pretty good story of a Highlandman and an English thorough Cockney in a row boat, away through the Highlands somewhere; and although it has no reference to the subject in hand, the story is good enough to be told anywhere and under any circumstances:

It appears the Highlandman was rowing a party across one of the lakes, and in the party was a thorough Cockney, who thought it would be good fun to stand up and rock the boat. The Highlander said to Mr. Englishman, "Tu had better sit doon or tu will fall oot." But the rocking continued until, sure enough, Mr. Englishman did " fall oot," and being unable to swim, the Highlander reached for him, grabbing him by the top of the head, pulling away the wig of the Cockney. He reached for him as he was disappearing for the second time, catching him by the breast, this time pulling away his paper "dickey," which so surprised the "Heelandman" that he threw the imitation shirt and scalp into the bottom of the boat and exclaimed, "My God, the man's made o' remnants!"

We were very sorry our time was so short here, for this seemed to us to be our real home, and we should have loved to have remained longer, so taking train we returned to Glasgow, only ten miles distant from Hamilton, and returning to the hotel somewhat tired, we sat down to enjoy a cigar, when in came a party of about one hundred, which proved to be the Young Men's Christian Association from America, among whom was our fellow-townsman, Mr. Robert Orr, who was looking well. Of course the hotel that evening was of a thoroughly religious character, and it was a gratification indeed, to see so many young men engaged in this good work, all on their way to Geneva, we believe, to exchange congratulations with their brethren of the Old World over their reformation of the wicked and worldly. Next day we enjoyed in visiting friends in Glasgow, and we were very sorry at being compelled to leave without shaking hands with our friend, Mr. Hume. Through the kindness of Mr. John B. Main, we were shown through the enormous business house of Messrs. Arthur & Company, engaged in the general dry goods line. At 4 P. M. we bade good-bye to our friend, Mr. Stilwell— he to sail that evening on S. S. "Anchoria," of Anchor Line, for home, and I to rejoin the party at Edinburgh.

Calling at the office of the hotel for the aforesaid "washing bill," which being presented, each separate item was carefully scrutinized—the Colonel's, one pound fifteen; the Major's, one pound fourteen and two pence ha'penny: and the Doctor's, one pound nine and a penny three farthings; which "bills of particulars" led us fully to believe no "cleansing" had been done for either of those three renowned personages for the past seventeen years, as was the self-confessed case of our Teutonic friend engaged in the jewelry business. "Carlisle" demurred at the payment of these gross amounts, and seeing no way to compromise on their confounded "soiled linen," he determined to leave their collars and socks and "sich" for the benefit of the poor; we wanted to compromise by having the hotel people keep the "furnishing goods" aforesaid if I would pay for the white ties these plebeians had "embezzled" from "Carlisle's" satchels; but, evidently anticipating something of this kind, they attached "Carlisle's" baggage, and as the hour for leaving had come, we were compelled to pay up, and take their abominable luggage along.

Let us say here, that nowhere on our trip did we enjoy ourselves more, have a better place to stop at, and more kind attention, than from Mr. and Mrs. Philp, the proprietors of the New Cockburn Hotel, of Glasgow —the latter being a native of Louisiana, and her genial husband we have frequently met in our own city of Allegheny. The hotel is newly built, newly furnished, and is a model in every respect.

Seated in the cars were soon sound asleep, and awakened only as we were entering the renowned old city and capital of Edinburgh, Scotland, and, on looking out of the windows of the cars, we saw Clinton and Fullerton and Moreland and Baxter linked arm-in-arm strolling toward the hotel. We soon rejoined them.

Letter No. 6.

Edinburgh.—Presentation of Bills to the Trio of the "Quartette."—Reception and Banquet by the Provincial Grand Lodge.—Melrose and Abbottsford.—Recherche Banquet at Leeds.—To London, and the Doctor and "Carlisle," now two poor and weary pilgrims, traveling alone.—Incidents by the Way.

As it was almost evening when we arrived in this good old capital city of Scotland, and the Commandery had arrived there during the night before, they had had the opportunity of seeing all the objects of local and historical points of interest which Edinburgh presents, the writer having more than once visited its attractive features, we did not care to again go over oft trodden ground, so we need not, therefore, enter into any detail of its palaces, castles, monuments, etc., further than a casual glance of a few of the many points which would interest the sight-seer for weeks, in following the wonderful history of Scotland, especially this ancient city of that good old country, whose wars and fame rank with those of the Romans, and have formed some remarkable historical annals in the history of the world.

The site of Edinburgh is generally admitted to be one of the most striking of any of the European capitals, and a more charming prospect than its hills present cannot be conceived, and David Macbeth beautifully and comprehensively describes its view and situation in the following words:

> "Traced like a map the landscape lies,
> In cultured beauty stretching wide;
> There Pentland's green acclivities;
> There Ocean with its azure tide;
> There Arthur's seat; and gleaming through
> Thy southern wing, Dunedin blue!
> While in the Orient, Lammer's daughters,
> A distant giant range are seen,
> North Berwick law, with cone of green,
> And Bass amid the waters."

In Princes street, a beautiful avenue, built only upon one side, with pleasure gardens upon the other side, stands the elegant monument to Sir Walter Scott, a magnificent piece of work costing £16,000. The Royal Institution, the National Gallery of Painting, the High School, the Philosophical Institution, etc., in the new town, are all worthy a visit, and much time can pleasantly and profitably be spent visiting them.

In close alliance to history, however, is the old town of Edinburgh, and while the new is beautifully laid out, terraced, and massively built with elegant modern buildings, with magnificent streets and drives, we will with the reader take a little walk through the old town, and take a hasty glimpse into a few of its famed courts and nooks; as every inch of this ground covers pages in history we cannot dwell long with any, nor speak of but a limited number. First, we come to the Castle, which stands upon a precipitous rock three hundred and eighty-three feet above the level of the sea, and commands a splendid view of the city and the surrounding country. Before gunpowder was invented, it was considered entirely impregnable, but with Gatling and Krupp guns of to-day, we fear sad havoc would be made of the walls and the valuable inner apartments. This old Castle is associated with many wonderful events, as doubtless all are familiar with its history, the attack upon it, in 1313, by Randolph, Earl of Moray, the defense of it, in Queen Mary's behalf by Sir William Kircaldy, and in 1650 its surrender to Oliver Cromwell. In the Crown Room are deposited the regalia, the insignia of Scottish royalty, consisting of the crown, sceptre, sword of state, and Lord Treasurer's rod of office. Adjoining the Crown Room is Queen Mary's Room, where Queen Mary gave birth to James VI, in whom the crowns of England and Scotland were united, On the wall is the following inscription, surmounted by the Scottish arms:

> "Lord Jesu Chryst, that crounit was with thornse,
> Preserve the birth, quhais Badgie heir is borne,
> And send Hir sonne successione, to reigne still,
> Lang in this realm, if that it be thy will.
> Als grant, O Lord, quhat ever of Hir proceed,
> Be to thy honer, and Praise, sobied.
>   19th, IVNII, 1566.

Upon the highest point of rock is Saint Margaret's Chapel, the oldest in Scotland, as Queen Margaret died in 1093, and close by this is famous old "Mons

Meg," a gigantic piece of artillery, cast in Belgium, in 1476, and having a history dating with the James's of Scotland. It is at the bore twenty inches in diameter, was used at the siege of Dumbarton in 1489, and Worham in the reign of James IV, in 1497; was burst in 1683, in firing a salute of honor, removed to the tower of London in 1684, and on the petition of Sir Walter Scott, was restored to the Castle by the Duke of Wellington in 1829.

Going down the High street, built up on either side are houses with ten, eleven and twelve stories to each, and it is no little source of amusement to see "washings" hanging out from the topmost stories from one side of the street to the other, with a pair of hose looking like a dot in the heavens, and articles of unmentionable nature resembling but the very small end of an American boy's kite-tail on one of our fire alarm telegraph wires.

Every building and dilapidated house and court upon this street has a history, and was the residence of some of the royalty, living in those disturbing days, and whose lives and characters go to make up that history. Upon the site of the Free Church Assembly Hall stood the house of Mary of Guise, Queen of James V, and mother of Queen Mary. Then there is a small remnant of the famous West Bow, which was ascended by Anne of Denmark, James I, Charles I, Oliver Cromwell, Charles II, James VII, and was the route by which the Marquis of Montrose and the Earl of Argyle were conveyed in the hangman's cart to their place of execution in the Grassmarket, and through this West Bow the murderers of Captain Porteus hurled their victim, which incident forms one of the most striking incidents in Sir Walter Scott's *Midlothian*. Then we come to St. Giles Church, a very ancient building, and belongs architecturally to various times. It was in the choir of this church, in 1637, that Jenny Geddes, a very devout lady indeed, threw her cutty stool at the Dean of Edinburgh, on his attempting to read the new Episcopal service book.

In Parliament Square also is the Parliament House, the ancient meeting place of the Scottish Parliament, but which has been appropriated since the Union for the use of the Supreme Courts, in connection with which is the Advocates' Library, containing the most valuable collection of books in Scotland, numbering upwards of 200,000 volumes, including very rare and curious works in Scottish poetry.

John Knox's house, provided for him in 1559, when he was elected minister of Edinburgh, is also in High street, where the great reformer resided from 1560 to 1572, and passing on down by many objects of interest, we come to Holyrood Palace. No building has ever, before its foundation or since, passed through such scenes of ambition, strife and bloodshed as has done the original church of the Holy Rood. Founded and richly endowed by King David I, as a church, it passes through years of worship within its walls, is burned, rebuilt, becomes the seat and home of royalty and the scene and seat of conspiracy, bloodshed, murder, crime, arson, &c., with such rapidity as to make its history a startling panorama.

Here resided the Duke of York, afterwards James II, of England, the adventurous Charles Edward Stuart, and the exiled Comte d'Artois, afterwards Charles X, of France; and George IV, on his visit to Edinburgh in 1822, held levees in the Palace, and it is still used by the present Queen Victoria as her residence on her visits to and from the Highlands of Scotland.

The most interesting portion of the Palace of course is Queen Mary's apartments; we enter Queen Mary's bed-room containing an ancient bed and some furniture. On one side of the room is the door of the secret passage by which the conspirators entered, and adjoining is the cabinet where they found their victim, Rizzio. It is said he was dragged from this to the door of the Audience Chamber, where he was finally despatched, and the exact spot where the body lay is identified by a stain of blood, still visible. Darnley, who headed the conspirators, entered first, and casting his arm fondly round the Queen's waist, seated himself beside her at a table, Lord Ruthven followed in complete armor, looking pale and ghastly, as one scarcely recovered from long sickness. Others crowded in after them, till the closet was filled with armed men. While the Queen demanded the purpose of their coming, Rizzio, who saw that his life was aimed at, got behind her and clasped the folds of her gown, that the respect due to her person might protect him. The assassins threw down the table, and seized upon the unfortunate object of their vengeance, while Darnley himself took hold of the Queen, and forced Rizzio and her asunder. It was their intention, doubtless, to have dragged Rizzio out of Mary's presence, and to have killed him elsewhere, but their fierce impatience hurried them into instant murder. They dragged him through the bed-room and ante-room and despatched him at the head of the staircase with no less than fifty-six wounds. Then there is the Abbey of Holyrood and Queen Mary's bath, &c. Arthur's seat is a beautiful drive, it being entirely surrounded by a magnificent roadway called the "Queen's Drive." We hastily glance at the University, Greyfriars' Church and Churchyard, Heriot's Hospital, the Dean Bridge, the Fettes College and a drive through the beautiful streets in the new town of Edinburgh, and you have been with us on one of the most delightful drives and walks possible in any country. With a closely read history of Scotland, you have here in Edinburgh much food for memory and thought, and we need speak no farther than we have already hastily done, as but few can exist, who are not as entirely familiar with its sights and historical objects as though they had gone over the ground in person, if they have have never done so in fact.

Upon entering the hotel, the "quartette" were soon reunited, tears of joy flowed free as a never-failing mountain stream, and mirth, merriment and rejoicing were the order of the hour over the wandering "Carlisle's" return. Just think of it, "Carlisle" had been absent from them for over two days, or as you like it, they had been absent from "Carlisle" for over two days.

"O! my, how glad we are to see you once more, my dear 'Carlisle'!" "How, oh! how we have missed you, 'Carlisle'!" and such expressions gushed forth from the mouths and hearts of these scheming plebeians; and while this "taffy" business was going on, "Carlisle" inwardly chuckled over the "Sweet Williams" in his pocket, which would soon bring forth such "blessings" as the Irish women of Queenstown pour out upon you when you refuse to buy any of their sweet little shamrock or gooseberries, etc. Tapping the Doctor on the watch-chain, for we couldn't reach up to his shoulder, we called him over to one side, and, in a low tone, said: "One pound, nine and a penny three farthings?" "What for?" yelled the Doctor, his joyous expression of face over "Carlisle's" return, changing to one of savage madness. "Washing!" whispered "Carlisle." "Washing?" yelled the now almost maniac, and said he never would pay it. "All right, Doctor, if it suits you, we can stand it," we replied. Fearing to further disturb the guests of the hotel, we called the Major and our gallant Colonel out, and wandering away up to old "Mons Meg" (the aforementioned small sized cannon in the Castle,) we got the commander to load old "Mons" up, and to fire her off when the "Majah" and the Colonel were about to reply. Putting a cart-load of powder into old "Mons," we seated ourselves on that high eminence on which the Castle is situated, covering that magnificent view, and calling their attention, we whispered to the Major, " One pound fourteen and two-pence ha'penny;" and to the Colonel, "One pound, fifteen;" when up jumped the two with a ferocious, demoniacal yell. " Ah!——" but we could n't hear the remainder of the sentence, as our scheme with old "Mons Meg" worked like a charm; for at that moment she belched forth her fire and smoke, drowning at least a little of the soft intonations of the gentlemen's voices. " Never pay it —never would!" echoed from them. We chuckled still further when we thought of about a hundred pounds' worth of new clothing in our trunk as "collateral" for their battle-worn linen, without buttons even; and we thought the "collateral" good, too, remembering that one coat of the Doctor's would make us a suit for summer and an overcoat for winter. Hinting the same, and stating we would immediately foreclose on the security, the gentlemen " came down " handsomely, paid their just bills, and, *sotto voce,* " Carlisle " was in another " pound, seven and six."

At eight o'clock on this evening, we were waited upon by an escort, or rather a committee, from the Grand Lodge of Masons of Edinburgh, Scotland, and taken to Freemasons' Hall, where another reception was tendered us; and coming as it did entirely spontaneously, and without any previous notice, was one of the most enjoyable affairs of the kind occurring on our tour. We were shown the beauties of the Grand Lodge room, the beauty and skill of the portraitures on the walls and ceiling, after which an exchange of congratulations with our newly-made friends, for we soon all knew each other as well as though we had been acquainted for years. We were conducted into the Board Room, and there sat down to a magnificent banquet table, covered with the good things of this life. Toasts, speeches, song and pleasant conversation soon passed the hours away. Of this reception and banquet the *Edinburgh Courant* with others speak thus: "Another Masonic meeting similar to the one held on Tuesday evening, (alluding to one tendered upon invitation to Mary Commandery, No. 36, of Philadelphia,) took place in Freemasons' Hall last night for the purpose of welcoming a 'Masonic Pilgrimage' from America. Brother William Mann, Past Senior Grand Warden, occupied the throne on the occasion; Brother Dr. J. Carmichael, R. W. M. of St. Andrew's, No. 48, acting as Senior Grand Warden; and Brother W. Greig, Grand Master of St. Stephen's, No. 145, acting as Junior Grand Warden; and these were supported by representatives of Grand Lodge and Masters of Lodges in the metropolitan province, who received the pilgrims as Master Masons. Amongst the members of Grand Lodge present were—Brothers D. Murray Lyon, Grand Secretary; David Kinnear, Grand Cashier; R. S. Brown, representative of the Grand Lodge of Kentucky; Dr. Loth, representative of the Grand Orient of France; Dr. Walter S. Carmichael, Dr. Dickson, Lindsay Mackersey,

Schopp, and Kay, &c. The visitors were members of the Allegheny Commandery, No. 35, of Knights Templar, of Pennsylvania, at present on a pilgrimage from America to Ireland, Scotland, England, Holland, Belgium, the Rhine, Switzerland, Italy, and the Paris Exposition. About thirty of them attended the meeting. On the arrival of the members, Grand Lodge was opened in the first degree, and the visitors were received with the customary honors, when a few words of hearty welcome were addressed to them from the throne. The Grand Master extended to each a fraternal greeting on the part of the brethren present, and the Eminent Commander Brother Smith suitably acknowledged the welcome, expressed the gratitude of his brethren for the manner in which they had been received, and the hope that in America they would soon have an opportunity of receiving visitors from the Grand Lodge of Scotland. Brother Hay then in a few sentences referred to the presence of Brother Dr. Morris, whose name as an author in Masonic literature was so well known to every reading Mason, and craved leave specially to thank the learned brother for his visit. This was carried with acclamation, and Brother Hay tastefully discharged the duty thus placed upon him. Dr. Morris, in the course of his reply, directed the attention of the visitors to the hall of Grand Lodge. Its beauty, and the skill displayed in the portraiture on its walls, would not, he assured them, be excelled in any Masonic temple they might visit, though some would be seen more costly and more elaborate; and he congratulated Grand Lodge on the possession of such a gem. Grand Lodge was then closed, and the brethren thereafter adjourned to the board-room, where they sat down to a banquet. After some time had been spent in friendly conversation, a number of toasts were given from the chair, comprising " The Queen," " The President of the United States," and then the toast of the evening—" The Visiting Brethren." In speaking to the latter the acting Grand Master expressed the pleasure which it afforded the brethren to see the visitors in Scotland, and the hope that their " pilgrimage " would tend to many private fraternal friendships, and to the benefit of the craft throughout the universe. Brother Smith made a very happy reply, enumerating the many invitations they had received since the idea of their trip across the Great Pond first oozed out, and the kindly, enthusiastic manner in which those already implemented had been fulfilled. He trusted that these meetings would be like ripples on the water, which would ever increase, and would still be growing after their return to America. In concluding, he proposed " The Grand Lodge of Scotland," and that toast was drank with all honors, including what the Americans styled a " sky-rocket." Brother Hay acknowledged the toast, and expressed the pride with which they found at Grand Lodge representatives from the most of the Grand Lodges of all America. He trusted that their brethren would appreciate the welcome now given them by Scottish Masons, would appreciate Scottish hospitality, and also Scottish whiskey, although there did not happen to be any of it on the table.

(Applause and laughter.) Brother Dr. Morris proposed "The music and poetry of Freemasonry," and in the course of his speech remarked that nothing had ever surprised him more when he began to study the subject than to find that while they had in their order such men as Scott, Ferguson, James Hogg, and Tom ·Moore, and many other writers, none of them, with the exception of Burns, had ever written a single line of Masonic verse. How Scotland's great poet and novelist, Sir Walter Scott, could have written so much poetry as he did, and never have found anything in the symbols and ceremonies of Masonry to write about was marvelous to him— (Hear, hear)—and he thought sometimes that these portions of his works must have been suppressed. In conclusion, Dr. Morris recited some verses of his own, which were afterwards excellently sung by Brother Slack, and were much admired. Brother Mackersey next proposed "The Grand Lodges of America." He remarked that there was one in every State, and that all of them were in a most flourishing condition, and were conducted in a most creditable manner. He expressed towards them the best wishes of the brethren in Scotland, and the hope that mutual good feeling would long continue, and would be cemented by many such meetings as the present. Brother Major Moreland replied in an eloquent address, in the course of which he said he had no doubt that when they went back to America they would give to each country visited by them that niche in their memory and that part in their hearts which such acts of hospitality as they were now receiving so richly and warmly warranted them in assigning. Brother R. S. Brown then gave "The Masonic Literature of America," in replying for which Dr. Morris referred to the position in Masonic literature taken by Brother D. Murray Lyon, and congratulated the Grand Lodge in having appointed him as Grand Secretary at a time when that office was so anxiously looked to in America as in other parts. Brother Smith then proposed "The Chairman;" the "Health of the Croupiers" was given from the chair; and afterwards, at the close of "Auld Lang Syne," the company separated. Several songs were given in the course of the evening in excellent style, particularly by the American brethren, and altogether the meeting was voted a most successful gathering. The general arrangements by Brother D. Murray Lyon for the two receptions that have taken place this week, and the purveying by Brother Theim, were admirable.

But before passing over this happy evening, happily spent, among happy friends and brethren, we must insert a remark made by a venerable and worthy brother of the Grand Lodge, holding a high position therein, in the course of his speech when he alluded to the Grand Lodge having tendered Mary Commandery, No. 36, of Philadelphia, a reception an evening or so previous, he said "he thought that Allegheny Commandery, No. 35, had rather the nicer body of men." Oh! now we have gone and done it sure. We did not intend to insert that, actually, but now that it is done, there is no use crying over spilled milk at all. We have always had since childhood' the strongest kind of an inclination to make some person or persons angry, and we did not know a better place to commence than on the good nature of Mary Commandery. Of her members we can truthfully say, they are as fine a body of men as ever stepped from the Templar Asylum, and we know Mary, No. 36, loves Allegheny No. 35 from the bottom of her large heart; but oh, what a pity No. 35 ever made two European Crusades, and has been made the recipients of so much distinction and so many favors in Europe. Just think— Allegheny Commandery ahead all the time. But we pray thee, Mary, darling, don't be angry with us, dear; it wasn't Allegheny Commandery's fault made that brother say that. "Carlisle" was along; that did the business. The worthy brother couldn't help it. Don't take it too hard, Mary. Allegheny No. 35 can't help having these good things said of her.

Next morning at 6:20 we were on our way to Melrose and Abbottsford—the ride thither being of a most pleasing character. On emerging from the tunnel after leaving the station at Edinburgh, a view is obtained on the right, of Arthur's Seat, Holyrood Palace, and ruins of St. Anthony's Chapel. Passing Portobello and the grounds of Dalhousie Castle, we obtain a beautiful prospect of the Pentland Hills. All along the route we pass places, points and spots of historic interest, as we believe every inch of Scottish soil is historic at any rate.

Arriving at Melrose, our two railway carriages are uncoupled and switched to a side track to await our return from a visit to Melrose, the Abbey and Abbottsford.

Melrose is a neat little city of some fifteen hundred inhabitants. In the centre of the market place is a stone cross bearing date of 1642, and opposite the King's Arms Hotel is a gabled house, of date 1635, where General Leslie slept on the night before the battle of Philliphaugh.

The Abbey is about five minutes walk from the station. It was founded by David I., in 1136, but not completed until 1146, and we may be permitted to say here, for a founder of churches and monasteries, &c., David I. bears away the palm, as nearly all claim to have been founded by that religiously inclined individual. It was destroyed by the English in 1322, and four years later was rebuilt from a fund of £2,000, equal to £50,000 of the money of the present day, by King Robert Bruce. It is a beautiful ruin, its style of magnificence entitling it to be classed among the most perfect work of the best age of ecclesiastical architecture.

In 1385 it was partially burnt by Richard II.; in 1545 it was despoiled by Evers and Latoun; and again in the same year by the Earl of Hetford. Oliver Cromwell amused himself a little while also by bombarding it from Gatton side, on the other side of the river.

The estates of the Abbey were granted by Queen Mary in 1566, to James Hepburn, Earl of Bothwell, by whose forfeiture, in 1567, they reverted again to the crown, and the usufruct, with the title of commendator, was conferred the following year upon James Douglass, second son to Sir William Douglass of Lochleven. Sir Walter Scott retains some of the lines of a popular satire on the monks of Melrose Abbey, which probably explains the reason of their mode of life being obnoxious to the Reformers:

"The monks of Melrose made fat kail
On *Fridays* when they fasted;
And neither wanted beef nor ale,
As long as their neighbor's lasted."

The Duke of Buccleuch is its present custodian, and to him the public is indebted for its careful preservation. The church is in the usual form of a Latin cross, with a square tower in the centre eighty-four feet in height. The entire length of the building is 258 feet, and the breadth of its transepts 137 feet.

The parts in best preservation are the choir, transept, part of the nave and nearly the whole of the southern aisle. The nave is bordered by two aisles, and intersected by what was formerly an organ loft. In the right or south aisle are eight small chapels, lighted by richly traceried windows and supported by double flying buttresses. In one of the niches of these buttresses there is a mutilated figure of the Virgin Mary and child, and in another, to the east, a statue of St. Andrew, the patron saint of Scotland.

The north transept, beautifully lighted by a circular or oriel window, representing the crown of thorns is one of its beauties. The window is one of rare beauty in the specimen of that style of ancient art, and the late Sir Walter Scott alludes to it in his Lay of the Last Minstrel, thus beautifully:

> "Thou wouldst have thought some fairy hand
> Twixt poplars straight the osier wand
> In many a freakish knot had twined;
> Then framed a spell when the work was done,
> And changed the willow wreath to stone."

The heart of the Bruce was deposited in this place after the attempt of the good Sir James of Douglass to carry it to the Holy Land, although the King's body had been interred at Dunfermline.

Among the many curious epitaphs in the graveyard is the following:

The earth goeth	The earth builds
on the earth	on the earth
Glistring like gold.	Castles and touers;
The earth goes	The earth says
to the earth	to the earth
Sooner than it wold.	All shall be ours.

Leaving this handsome old ruin, we found carriages in waiting for us, and were at once driven to Abbottsford, the abode of the wonderful poet and novelist, Sir Walter Scott, which is beautifully situated, overlooking the fine sweep of the river, and all through the thick woods surrounding Abbottsford are winding walks planned and laid out by Sir Walter Scott himself.

It is a beautifully made up building—Abbottsford—as almost every building celebrated in ancient history have contributed something to its erection; pieces from Holyrood, Dunfermline, Linlithgow, and the churches of Melrose and Roslin have furnished their share. In the armory are collections of warlike instruments, old trophies, curiosities, &c., among which may be mentioned Rob Roy's gun, Montrose's sword, the gift of Charles I., Grahame of Claverhouse's pistol; pistols found in Napoleon's carriage after Waterloo; Hofer's blunderbuss, James the Sixth's hunting flask, Roman spear head, thumbkins and other instruments of torture. Then there is the Library, the Study with his old chair in which we all sat, the dining hall, &c., all full of interesting objects. The present proprietor of Abbottsford is J. R. Hope Scott, Esq.

Our time being up, we hurried back to the station, only to find an accident had occurred somewhere along the railroad, and our train was some two hours late. Becoming hungry, we wandered back into the town, and James Milliken, Clinton, Fullerton, Moreland, Smith, the Colonel, and "Carlisle" cleared out the two bakeries of the village in little less than no time. Poor Mrs. Mifflin, delicate as she was, had gotten about half-a-crown's worth "cookies," and was sitting all by her little lone self, getting away with them. Poor Mrs. M.! how our hearts went out to her in her being so delicate! We spoke of the same in a former letter.

Finally, the train came along, the Knights of Submission business was reopened more vigorously than ever before; Mrs. Slack, our mother, sat up two nights endeavoring to rebuild the Doctor's duster, and at 6 P. M. we arrived in Leeds, in " Merrie Old England," two hours and a half late, in which we were sadly disappointed, as Leeds Priory had called a special conclave at a special hour, that we might be received in open Priory, as will be seen by the following orders issued by the officers of Leeds Priory:

FIDELITY PRECEPTORY

OF THE

ROYAL AND UNITED RELIGIOUS AND MILITARY ORDERS OF THE

TEMPLE AND MALTA.

Sir Knight S. E. SEANOR, E. P.

DEAR SIR KNIGHT:

An emergency meeting will be held on Friday, the 26th inst., at 5:30 P. M., at the Fidelity Rooms, Carlton Hill, Leeds, at which the members of Allegheny Commandery, No. 35, Knights Templar, of Pennsylvania, America, will be present.

A banquet will be given by the Preceptory to the American visitors at the Great Northern Hotel, Leeds, at eight o'clock, to which you are invited to be present, and may introduce a lady. Tickets for which may be obtained of myself, 29 Bond Street, not later than Thursday, the 25th inst.

I am, dear Sir Knight,

Fraternally yours,

J. J. BOSWELL, 18°,

Registrar.

As stated, owing to our arriving late, we could not visit their Priory, much as we desired to do so; so barber shops were hunted down, barbers made wealthy, and at 8 P. M. we were escorted to the Great Northern Hotel, where we received another reception, the most *recherche* affair we had the pleasure of attending.

Every arrangement was so complete, a drawing-room had been set apart for a cloak-room, and the spacious dining-hall, with its rows of tables covered with beautiful white linen and decorated in the highest style, and being so profusely and richly laden with the luxuries spread upon them, it was a most beautiful sight. It was a full dress reception, the gentlemanly Knights of Leeds Priory being accompanied, and the occasion graced, by the wives, daughters, and most beautiful ladies of Leeds. A very handsomely gotten up *menu* was prepared, and the following toasts printed upon the other side was in each plate:

BANQUET, JULY 26TH, 1878.

I. Her Gracious Majesty, the Queen.
II. The President of the United States.
III. The Grand Patron of English and the Most Eminent Commander of American Knights Templar.
IV. To All Eminent Knights Templar and Freemasons of Every Grade.
V. Our American Visitors.
VI. The Ladies.

During the banquet these toasts were severally announced from the chair by Eminent Sir Samuel E. Seanor, the E. P. of Fidelity Preceptory, and responded to by the various persons announced to respond to each. Kind words of welcome and congratulation came from the speakers. The order of toasts being " Her Most Gracious Majesty the Queen," " The President of the United States," " The Grand Patron of English and the Most Eminent Commander of American Knights Templar," " To all Eminent Knights Templar and Freemasons of every grade," " Our American Visitors," and " The Ladies," the latter being responded to by our Captain-General, Sir William C. Moreland. From his wonderful vocabulary of language, and in his beautiful oratory, was paid a lovely tribute to women in general—the ladies of Leeds—those present in particular. How kind those good fraters of Leeds were, none but those who participated in their hospitality on that occasion can know; and though years may roll round, and should many such occasions be enjoyed, never will the memory of that pleasant and happy evening be forgotten. Of one thing we are positive, that never shall we forget the hospitality, the hearty welcome, the knightly and friendly greeting of Sir Samuel Seanor and his good wife, and the kind and beautiful face of his charming daughter, our *vis-a-vis* on that evening, and our newly made but warm friend, J. Smiley Coey, Esq.; and as, since our pleasant visit to Leeds, venerable father Time has wrought happy changes in that assembly, so that our charming lady friend, the daughter of Eminent Sir Seanor is now the loving wife of our friend Mr. Coey, may we be permitted to wish in these lines, their lives to be long spared to each other, to go through this world with the very smallest portion of life's sorrows allotted to mankind as their share, and ever may their love be pure as the mountain air, clear and sparkling as the dewdrop, touched by the kisses of the glad morning sunbeam upon the leaf, and as refreshing as the cold mountain stream trickling from its hidden fountain in the rocks, is our earnest prayer and hearty wish.

At 11 P. M. we returned to our hotel, bade our friends good-bye, and the "Quartette" were soon comfortably ensconced in a decent car, known to us as a " Pullman Drawing-Room Sleeping Car," and, oh! how we enjoyed meeting a good old friend—a genuine, real Pullman Sleeper. Our berths being made up, we were soon fast in the "arms of Morpheus," to awaken at 7 A. M. in the Midland Grand Depot and Hotel in the great city of London, where we arrived at the appointed hour. On that day our company was to be in part broken—the "Quartette" was then and there to be finally split and separated. Before leaving England for the Continent, we can see—on looking back over our trip through Ireland, Scotland and England—in our receptions at these various places a cool, calm and premeditated determination on the part of our fraters of the Old World to massacre us in and under the guise of kindness. It was nothing but "come and eat," "come and eat," from the time we landed till the time we left; a pure case of attempt at murder by gorging, either for vengeance on the party of 1871 for having such men as Judge Heath,

Judge Sholes, Senator Rambo, &c., along, who had eaten them nearly out of house and home on that crusade, or to deter other bodies from making a similar pilgrimage in another year; and that our readers may judge of the way we were feasted, a few comparisons in weights will sufficiently prove. The Doctor at New York, one hundred and ten pounds, at London, two hundred and ten; the Major, at New York, one hundred and thirteen and a quarter pounds, at London, one hundred and ninety-six pounds fourteen ounces; the Colonel, at Utah, ninety-six pounds ten ounces, at London, two hundred and twenty-six pounds, seven and a half ounces; Jacob Laucks, Esq., at New York, one hundred and fourteen pounds, at London, forty-seven pounds. (We can only account for loss in the latter case from his excessive noise and boisterousness.) "Carlisle," at New York, one hundred and forty-four pounds, at London, one hundred and fifty. (It will be observed in this case that six pounds in addition to "Carlisle's" weight would be a bona fide increase, and no gorging there.) These will do as instances, and we dread giving additional ones. The day we arrived in London we spent in sight-seeing, and as the Doctor and "Carlisle" were pressed for time, we could not take all of the tour as laid down for the party for the Continent, so we booked as fellow-travelers from London alone, and as we came back to London before sailing for home, we will see what is to be seen there. At 8 P. M. we bade good-bye to all in our party, not without regret, for we had many of us met as strangers but were parting now as friends. We could not prevent the ladies of the party falling upon our necks and ——. Well, it's all right, we won't tell the rest. Mrs. M., of Philadelphia, did n't fall on us, however, for this trip would have been an unwritten history, so far as "Carlisle" or the Doctor were concerned, forever. Our recollections of all are most pleasant. True, every one has their little peculiarities—who hasn't? we have, we know—but these can be all overlooked; and we say again, that there never could have been thirty-eight persons more congenial and gentlemanly towards each other than were those of the Pilgrimage Party of Allegheny Commandery during 1878. To each one belongs more or less of the many pleasant days we all enjoyed together, and to each one we are indebted for his or her share of the pleasure during the crusade. On this point we will have something more to say a few pages further on in this work.

As stated, at 8 P. M. the Doctor and "Carlisle" took train—two fellow-travelers alone now—for Newhaven, Dieppe and Paris, and a royal good trip we did have.

Letter No. 7.

A Saturday Night's Ride to Paris.—The Two Pilgrims in Paris.—Meeting of Friends in Cologne.—Accident on the Rhine.—Bingen.—Mayence.—Heidleberg.—Bâle.—Lake Lucerne.—Brunig Pass and Brienz Valley.—Interlaken.—Berne.—Martigny to Chamouny, over the Tête-Noire.—Geneva.—To London.—Incidents by the Way.

WE were now " two poor and weary pilgrims " traveling alone, all by their own little and big selves and going into a country and countries, where the inhabitants thereof could speak their language in a much more proper and refined manner than could either of the aforesaid pilgrims, for neither of them could speak or understand one word of the French language.

Owing to the hour, darkness soon interrupted our seeing the country through which we were passing, so conversation was our pleasant pastime, and reflection of the many new friends and acquaintances made during the past three weeks, and the incidents transpiring, as related in our past letters.

In our compartment were two very pleasant and entertaining English gentlemen, who gave us much valuable information. With us also was a gentleman clad in navy-blue uniform, with gilt buttons, wearing a gondola hat, around which was a band lettered in gold, " Tourist Agent." We found him to be a conductor for that firm taking over a regular Saturday evening excursion to Paris, consisting of about four hundred persons. From him also we derived much important information, particularly the Doctor, he being compelled to carry out the " Colonel's " part of the programme—arranging and keeping the " itinerary " so faithfully executed by our friend of Appomattox fame.

Just prior to our arrival at Newhaven, Mr. Conductor Tourist gave us the valuable hint that, owing to the heavy train, some difficulty might ensue on our arrival at Newhaven in securing a berth on the Channel steamers; but as he knew all the ropes, by following him we might obtain an advantage over the rest; and one thing we might say here: an Englishman is away behind on taking up hints and dodging into places satisfactory to his own comfort.

It may be mean, and an evidence of a small spirit, but it is infinitely more pleasure to lay on the broad of your back in a berth, and hear two or three dozen men who have been " left " swear for an hour or so, and then have to lay out on the open deck, than it is to do the swearing and lay on the deck yourself. Oh! how much sweeter is the sleep, how much softer the bed, how refreshing the repose, with two or three growling around for some place to lay their weary heads, and yourself ensconced snugly in the "last berth to be had." How much more pleasure is it, though, to have this satisfaction when a full-blooded Londoner has been "squeezed out," *you know;* "it's perfectly scandalous, you know;" "ought to be reported to the *Times*, you know." We never have before nor since felt in any way under such deep and lasting obligations to anyone, as we have done towards that "Tourist Conductor." He was taking a regular Saturday night excursion to Paris, to spend the Sunday in that "City of all the World," and in his party alone were three hundred persons, and we presume there were as many as three times that number on the train not in the excursionist group, and but for our singular good luck, we should have had a very slim chance of sleeping comfortably on a bed for that night.

The people swarmed into the boats as flies would to New Orleans molasses spread on the Colonel's head, and found the Doctor occupying two berths, and the rest all gone, then did n't the Yankees catch some dash blessings; but when our master-stroke had been learned, a fearful outburst of applause went up from those two boats. It got noised abroad, and rumor was current that Disraeli and Bismarck and Gortschakoff and Schouvaloff and Wm. M. Evarts, were aboard; and unaware of the distinction we were thus receiving, we went looking for some of these celebrated personages, when we found the whole crowd following us, and of course, clapped our hands on our pocket-book and watch at once. The President of the railway and one or two owners of the boats were on board, and requested an interview, which we condescendingly granted, an offer of a few hundred thousand a year was offered, but we begged leave to remind them that an editor's chair was vacant, thousands and thousands of constituents in subscribers were awaiting our return, and the enormously lucrative position of editor was not to be bribed or incautiously led away by the offer of a few paltry hundred thousands offered by some petty English lords. We have no recollection of ever having seen such a crush and scrambling and jamming as on that occasion. It was all "big I and little you," and in that particular instance "might was right and did prevail." Soon after the boat left the pier, we found it very dark, and a heavy fog coming down, which made it exceedingly unpleasant, aside from the uncomfortable crowding of the decks, so we retired to our berths, and soon were fast asleep, not knowing, however, on closing our eyes, at what hour, as we crossed that dreaded channel, we would be called upon to go up on deck and take an astronomical view, or look upon the brilliant phosphorescence; but we did n't require to, fortunately, and so slept soundly on, dreaming of dear ones at home. About 6 A. M., we awoke refreshed, and looked around first for our care—for such the Doctor had now become; for at any of our banquets where a Commandery member did not eat, the

Doctor, as the Eminent Commander, had to do it for him, consequently, "Carlisle," from his legitimate increase in weight, had to manage now for the Doctor. Well, we looked around and could n't see the Doctor; we arose and made for the deck, and after threading our way among people spread out as though to dry, and tin pans and pails, and tubs, and so on, we came across our old friend, actually sitting on a camp-stool. There he sat, poor fellow, pale and emaciated, and an explanation is hardly necessary, we think; he *had* been up during the night, taking an astronomical observation, gazed upon the phosphorescence, and what else no man save himself knows.

Soon we were landed at Dieppe, and they run their trains on the " accommodation " plan from Dieppe to Paris. We were informed a train would leave at 7:45; so, after partaking of our first French breakfast, and paying the woman two sous for the privilege of washing our hands, we adjourned, to find written on the blackboard, " Train will leave at 11:45." Rather annoyed at this delay, we took a stroll the little and uncleanly town of Dieppe, on that beautiful Sunday morning.

All our conversations were conducted somewhat on the pantomime order, as our foreign and French brethren carried on a marvelous conversation with their hands, feet, shoulders and heads, while we as intelligently kept up any interesting conversation in which we were engaged by saying continuously and simply, " Oui," " Oui," " Oui," and yawning rather broadly; only this and nothing more.

The stores were all open. In front of the "greengrocer's" stood the baskets of cabbage, lettuce, spinach, &c., while the enterprising dry-goods merchant "flung to the breeze" his display of calicoes, flannels, pant stuffs, &c., across the hooks in front of his door as busily as we good people of Allegheny would do on our Saturday or Monday; while, passing the shops, were the more religious, prayer-books in hand, wending their peaceful way to their places of worship, returning from which they would stop in and make their purchase of a "couple of yards of five-cent calico" or a spool of "O. N. T." cotton, as do our good folks during the week. At 11:45, however, we took train for Paris, and enjoyed a delightful ride through that beautiful country, notwithstanding the intense heat of the day.

Reaching the "City of the World" about 3:30, on alighting from the cars we were immediately taken by the hand by our old friend and Sir Knight of Allegheny Commandery, William A. May, Esq., who conducted us to a carriage in waiting for us, and thence to our hotel, where two choice rooms had been secured for us. A wash, and we were off to one of the many handsome stores open, to purchase a chapeau; our genial old friend, Amsden, having run short a hat, had captured ours into his trunk, either for his own wear or for the benefit of a son he had left at home. Investing a Napoleon, we were soon taking a stroll along those magnificent boulevards; but owing to the lateness of the hour in arriving, we returned for dinner, preparatory to seeing this wonderful city by gaslight on a very lovely Sabbath evening. Taking a cab, we drive to the Palais Royal, the former residence of Napoleon I., thence to the Tuileries, the Louvre, the Tuileries Gardens, and then out the Champs Elysees—truly a wonderful sight, thousands of cabs upon this beautiful drive, with their little lamps burning on either side—and on looking up towards the Arc de Triomphe it resembles one vast torchlight procession, while on either side the grand cafes, with their millions of variegated lights, and beautiful strains coming from elegant bands of music, gives all the appearance of fairy-land. If we did not attempt a description of places of interest visited heretofore, certainly we cannot have space in this work to enter into one of all grandeur, elegance and magnificence of this most beautiful city of cities, further than a hasty and casual glance. As we looked upon all the art—the outcome of millions upon millions expended to make Paris the most attractive city of the world—we could scarcely realize that our most earnest anticipations had been fully realized as we drove through its broad, spacious and magnificent boulevards. Months would be requisite to see and know Paris with all its beauties and attractions, and we regret exceedingly to confess our time limited us to but about one week ; but to show during that period our time was profitably spent, we hastily review some of the points of interest coming under our observation.

First, securing a *fiacre* at the rate of two francs or forty cents an hour, we drive over some of the "Great Boulevards," which were formed, as many of our readers may know, by filling up the moats around the fortifications of Paris in 1670, during the reign of Louis XIV., and on the removal of these fortifications, were laid these magnificent wide streets or boulevards. We stop at the *Place de la Bastille,* where stood a castle and stronghold erected by Kings Charles V. and VI., and through the *Boulevard des Italiens* to the *Bourse* or Exchange, a very handsome building surrounded by a series of sixty-four Corinthian columns, and being an imitation of the Temple of Vespasian, in the forum at Rome.

At the corners stand four allegorical statues—Commerce, Commercial Equity, Industry and Agriculture. The hall of the Bourse is opened at twelve o'clock, and is soon crowded with eager men seeking to make a stroke of money, while in front of the building are numberless carriages awaiting the return of their owners, and from the hour of opening until three o'clock, the hour of closing, it is a scene of wild excitement which would make our lively Oil Exchange of Oil City a place of Quaker meeting in comparison. The building cost 8,149,000 francs.

Then we go to the Opera House, the most magnificent edifice of the kind in the world, erected at an estimated cost of 6,000,000 francs, but when finished cost just four times that amount. It covers nearly three acres of ground, was designed by Garnier, from competitive plans from the most eminent architects of France. The government contributes 800,000 francs per annum towards its support. Nothing can equal, certainly not surpass its elegance, grandeur and magnificence, being built from green and red granite from Sweden and Scotland, yellow and white marbles from Italy, red porphyry from Finland, "brocatello" from Spain, and other marbles from various parts of France. The finest works of art adorn it in statuary, paintings, &c., on every hand, such as statues of music, lyric poetry, idyllic poetry, declamation, song, lyric drama, dance, with medallion busts of Bach, Pergolese, Haydn, Cimarosa, Mozart, Beethoven, Spontini, Auber, Rossini, Meyerbeer, and Halevy. The steps are of white marble and the hand-rail formed of Algerian Onyx. The magnificent and curiously shaped chandelier contains three hundred and forty burners, and as seen from below presents the appearance of a crown of pearls. The stage is one hundred and ninety-six feet in height, one hundred and seventy-eight feet in width, and seventy-four feet in depth. At the back of the stage is the Ball Room, the end of which is formed by a mirror twenty-three feet in width and thirty-three feet in height, the largest ever made.

In the *Grand Foyer*, in large medallions above the door are groups of children carrying musical instruments, which are intended as emblems of the music of different nations. The cymbals refer to the Persians, the lyre and double flute to the Greeks, the horn, shell and tuba to the Romans, the organ to the Germans, the castanets and guitar to the Spaniards, the drum and cornet to the French, the harp to the English, the tambourine and mandoline to the Italians, the psaltery, sistrum and tintinnabulum to the Egyptians, and the triangle and darabuka to the barbarian races. Every nook and corner has its statue or emblem, representing some person or object alluding to or contributing to the cause of the erection of this truly magnificent structure. The building is fire-proof, iron used entirely in place of any timber, but it narrowly escaped destruction in 1871, when it was used by the communists as a magazine for gunpowder and other munitions of war.

The *Column Vendome* is an imitation of Trajan's column at Rome, one hundred and forty-two feet in height, and thirteen feet in diameter. The total weight of bronze employed in its construction is 1,800,000 pounds, supplied by twelve hundred cannons taken during a campaign of three months. It was erected by order of Napoleon I., in 1806, to commemorate his victories over the Russians and Austrians in 1805. The statue of Napoleon, which occupied the summit, was melted down by the Royalists in 1814, and the metal employed in casting the equestrian statue of Henri IV., on the Pont Neuf. Subsequently, in 1831, Louis Phillippe caused a new statue to be cast of the metal of guns captured at Algiers and to be placed on the summit. This was again removed in 1863, and replaced by a statue of the emperor in Roman costume, executed by Dumont. May 16th, 1871, the Commune pulled down the column, to the outer gallery of which the tri-colored flag of France was attached, in order to mark its downfall and the triumph of the insurrectionary red colors. Nothing was left standing but the pedestal, a master-piece of composition, twenty-one feet in height, and twenty in breadth. But the fragments of the column were fortunately saved, and employed in the reconstruction of the magnificent monument.

The Madeleine or Church of St. Mary Magdalene is our next object, and here we saw the congregation at communion, and without any disrespect intended to any one, we saw the pastor of the flock *literally* carry out the spiritual command, "Drink ye *all* of it," as he filled the goblet to participate in the Holy Communion, and he did drink *all* of it, if the bottom side of the goblet turned up while to his lips is any indication.

This splendid edifice was commenced in the reign of Louis XV. The Revolution found the building incompleted, and the works were suspended. It was restored to the uses of religion during the Restoration, and was completed in 1842. The carvings over the entrance in front are from the chisel of Lemaire, and represent the Last Judgment. The exterior of the edifice, with its fifty-two columns and its square form, rather resembles a Greek temple than a Catholic church. The niches in the walls contain statues of saints especially revered in France, all by modern sculptors. The church is

R

approached by a flight of twenty-eight steps, occupying the entire breadth of the edifice. The bronze doors are adorned with illustrations of the ten commandments, designed by Triqueti, and deserve especial notice. The interior is gorgeously gilded and ornamented with paintings by the most celebrated contemporary artists. Notice should be taken of the grand altar, the two handsome vases for holy water, the fonts, and the groups by Rude and Pradier. The light is unfortunately insufficient to display these fine groups to advantage. When the principal door and gate are closed, access may be obtained by the entrances on the eastern and western sides of the church.

In May, 1871, the insurgents had constructed one of their most formidable barricades across the Rue Royale, opposite to, and within a short distance of the Madeleine. The appalling scene enacted here on May 22d and 23d, baffles description. The houses in the Rue Royale which escaped destruction by fire were literally riddled with shells and bullets, but the church, owing to its massive construction, suffered comparatively little. This fearful battle ended in the Versailles army driving the Communists, after much loss on both sides, from their barricade. Three hundred of the insurgents, closely pursued by their enemies, sought refuge in the sacred edifice; the troops soon forced an entrance, and suffered not one of their victims to escape alive.

The *Palais Royal*, was erected in 1629 by Cardinal Richelieu, and originally was named by that personage the *Palais Cardinal*. It was occupied after his death by Anne of Austria, the widow of Louis XIII., with her two sons, Louis XIV. and Philip of Orleans. The garden is in the centre of the building, and is in a parallelogram form; a fountain stands in the middle, and there is a double row of trees round it. The covered promenade is very convenient during rainy weather, being in the shape of an arcade, all arched and covered over. A military band usually plays between five and six o'clock on fine evenings, in the middle of the garden. On May 22d, 1871, the Communists set the *Palais Royal* on fire, and the entire south wing, including most of the apartments in the *Cour d'Honneur*, with the exception of the south-western corner, became a prey to the flames, and was almost entirely destroyed. Had the galleries, with their attractive shops, been destroyed, the loss would have been incalculable.

The Palace has since been restored, the apartments being used now by the *Conseil d'Etat*, and are not shown to the public.

Now we come to Paris' pride and most important public building, the *Louvre*, and said to derive its name from an ancient hunting chateau called the *Louverie*.

The Palace was originally destined for the reception of foreign monarchs during their sojourn in the French capital. In 1528, Francis I. pulled down the old building in order to replace it by a new edifice, which was finished in the reign of his son Henry II., the sculptures which adorned it being the work of the celebrated Jean Goujon.

The older part of the Louvre has been the scene of many historical events. On August 19th, 1572, the marriage of the Princess Margaret of Valois with Henri IV., was solemnized here, most of the Huguenots being present on that occasion. Five days later, on the twenty-fourth of August, the signal was given for the massacre of the Huguenots.

A part of the modern structure was erected by the order of Louis XIV.; and it was during the life of this monarch that the superb eastern *facade* facing the church of St. Germain l'Auxerrois was executed after the designs of Claude Perrault. This masterpiece of architecture yields in nothing to the most beautiful productions of antique art.

The building was neglected after the death of Louis XIV. In 1805, Napoleon I. caused the whole of the Louvre buildings to be thoroughly restored, with a connecting gallery between the Tuileries and the Louvre.

That side of the Louvre which faces the river is decorated with some most admirable carvings, and the pavilions of *Rohan* and *Lesdiguieres* are marvellous instances of the power of the sculptor's chisel, while the innumerable monumental statues which decorate the building on every side are truly worthy of the place they occupy.

On the night of the 23d of May, 1871, the insurgents of the Commune entered the Louvre and set fire to the premises. Although the most precious *chefs d'œuvre* had been sent to Brest for safety before the siege of 1870, a valuable collection, comprising upwards of 90,000 volumes and a number of rare and interesting MSS. were entirely destroyed by the flames. It would take volume after volume to enumerate and describe the contents of the Louvre, which contains collections from the brushes and chisels of renowned artists dating back to the sixteenth century, and a person could linger and loiter about the spacious passages and galleries of the Louvre for weeks and never tire of its wonderful arts and beauties.

The Tuileries on the opposite side of the vast square between the Louvre and the Tuileries dates from the reign of Henri II. in 1589.

No edifice in Paris is so rich in historical associations as the Tuileries, and none, with the single exception of the Hotel de Ville, has ever been overtaken by so terrible a fate. On August 10th, 1792, after a fierce contest, the palace was taken by storm by an infuriated populace, and its defenders, consisting of a number of French nobles, one thousand Swiss guards and twenty-six officers, one hundred domestics of the palace, and two hundred national guards, mercilessly butchered. On July 29th, 1830, the Tuileries was again captured, and the furniture plundered or destroyed. But Louis Phillippe reinstated it in great splendor, and was in it when the Revolution of 1848 took place. Although there were abundance of troops to defend the palace, he preferred leaving it, and made his escape through the gardens. The capture of the palace was succeeded by the most frightful scenes of devastation. The royal carriages and furniture were burned in the courtyard, and the throne was carried to the Place de la Bastille and burnt also.

On May 20th, 1871, the Communists, aware of their desperate position and impending destruction, determined at one of their secret meetings to wreak their revenge on the ill-fated city by setting all the principal public buildings on fire. The prelude to the appalling scene which ensued consisted in placing combustibles soaked with petroleum, and barrels of gunpowder in the buildings doomed to destruction. The Tuileries was one of the first edifices subjected to this fearfully comprehensive and diabolical scheme. It was set on fire in a number of different places on the 22d May, the day after the Versailles troops had obtained an entrance into the city, but before they had gained possession of the palace. The conflagration soon assumed the most terrible dimensions, and all attempts to extinguish it were entirely fruitless. The whole of the western side of the palace facing the Jardin des Tuileries, and the pavilion on the north side next to the Rue de Rivoli, were reduced to a gigantic heap of smouldering ruins, after burning three days and nights.

In the square stands the Arc De Triomphe du Caroussel, erected by order of Napoleon I. to commemorate his victories of 1805 and 1806. It is forty-eight feet in height, sixty-three and a half in width, and twenty-one feet in thickness, flanked by Corinthian columns of red marble and with bases and capitals in bronze. On the marble entablature above the columns, in front and at the back, are placed marble statues representing the soldiers of the Empire, in the uniforms of their different corps; and on the four faces are marble reliefs, representing battles, &c., of the Imperial period. The arch was originally surmounted by the four bronze horses from the Basilica of St. Mark, at Venice; these, however, were restored to Venice in 1814, and have been replaced by a female figure in a chariot, designed to represent the Restoration.

The *Place de la Concorde* is the most beautiful place in the city, if not in the world. On the spot now occupied by the Obelisk, the guillotine was erected for the execution of Louis XVI. on January 21st, 1793. After a brief removal to the Place du Carrousel, the guillotine was again raised here, and more than 2,800 individuals were sacrificed to the bloodthirsty savages of 1793. Among those who terminated their career upon this awful spot were Charlotte Corday, the courageous patriot; Brissot, chief of the Girondins; Marie Antoinette, the beautiful queen; Philippe Egalité, Duke d'Orléans; Madame Roland, whose dying words were: "Oh, Liberty! what crimes are committed in thy name!" Hébert; Danton; Camille Desmoulins; Chaumette; Madame Elisabeth, sister of Louis XVI.; Robespierre; St. Just; and hundreds of the French nobility.

The Obelisk now in the Place de la Concorde ornamented the palace of the kings of Egypt, at Thebes, about 1,500 years before the Christian era, and was a gift of Mehemet Ali, Pacha of Egypt, to the French government, at the same time that he gave a similar one to the English (the Cleopatra Needle.) The expenses entailed by the transport to Paris and elevation of the obelisk in its present position amounted to two millions of francs, and as the obelisk is 500,000 lbs. in weight, the stone of which it consists has cost four francs per pound! The pedestal on which it stands is a single block of grey granite from the quarries of Laber, in Brittany, weighing 240,000 lbs. Upon the northern side of this pedestal is represented the apparatus employed in the removal and embarkation of the beautiful Egyptian relic, and on the southern side that used in raising it in position. The obelisk itself is a magnificent monolith, a monument of solid, reddish granite, and is inscribed with three rows of deep, sharply cut, and well-preserved hieroglyphics on each side. On either side of this prodigious stone is a fountain executed in the best taste.

The eight statues placed round the Place de la Concorde represent the eight principal towns of France—Lyons, Marseilles, Bordeaux, Nantes, Rouen, Brest, Lille and Strasburg, the latter now, however, belonging to their beloved neighbors the Germans.

The *Champs Elysees* is a magnificent avenue, one of the most fashionable promenades of Paris, and flanked by the most handsome buildings, and presents a most striking and animated appearance say from three to six o'clock, when elegant equipages and noble horses, with their elegantly attired and fashionable occupants and riders are on their way to and from the Bois de Bologne.

On this avenue are the *Palais de l'Elysee* which has been the residence of Madame de Pompadour, a government printing office, ball-rooms, gaming tables, occupied by Murat, Napoleon 1., Louis Bonaparte, Emperor Alexander I., of Russia, and so on, and was the residence of President McMahon; also the *Palais de l'Industrie*, and proceeding out to the end of the Champs Elysees, we come to the Arc de Triomphe de l'Etoile, the most imposing structure of the kind in existence. It stands on a slight eminence and is visible from almost any part of the city. From this magnificent and triumphal arch diverge twelve different avenues, in star shape. It is a handsome arch, costing ten millions of francs, is one hundred and sixty feet in height, one hundred and forty-six in width and seventy-two feet in depth, and was one of four triumphal arches Napoleon I. determined to erect in commemoration of his victories, but he accomplished but two. We would fail to even attempt a description of its wonderful traceries, the hand of the chisel in its carvings of those unusually handsome representations of important points in the first Napoleon's career.

The famous *Bois de Bologne*, formerly a forest abounding in game, the resort of duelists, persons inclined to suicide, garroters and midnight marauders, is now a beautiful park containing twenty-two hundred and fifty acres.

The *Hotel de Ville*, or town hall of Paris, is in utter ruin, having been burned to the ground by the bloodthirsty Communists on May 24th, 1871, including a library of over 100,000 volumes, and an incalculable loss in the destruction of a great many very important public documents. We are informed that the ball and reception rooms on the first floor of this once interesting building were so gorgeously and magnificently fitted up as to eclipse entirely the imperial palaces.

We visit famous *Notre Dame Cathedral*, where a very plain and fluent English speaker gives us briskly and fully this old church's history. It was founded in 1163 and consecrated in 1182. It is one hundred and thirty-nine yards long and fifty-two and a half yards broad. The organ in the church was built in 1750 and enlarged in 1868, and has fifty-two hundred and forty-six pipes and eighty-six stops. The choir stalls and the reliefs in wood represent scenes from the history of Christ and the Virgin, and are marvels of wood carving. Here are shown mementos of former archbishops of Paris with monuments to their memories; among others the good archbishop Darboy, who, it will be remembered, in 1871, was confined in the Prison de la Roquette, and being entirely innocent and unoffending, with five others were taken to a place in front of the infirmary of the prison, and after being subjected to gross insults from the National guards were cruelly and brutally murdered by the red-handed assassins in possession of the city at the time.

Then the *Morgue*, where are exposed from five to six hundred persons annually, who have either been drowned, or drowned themselves, and when found, are taken to this place, laid upon marble slabs, and their clothing hung above them, and their bodies kept cool by a constant flow of water.

The *Palais du Luxembourg* was founded in 1612, and continued to be a royal residence down to the time of the Revolution. The *Pantheon* resembles a heathen temple much more than a church, its form being a Greek cross, surmounted by a dome two hundred and seventy-two feet high. The *Hotel des Monnaies*, or the Parisian Mint, is another exceedingly fine building; on the ground floor are five entrance arcades, above which, on the first and second floors, is a handsome colonnade of six Ionic columns. Above the cornice are placed statues of Peace, Plenty, Commerce, Power, Wisdom and Law. The numerous glass cases in the principal saloon contains an interesting collection of French coins, arranged chronologically from the earliest times down to the present day, and a collection of foreign coins, including a Chinese coin of the year 1700, B. C. The machines turn out seventy pieces of money per minute, while the whole of them in operation at once are capable of yielding two millions of francs per day.

As we entered the *Hotel des Invalides* we could hardly lead ourselves to believe that all our anticipations had actually been realized; we had read over and over again the life and history of the great Napoleon, the little Corporal, and we had sighed often and often that we might look upon the tomb which contains the mortal dust of the greatest warrior the world has ever seen. This building was founded in 1670, by Louis XIV., and was completed in 1675. Soldiers disabled by wounds, and those who have served over thirty years are admitted to the Invalides. The Musée d'Artillerie in the the building contains over four thousand specimens of weapons of all kinds. The magnificent tomb of Napoleon I. is situated beneath the dome in an open circular crypt, and on the mosaic pavement, which represents a wreath of laurels, rises the splendid sarcophagus, thirteen feet long, six and a half wide and fourteen and a half in height, and consists of a single huge block of red sandstone, weighing upwards of sixty-seven tons, brought from Finland, and cost one hundred and forty thousand francs. And so we might go on, never tiring of the beauties of magnificent, worldly Paris, with its Palais Pompeien, Jardin d'Acclimatation, Russian Church, Tour St. Jacques, Churches of Ste Gervais and St. Eustache, Bibliothèque Nationale, Conservatoire des Arts, Palais de Justice, Saint Chapelle, Musée de Luxembourg, Musée de Cluny, Jardin des Plantes, St. Sulpice, Palais des Beaux Arts, its cemeteries, its parks, its fountains, its broad and smooth avenues, but we could not do it the justice it deserves; we can only say, that we employed every moment of our time to the very best advantage possible, spending, in addition to the places previously mentioned, two days in the Paris Exposition, which in fine fabrics and fine arts excelled our own '76 Centennial, in our opinion, but in all the other departments we exceeded the French display.

Taking a train we run out to Versailles, the seat of government of France, fourteen miles from the city of Paris, and its site is certainly anything but favorable. The Palace and Park cost the treasury of Louis XIV. the enormous sum of one thousand million francs. It is stated no fewer than thirty-six thousand men and six thousand horses were employed at one time in forming the terraces of the gardens and improving the parks.

During the time of the unfortunate Louis XVI., the Palace of Versailles was sacked by a Parisian mob, largely made up of women, and ever since that time it has been uninhabited. From the 19th of September, 1870, to March 6th, 1871, the palace was the headquarters of the King of Prussia, and a great portion of the edifice was used as a military hospital, the pictures having been carefully covered to protect them from injury. A most impressive ceremony in the history of Versailles took place there on January 18th, 1871, when the Prussian monarch, with the unanimous consent of the German States was saluted as the Emperor of United Germany.

The Palace is a very plain looking building, dating from the time of Louis XIII. On the first floor are the apartments of Louis XIV. The Gallerie de Louis

XIV. is a magnificent hall eighty yards in length and forty-one feet in height, and commands a beautiful view of the gardens. In this room King William was proclaimed Emperor of Germany. In this are some most superb paintings by some of the most renowned artists.

The gardens of Versailles are the finest perhaps the world has ever seen, and are nearly in the same condition as when originally laid out by *Le Notre*, the most famous landscape gardener of his day. They are adorned with numerous statues and vases, and ornamental sheets of water. The playing of the famous fountains in these gardens, which we had the pleasure to see, always attracts large crowds of spectators, which may be seen only on the first Sunday of each month from May to October, and costs eight to ten thousand francs to exhibit on every occasion, or about two thousand dollars every time they play, and this sight alone is almost worth the trouble and expense of crossing the Atlantic to witness.

Having completed our sight-seeing in Paris, we can not but admire the late Emperor Napoleon III., who did so much, expended so much, and manifested such an interest in constantly adding to the beauties of this metropolis; whatever may have been his faults, they should be covered up and hidden from sight, only thinking of the good he has done, in aiding by every means within his power, to please the eye of the beautiful; and seeing all this vast wealth expended in magnificent buildings, in fine works of art, in elegant boulevards and avenues, how any mob, no matter how low their birth, their origin, their surroundings, even though they be thoroughly tutored in the school of crime, could become so debased in everything human, as to commit the bloody work, cruel butchery, and high-handed villainies as perpetrated by the Communists in 1871, is only something at which we can marvel.

With deep and much regret we returned to our hotel, packed our traps, paid our bills, bade our friend William A. May, Esq., good-bye; and, we may say, to that gentleman we are much indebted for courtesies and kindness while in Paris, he having been there for almost a year in the interest of the Westinghouse Air Brake Company, of Pittsburgh, and perfectly familiar with the city, what would necessarily have been a visit of some annoyance, owing to our lack of knowledge of the French vernacular, was made through that gentleman one of pleasure and of interest.

After a pleasant ride, on a beautiful day, of eleven hours, the Doctor and "Carlisle" were to be found in the city of Cologne, in good old Faderland, and in our rooms facing the beautiful Rhine.

Here we had the pleasure of meeting dear friends, Mr. William Semple, of Allegheny City, who was on his semi-annual trip to Europe, seeking a few weeks' recreation and recuperation, and accompanied by John B. Main, Esq., of Glasgow, Scotland, who was hale, hearty, and stout, and very anxiously looking for a "rest," otherwise, as customary with nearly all in Britain, accustomed to short distance traveling, and not exactly up to the "pick-up-your-satchel-and-run" business, Mr. Main was slightly fatigued, and we are prone to think would quite as soon have remained a day or so "resting" at Cologne.

Cologne is the largest town in the Rhenish Province of Prussia, is one of the most important commercial towns in Germany, has about 136,000 inhabitants, including a garrison of seven thousand men. Its age anti-dates Roman times, for it is known that in the year A. D. 50, Agrippina, daughter of Germanicus and mother of Nero, founded a colony of Roman veterans on the site of Cologne, and was known as Colonia Agrippinensis.

The Cathedral in Cologne is probably the most magnificent Gothic edifice in the world, it was commenced in 1244, and they are still completing it, and is expected to be finished in about two years from this date. It covers 66,800 square feet of room, is surmounted by a spire now three hundred feet in height, to which is to be added yet two hundred and thirty-two feet, making it five hundred and thirty-two feet in all, and eighteen feet higher than the highest pyramid of Egypt; its roof has some five thousand spires or pinnacles, the nave is one hundred and sixty feet from floor to ceiling, and this vast church will seat comfortably 42,500 persons. It contains the remains of many illustrious dead, and also very fine tombs, some of which were damaged by the French soldiers in 1803-7.

The largest of the bells in the tower is called the *Kaiserglocke*, which was cast in 1874 with the metal of French guns, and weighs twenty-five tons. Fine stained-glass windows adorn this magnificent building, some of which represent John the Baptist, Nativity, Lord's Supper, Death of Christ, Descent of the Holy Ghost, Stoning of St. Stephen, and one commemorating the elevation of Archbishop Geissel, of Cologne, to the rank of Cardinal. The walls behind the choir stalls are covered with tapestry worked by the ladies of Cologne, illustrative of the Nicene creed and the seven sacraments. There are several other very fine churches in Cologne, but of course the Cathedral is the one of main interest.

It is a singular sight early in the morning to see the strong, hearty, red-faced, jolly German women come marching along—dear knows how far they have walked—carrying heavy baskets of marketing upon their heads, and as they walk rapidly on, knitting a stocking at the same time, their cheeks red, and bearing a glow such as is seldom seen in America.

At 8:45 A. M. on a bright sunny morning we, meaning Mr. William Semple, John B. Main, the Doctor and " Carlisle," stepped aboard the fine steamer " Kaiser and Kœnig Wilhelm," on the famed river Rhine, and soon were on our way up this beautiful stream, the pride—and well may it be—of the grand and good old German nation. A fine list of passengers were aboard, the day was all that could be desired, and we anticipated a day of rich treat and rare pleasure.

Soon after leaving Cologne, we come in sight, on our left, of the Château Bensberg, a Prussian military school, at the foot of which building stands a monument to the memory of two thousand Austrian soldiers who fell at Jemappes in 1794, and erected by the Emperor of Austria in 1854. On the right a little further up is the suppressed Benedictine Abbey of Siegburg. Passing on up we came to *Bonn*, frequently mentioned by Tacitus, and was one of the first Roman fortresses on the Rhine, and was probably founded by Drusus; and at Bonn we see some of the most handsome residences to be seen on the Rhine, and passing this city we come to the most picturesque and famous scenery on the river. We pass the islands of *Nonnenwerth* and *Grafenwerth*, on the former of which stands an extensive nunnery, very ancient, being mentioned in a document of the twelfth century. The nunnery was suppressed in 1802 but was re-opened in 1845 as a girls' school under the auspices of Franciscan nuns.

Rolandseck is the next point passed, and is one of the most beautiful spots on the river, surrounded by numerous villas and pleasant gardens, chiefly belonging to wealthy merchants from the Lower Rhine. Here, on a Basaltic rock, stood Roland's Castle; in connection with this is told this tradition : "The brave Knight Roland, scouring the Rhine in search of adventure, found himself the guest of Count Herbert, lord of the Seven Mountains, at his castle of Drachenburg. According to custom the daughter of the host, the peerless Hildegunde, welcomed him with the offering of bread, wine and fish. Her beauty riveted the gaze of the young knight, and Hildegunde and Roland were soon affianced lovers, but their happiness was brief. Roland was summoned by Charlemagne to the crusade. Time sped on and anxiously did Hildegunde await his return. But sad rumors came. The brave Roland was said to have fallen by the hands of the infidels, and the world no longer possessing any charm for the inconsolable Hildegunde, she took refuge in the 'kloster' in the adjacent island of Nonnenwerth. The rumors, however, of the death of her betrothed were unfounded. Although desperately wounded he recovered, and hastened to the halls of Drachenburg to claim his bride; but instead of being welcomed back by her fond smile, he found that she was forever lost to him. In despair he built the castle, of which one crumbling arch remains, and there lived in solitude, catching an occasional glimpse of a fair form passing to and fro to her devotions in the little chapel of the 'kloster.' At length he missed her, and soon the tolling of the bell and a mournful procession conveyed to him the heart-rending intelligence that his beloved Hildegunde was now indeed removed forever. From that moment Roland never spoke again; for a short time he dragged on his weary existence, but his heart was broken, and one morning he was found rigid and lifeless, his glassy eye still turned towards the convent chapel."

At every turn in the river the scenery was becoming more and more interesting, new features and attractions were continually presenting themselves, and we were thoroughly intent on all the beauties now surrounding us and coming to view; we were now approaching Godesburg, situated at a point where the river expands, and which place is a favorite summer resort, where wealthy merchants of Cologne, Elberfield, and Crefeld have erected a number of handsome villas, surrounded by pleasant gardens; upon the deck of the fine steamer, friend sat chatting with friend; children played lively around the spacious deck of the handsome steamer; Mr. William Semple and John Main were away forward at the bow of the boat, the Doctor was down looking over the railing at the beautiful working engine, and "Carlisle" was sitting near the stern of the boat taking notes and writing home. Everybody was joyous, joking and laughing—everything around us enchanting, and, owing to the very swift current at this point, the engines of the steamer were working hard and raising steam fast—when suddenly, boom!! a loud report, followed by another, and steam shot away up into the air, the engineers driven out with cuts and bruises! The laughing changed to crying, the rosiest cheeks were blanched, and faces were pale; friends running to and fro seeking friends; a mother screaming for her child she had placed to sleep in the cabin below, and no means of reaching it, owing to the escaping steam. "What is the matter?" came from the lips of one and all. The steam rushed and roared, and the engineers could not get at the throttle-valve to shut off steam, and there we were, in the middle of the Rhine, a strong current against us, a very heavy head of steam on, and it still raising rapidly, so much so that the magnificent boat shivered all over as does a person chilled, we looking every moment to see her blown into atoms; but at last, by being wrapped in wet blankets and cloths, the engineers were enabled to rush in, and, shutting off steam, it was found she had broken her connecting rod and blown out a cylinder head, and when her engines were stopped, the broken piece of the connecting rod was revolving on her shaft at frightful speed. All this occurred in less time than it takes to write it, and a feeling of relief was only obtained when the four of us got off in a little boat, walked inland to the railway, and took train at once from the station at Godesburg for Bingen. It was quite an excitement, and all things considered, was a narrow and lucky enough escape. We cannot pass over the remaining portion of our tour without attempting a description of the wonderful beauties as nature has laid them down and painted them in her mountains, valleys, lakes and rivers, and we would not exchange the rapid tour of these beauties for all former visits to Britain put together, exclusive of this one, of course, spent among our many Masonic friends.

From Godesburg to Mayence, of course, owing to the more rapid traveling by railroad than on the boat, and being on one side of the bank all the way up, and on the edge of hills, our anticipations of viewing the scenery of the Rhine, were from this accident to the

'Kaiser Wilhelm' unrealized, further than the very provoking and unsatisfactory view of one side.

Leaving Godesburg, we approach the Rhine's most interesting scenery, which attracts at once the artist's and tourist's eye; on our right hand, towering away far above us are high hills, bare at places—but let us look to the left. Down through the ravine flows the swift running Rhine, in its beautiful bed, its banks on either side so rich and green; on the far side is a lovely picturesque country, suddenly coming up against as it were a high mountain, and all that the eye can take in, down their broad sides, are the grape vines, for which the Rhine country is so famous, every inch of ground being utilized for that cultivation, even to banking up the earth with walls, so as to maintain maybe a little patch of ground ten or twelve feet in area; then will appear another mountain whose face-side slopes so gracefully, and from its base to its summit will be row upon row of terraces bearing the purple bunches of autumn's fruit; occasionally the grand scenery will melt away and give place to some of the most lovely picturesque scenery man's eye could wish to behold; the sun's rays pouring down so warmly upon the hills and valleys makes the looker-on an admirer of the German nation, makes him love those good old honest people more and more; and, we say how can they help loving their beautiful river, guarding it jealously, and warm with enthusiasm sing their "Wacht am Rhine." No wonder when they heard or saw their Rhine and its beautiful banks about to be invaded by their grasping neighbors, that the whole noble German Empire, with its sterling people, handsome, manly men, particularly their soldiers, rise *en masse*, and by their masterly education, their unapproachable discipline, filled with patriotism and love for what is and should be their pride, drove back, repulsed, and broke down a mighty and prosperous nation whom others had long feared.

The scenery here is perfectly grand ; we pass on our right the summer residence of the Empress of Germany, which from our train we could barely catch a glimpse, and then we come to " Bingen, fair Bingen on the Rhine."

Bingen is a little Hessian town of some 6,500 inhabitants, was known to the Romans, who erected a castle here. During the thirty years war it was repeatedly captured, and totally destroyed in 1689 by the French. The town carries on considerable trade in wine and a busy river and railway traffic.

From Bingen we proceed to Mayence, and here the Doctor cruelly concluded to leave " Carlisle," and at this point we parted company for a little while, for having spent all of his own money, and having begged, borrowed and—from us all we could advance him, he said he thought he would like to meet the party once more, and would therefore go and meet them at Brussels. We, poor, innocent mortal, took it all in good faith, appreciated his motives of going to shake hands with our companions once more, and considered it all as coming from the goodness of the Doctor's heart, that he would sacrifice the beauties of Switzerland just to greet our fellow travelers once more; we wished him God speed, to meet him a week or so later in London. But the deep scheming of this gentleman was only brought to light since our appointment as "Notary Public" by Prof. Slack, Hon. J. Fred. Beilstein, the juicy beef-slayer; James Milliken, Esq.; James Rafferty, Esq.; Judge Major, Hon. W. C. Moreland, coming to our office to have some lengthy accounts probated against this dealer in "amalgam and sich," as well as letters from poor Mrs. Mifflin, Mrs. Frohock, Rev. O. H. Brusie, Dr. Isaac Landis, Solomon McConihe, D. D., and many others, offering me half the claim if we could collect part of the sovereigns, centimes and pfennings he had fleeced them of in Brussels. Some offered to take "Dental chairs," "forceps," "double uppers," "half soles," or anything else, to square up accounts.

Mayence, or Mainz, is a strongly fortified town of 57,000 inhabitants, with a garrison of 8,000 soldiers, and is historically one of the most interesting towns of the Rhenish provinces. In the year 14, B. C., Augustus sent his son-in-law Drusus to the Rhine, as commander-in-chief, and by him was Mayence founded. It has a Cathedral, commenced in 978, but was burned down in 1009. It was restored, but again destroyed by fire in 1081, 1137 and 1191, after each of which occasions it was re-erected on a grander scale than before.

From Mayence we proceed to Heidleberg, and 'tis here the beauties of an Almighty Creator begins to show His Omnipotent grandeur in nature's architecture and paintings. We approach Heidleberg on level ground, and taking a carriage, drive up to the top of the mountain, at the base and lower side of which is situated this beautiful town, and arrive at the Koenig's stool, through and over one of the most enchanting drives, shaded over by beautiful trees, their branches interwoven and connected, forming a wonderfully fine arch of living green, and making it so cool, pleasant and enjoyable; the drive winding up the mountain side in serpentine manner, while occasionally an opening in the trees permits us to have, as we might say, only a tantalizing and tormenting glance at the panorama in the valley below.

But at last we reach the summit, and oh! what a sight awaits our coming. Standing in an open space, we look down the mighty mountain side, bearing all the shades of green, contrasting and harmonizing together as nature only can arrange her bouquets, and away down at the base so quietly and beautifully lay the white houses which make the pretty village of Heidleberg, through which we can see its charming walks and trysting places, for lovers, for families, or for any one who desires to sit in reverie, and take in, in an unbreaking clasp, the beauties he has seen. Raising our eyes, what a lovely valley we see as far as sight almost can carry, divided and subdivided by the various kinds of grain in their various shades of ripening, and down through its centre flows the little Neckar, winding its narrow, serpentine path to the mother of German rivers, and we are enchanted with the scene. Now let us move down the mountain side a little and we come to Heidleberg Castle, and having seen this castle let us see no more ruins bearing so formidable a name. What a grand old ruin, the largest and finest in all Europe, its symmetry and proportions, and the beauty of its workmanship, still plainly visible, having stood the storms and wars of ages, the elegant carvings still the admiration of all and defying the crumbling effects of time and season; and then its position, commanding a view of the entire valley we have just seen, and situated directly above and over the town. As we sat or leaned over the balustrade on that beautiful summer evening and heard the music from a fine band at one of the hotels, wafted through those trees and up that valley, it had all the appearance of fairy-land. In the cellar of the castle is a vat or tun, which held 360,000 bottles of wine, from which the king's jester, a dwarf, drank fifteen bottles per day. It wasn't a very good day for drinking, either! Where, oh! where was local option in those days? Echo answers—where?

Few towns if any can vie with Heidleberg in the beauties of its environs and historical interest. It contains about 22,000 inhabitants. The University is among the oldest in Germany, was founded in 1386, by Elector Rupert I., and is attended by about seven hundred students. The library contains upwards of three hundred thousand volumes, seventy thousand pamphlets, eighteen hundred MSS., and fifteen hundred diplomas.

Taking a "schlaf-waggon" we continue our tour, arriving the following morning at an early hour in the pretty little enterprising city of *Bâle*, the principal city of half-canton of Bâleville, having a population of some forty-five thousand inhabitants—all enterprising—making the town of Bâle a place of commercial interest of no small note, and may be marked down with a history dating from the ancients, as we find Bâle first named as Basilea, in the year 374, and founded by the Romans, who had the cheerful habit of founding cities and towns for about the first five hundred years after the Christian era, when they were pleased to pay their poor and unoffending neighbors all over Europe, some and frequent calls to borrow a piece of territory to add to their empire just for amusement's sake.

We did not tarry long at Bâle but went direct to Lucerne, a very pretty little town on the lake of the same name. The well preserved walls and watch towers about and in Lucerne, which were erected in 1385, give the town an imposing appearance, while its amphitheatrical situation on the lake, invests it with a peculiar charm.

We take boat on the lake for Alpnacht, and the scenery around this beautiful sheet of water is not surpassed, if equaled, in the whole of Europe. Before us as we leave the pier is the grand old Rigi, stern old Pilatus, the fine old peaks called the Bürgenstock, the Buochser Horn, and the Stauser Horn; on our left the Schreckhörner, Mönch, Eiger, and Jungfrau with its barren peak capped with snow in the month of August; and there, nestling among those magnificent mountains, their heads hoary with age, lies the pretty little town of Lucerne, with its towers and battlements. Very unfortunately, from lack of time, we were denied the pleasure of ascending the Rigi, much as we were led into temptation to do so. As we approach the Rigi and its sister mountains we are at once struck with their majesty and grandeur, our strongest portions of admiration are called upon, and here, amid those majestic mountains, in whose bosom we might say lays calmly and peacefully this little sheet of water called Lake Lucerne, in trust as we might say of their guardians, the mountains—and how well we see do those guardians keep their vigilant watch, they shelter the little lake, so that no evil may come in, as a wolf to the fold, to disturb the calm repose in which it sleeps, not a ripple on its surface—and there, in front of us, behind us and around us, rising up high into the pure mountain air, are those mountains of nature, while occasionally on their sides, far up, may be seen a little, rich green place cultivated by the sturdy mountaineers, and the lake kisses their sides so softly and beautifully!

We arrive at Alpnacht, where we take diligence through the Brunig Pass, and, as we near it, our vocabulary of adjectives falls far short to qualify and words to describe the beauty here. We pass up and around the mountain side, and between large mountains whose heads are seemingly blushing to appear from beneath the white and fleecy clouds which hover around and rest upon the tree tops, just like pretty white wool—so much so, that we had the feeling that we should love to have gone up thither and brought down a big armful. But let us look back—a new panorama has been placed there; we again see the pretty little lake and the well cultivated valley; but the climax of all this is to be reached as we near the summit. We ascend slowly as it is very steep; we are going through a narrow pass, on the summit of those mountains, one on either side, like horns, until at last we are on level ground, through which we run, until, turning suddenly to the right, and there—oh! there, what a sight!—nature has given her kaleidoscope another turn, and though we think she has been kindly showing us her best architectural piles in her mountains, and her best paintings in her valleys and plains, we find she has only been leading us on, tantalizing our appetites for more of her beauties, leading us farther into her meshes, just as many are led into vice— for, having seen one picture we want to go on and see more. Here she has placed her finest picture. On our right hand, and on our way down, is the steep mountain side, round which the road, smooth as a table, gracefully winds; just over the precipices on our left, and away in front, from directly under our position, lays the unspeakable charming Brienz Valley, as level as can be, and so cultivated and mapped out as to resemble a vast checkerboard of squares, composed of such greens as may be seen only in Switzerland; and then, directly down its centre, runs the little river Aar, entering into the small but picturesque Brienz Lake in the distance. Down the steep side of the mountain on which we are is one side of the background, of thickly wooded pines, and then, over on our left, are two sturdy mountains looming haughtily into the air. From a side base, in cone shape, and just in between the tops of these two cones, stands a barren, rugged, bald-faced mountain, with a head gear of the purest white snow, made brilliant like diamonds by the sun's rays, and what a grand and lovely background all this makes to the modest yet beautiful valley at these haughty mountains' feet; yet they all seem to me like a happy family. The mountain, with its hoary, white head covered with its perpetual wig of snow, keeps its place, and does not seem jealous of its sister mountains, who, with their luxuriant foliage, do not seem to envy their taller sister, which bears her peculiar mark of admiration, that of snow in summer, but all seem to clasp hands round their little *protege*— the valley—as much as to say, in the strong voice of nature, "Our little daughter is beautiful, her pretty face we will guard and shelter from winter's cold blast, she shall be nice and warm, and from our tops we will let our little streams of clear, cold, sparkling water pour down our sides, and give her refreshing food and drink, so that she shall be beautiful always, and we will reflect credit upon her by appearing here as a background for her," and the beautiful valley would seem to say in response: "My big sisters are so kind, I will try and be more beautiful than ever, and try to reflect beauty back upon my more striking sisters, who have grown so tall, yet would lack their grandeur were I to fade and die away." Then, as we pass on down high, rugged rocks, perpendicular, and, at times, hanging over us, until, as we near the base, and are about to enter the plain, we find we are in an immense colosseum—a great, vast, close amphitheatre of hills —the niches in whose sides form a gallery, that man, in all his power and strength of mind, can never hope to accomplish in imitating. How very small are we poor traveling, toiling, or indolent ants in comparison with the other works of nature! True, the human being has an immortal soul that poor, dumb nature has not; but, oh! how she, in her beauty and wonders, speaks to us in words far more powerful and expressive than any in the vocabulary of any human tongue.

When we take the little boat at Brienz, on the little Brienz Lake, which is much smaller, but no less beautiful than Lake Lucerne, we find ourselves landlocked, we can scarcely trace the road through which we came, and this is wholly the feature with Swiss scenery; it is a picture that is ever and constantly changing at every step we advance—a peak pops out its bare or beautifully covered head, if only for a peep, or a valley shows its pretty face in some kindly opening nook in the mountain, or some grand old barren rock struts forward boldly and commands attention at once.

As we leave Brienz on the little steamer, across the lake stands a very high mountain, entirely covered with pine trees, and about half way up in a little crevice in the mountain stands the Giessbach hotel, an elegant building, in just such a situation as the shrewd old ancients selected for their castles. The situation is delightful, commanding a fine view of all the surrounding country; a little above it are the Giessbach Waterfall and Cascade, which are known as the illuminated falls.

The Lake of Brienz is seven and a half miles long and two miles in width, surrounded entirely and completely by lofty wooded mountains and rocks. We stop at Bönigen, and are conveyed by railway about a quarter of an hour's ride to Interlaken, which is a delightful ride; seated in comfortable seats on the tops of the cars, an ample opportunity is afforded to take in the surrounding scenery.

Proceeding to the Royal Victoria Hotel, at Interlaken, one of the finest hotels visited on our tour, after dinner—and a rare one too—we had the pleasure of seeing some very elegant costumes at a full dress hop that was given in the parlors of the hotel on that same evening. Interlaken lies between the Lakes of Thun and Brienz, and in the centre of the town is a handsome avenue of walnut trees, and from its centre a fine view is obtained of the snow-capped Jungfrau.

The town is a great resort for summer visitors from almost all quarters, and is noted for its even and mild temperature. From Interlaken we travel to Thun and Berne, starting on the steamer on Lake of Thun, which is ten and a half miles long and two in width, with picturesque villas and gardens at first on either bank, and then becoming high and precipitous.

From Thun on a lovely Sabbath morning we travel to and arrive at *Berne*, a very pretty little Swiss town, crossing the *Nydeckbrucke*, a handsome railroad bridge of three arches, completed in 1844, at the end of which is the Bear's Den; here the bear, which is the heraldic emblem of Berne is maintained, according to immemorial custom at the expense of the municipality, and no persons are permitted to make old Bruin any offerings except bread and fruit. An English officer in 1861 fell into the home and arms of Bruin, and was torn in pieces, after a desperate struggle.

Berne is a place of much interest, containing about 40,000 inhabitants. It is built on a peninsula of sandstone rock, and the fine stone houses are mostly all built over arcades, the pavements nearly all being under cover. As Brooklyn is the city of churches,

T

so Berne might properly be called the city of fountains, most of which are adorned with statues in which the bear is always a prominent and recurring object. While passing round the city we saw the most singular and ingenious mechanical figures in the Clock Tower. At three minutes of any hour a cock flaps its wings and crows; near it, in a circle, like a circus ring, comes out a number of animals and grotesque figures, which run around five or six times; while this is going on a devil sits up on a stool, each hand on a bell-rope, and rings two bells, kicks up his feet, and laughs; then, as the hour is reached, a large iron figure of a man raises his arms and strikes the hour on the large bell with a hammer; at the same time a man with a long white beard, representing Old Age, turns over a sand-glass, slowly nodding his head, and a bear his.

A fine building is the Cathedral, which was commenced in 1421, and completed fifty-two years later. It has some particularly fine decorations, the sculptures representing the Last Judgment, the Prophets, the Apostles and the Wise and Foolish Virgins. Among other prominent buildings are the Museum, the University, the Corn Hall, the Federal Council, &c.

From Berne we take train to Lausanne, but do not stop here longer than to change cars; and securing a seat on the right side, we continue our journeying, skirting for a number of miles the beautiful Lake of Geneva, which is a singular and very deep blue color, and on its banks grow the sweet and wild chestnut, the walnut, the magnolia, the cedar of Lebanon and the omnipresent grapevine. There is a very singular feature in connection with the Lake of Geneva; at particular spots the water rises several feet without any apparent cause or previous commotion, remains so for about half an hour, and then subsides to its original level. This is a singular phenomenon, and occurs mostly in spring and autumn, and at night. The currents caused by the rising of subterranean springs are frequently so strong that no oarsman can make headway against them. We next come to the Castle of Chillon, where Bonivard was confined in 1530, by the Duke of Savoy. From near this point we enter the picturesque valley of the Rhone, which is only three miles wide, and hemmed in on either side by very high mountains, while down the valley flows the Rhone river, a dark grey colored water, and shortly after we arrive at Martigny and proceed to the *Hotel Clerc*, where we remain for the night, preparatory to crossing over the Tete-Noire to Chamouny. Hardly any feature of Martigny is worth mentioning, save the very prevalent and repulsive form of cretinism, of which almost every inhabitant is afflicted, and are the most disgusting looking people as a rule to be seen anywhere, with large heads, squat and bloated figures, bleared and hollow eyes, flat noses, limbs short and misshapen, knees thick, feet flat and an immense gathering at the throat, and generally have the sexual instincts developed in the most brutal form. It is a rare exception to find one not afflicted with goitre or incipient cretinism in male and female, young or old.

Retiring early, we were up with the sun, and on our way over the Tete-Noire, which we proceed to ascend through vineyards and orchards, and meadows, where may be seen men cutting hay and grain, and women, girls and boys raking and binding, and on the mountain side we have a most magnificent and extensive view of the valley of the Rhone, and continuing our ascent, a good healthy one at that, we arrive at the summit, and have one of the grandest views we have yet seen; on our left having the *Col de Balme*, behind us the snow capped *Buet*, and on the right the Aiguilles Rouges, with Mont Blanc, the Gemmi, the Jungfrau, the Finster-Aarhorn, Grimsell and Furca, all in view in the distance and all beautifully topped with snow. From here we descend the steep side of the mountain, through the famous forest of Trient, and over a rough and rugged road cut out from the solid rock to Châtelard, and through the grandest of scenery, wild and romantic in appearance; and after dinner and changing horses we continue our ride to Chamouny, where we arrive late in the afternoon, and from our room windows in the Angletevie we look up to old Mont Blanc, with its wonderful glaciers, the *Glacier du Tour, d'Argentieve, Mer De Glace*, and *des Bossons*.

Any attempt at description of this grand and gorgeous scenery would be simply a failure upon our part, and words inadequate to its beauty, as one can scarcely conceive of this grand old mountain rising to the height of 15,732 feet, covered with its aforementioned glaciers and beautiful white snow, while down in the pretty valley of Chamouny but a short distance from the lower portion of the glaciers, may be seen the Swiss reaping their golden grain. With a contrast so great, summer wedded to winter, heat to frost, harvest to harvest's death, the scenery can better be imagined than described.

At 7 A. M. we take the express coach, an eight-horse immense vehicle, and journey through picturesque and beautiful valleys, the views upon the road constantly changing; one high old mountain on either side playing "peep" round the corner of another, so that one could almost continue traveling over Switzerland and never weary in all the beauties which are constantly presented, and passing lovely grounds and handsome suburbs, we enter the beautiful city of Geneva.

Geneva is one of the prettiest situated and prettiest looking cities of Europe, containing about 48,000 inhabitants, about one-half of whom are Catholics. The river Rhone emerges from the lake and shoots swiftly through the town. The old city which lies on the left bank of the Rhone, is narrow and hilly and rather unsightly, but upon the removal of the fortifications, which were converted into promenades and quays, it has been made a very handsome elegantly built city.

From the grand quay which fronts on the lake, a splendid view is to be had of the Mont Blanc range of mountains, and on a summer evening the appearance is certainly the most handsome conceivable.

It was in this town that John Calvin, the founder of Presbyterianism, while advocating the principles and doctrines with which he was imbued, and liberty of conscience and religious thought, performed the charitable, Christianlike and humane act of banishing one of his friends for differing with him on a little point of predestination, banished him, and carried out the more interesting and cheerful act of burning at the stake another poor fellow who differed with him on the doctrine of the Trinity, who on account of Calvin's charitable teachings, had fled to the city of Geneva where he expected he would receive encouragement and shelter from those whom he was led to believe would give such, only to meet his horrible fate of slowly roasting to death tied to a stake.

The Cathedral is a fine building dedicated to St. Peter, and is supposed to occupy the site of an ancient temple of Apollo. The public library contains about sixty thousand volumes. The University, founded in 1368, was reorganized by Calvin and Beza; in it are taught belles-lettres, philosophy, science, divinity, and law, the new building costing one-and-a-quarter million francs.

Over three thousand persons are employed in Geneva, in the manufacture of watches, jewelry and musical boxes, and some conception of the chronometers, &c., turned out in this city may be had when we give the figures of over one hundred thousand watches being made annually, using seventy-five thousand ounces of gold, five thousand marks of silver, and over two hundred thousand dollars worth of precious stones, and in addition to these are manufactured velvets, silks, leather, cutlery, firearms, mathematical, astronomical, and surgical instruments.

The history of Geneva can almost be dated back to 122, B. C. and was burned during the reign of Heliogabalus, and rebuilt by Aurelian. John Knox was made a citizen of Geneva in 1558. In 1782, about one thousand of the citizens of Geneva applied for permission to settle in Ireland, and the Irish Parliament voted £50,000 to defray their expenses and granted them settlements of land near Waterford, but this never succeeded. It will also be remembered that the court of arbitration appointed by the United States, Great Britain, Italy, Switzerland, and Brazil, met in this city to settle the Alabama question, arising between the United States and Great Britain. In 1873, the Duke of Brunswick, who died in that year, left his entire fortune of one hundred million francs to the city, which makes us think what a feast it would be for Pittsburgh, had she about half a dozen dukes as her residents, who would take it cheerfully into their heads to die and leave a few millions for the city's benefit. She needs it badly.

From Geneva we take train for Paris, a long and tedious ride of about seventeen hours, and we encountered rather an amusing incident on our journey thither. Mr. John Main and " Carlisle " were comfortably spread out the entire length of the three seats of the compartment, locked tightly in the arms of Morpheus, the hour was about two o'clock in the morning, and dark as the darkness of Egypt. To our train was attached a very elegantly fitted-up directors' car, in which was a party of handsomely dressed English ladies and stylishly made-up gentlemen. "Carlisle" was awakened from his sound and peaceful slumbers by feeling some person or persons pulling vigorously at his clothing, and a full round voice of pure broad English, saying, "Get up, young man; wake up, young man, h'and don't keep the ladies standing, you know." We did as directed and awakened to find us in a perfect bedlam of chatter and noise. There was an elderly gentleman with evidently a liver that was in very bad condition, judging from his countenance; an elderly lady, his wife, with the similar necessary portion of her living apparatus in about the same condition; a younger gentlemen and lady. These we recognize as the party occupying the special car, the journals and wheel works of which had become red-hot from fast running, and had to be cut off at a side station and its occupants transferred to our carriage and compartment, into which they were placed, each carrying band-boxes, hat-boxes, valises, satchels, coats, wraps, &c., while the elderly lady carried in her hands an article of ladies' wearing apparel usually purchased by number, and they jabbered away in about this style: Old gent—"Why, my deah, you'll catch your death of cold, you av'n't even got your stays on, my deah!" Old lady—"Perfectly scandalous this, taken from one's bed at two o'clock in the morning in a perfect state of prespiration; terrible, indeed, h'and then thrust into a compartment with perfect strangers, h'and they occupying the entire seats!" while the younger lady relieved herself about thusly: "Perfect shame, this, ought to be written to *Times*, you know; no place in Britain would we be treated like this; perfectly scandalous to be taken from one's couch in their sleeping garments," &c. All this given in true English accent, it was, we thought the funniest thing we had ever seen, and should have been seen to have been fully enjoyed. Of course the remarks of the O. L. were a little rough on Mr. Main and " Carlisle," still we are always ready to forgive the ignorant for they never know any better.

Arriving in Paris, we spend two or three days, and then, *via* Calais and Dover, we proceed to London, where we arrive about 7 A. M.

Letter No. 8.

London and its Sights.—The Unfortunate Loss of a Watch.—Pilgrims Turn Their Weary Feet Homewards.—"Carlisle" and the Doctor Badly Used Up on the Homeward Voyage.—Particularly "Carlisle."—Arrival Home.—Incidents by the Way.

On our arrival at the station at London, we here hastily bade good-bye to Mr. Wm. Semple, who drove to Pancross Station, to take train at once for other cities in England, Scotland and Ireland for business purposes, and Mr. Main and "Carlisle" wended their way to the Midland Grand Hotel, where we found our old friend, the Doctor, domiciled in his room and fast asleep, he having as stated, "raised" sufficient on his tour, solitary and alone, having spent a few days with our party in Brussells, and found his way back through Holland and Belgium, to London. We soon had him awake, and inquiries made relative to our baggage and some purchases we had made on the continent and sent per *Express* to London from Cologne, paying ten francs for the same in order to secure promptness and security in delivery. The Doctor cheerfully informed us our baggage had not yet arrived, and we spent one entire day in a "hansom" and in the neighborhood of three or four thousand pounds in fees in looking it up, finally succeeding in finding it about six o'clock in the evening.

They conduct their *Express* companies on the most scientific mule plan of anything we have ever seen. If we wished to send a package, say to Sewickley, about thirteen miles from the city of Allegheny, on the European plan, it would be forwarded in the lightning time of about *four days* from the office in Allegheny to that of Sewickley, while, allowing all due time for delays in carrying packages to express office, by ordering some goods by telegraph from New York a person might reasonably expect that the order given in the spring the goods would come to hand by the fall at any rate, so *expeditious* and *systematic* are they in the good " Old Countrie."

Starting out to see London is like going to visit a country of itself; however, securing a " hansom" we go over the main part of the ground. London, in the twelfth century had about 50,000 inhabitants, in the seventeenth, about 200,000 ; in 1801, about 1,000,000 ; in 1821, about 1,350,000 ; in 1841, about 2,000,000 ; in 1861, almost 3,000,000, and in 1871, about 4,000,000 ; almost as many as the entire State of Pennsylvania, most of whom also were born in England. The city of London has about 7,400 streets, which, if laid end to end would form a line 2,600 miles long, or to give an idea of distance, would stretch almost across the American continent. It is lighted by 1,000,000 gas lamps, and consumes 28,000,000 cubic feet of gas daily. The annual value of house property is about £24,000,000 pounds sterling. A singular fact is that there are more Scotchmen in London than are in Edinburgh, more

Irish than in Dublin, more Jews than in Palestine, and more Roman Catholics than in Rome! It is estimated that there are annually consumed about 2,000,000 quarters of wheat, 400,000 oxen, 1,500,000 sheep, 130,000 calves, 250,000 swine, 8,000,000 head of poultry and game, 400,000,000 pounds of fish, 500,000,000 oysters, 1,250,000 lobsters, and 3,000,000 salmon, and wash all this down with 180,000,000 quarts of porter and ale, 8,000,000 quarts of spirits, and 31,000,000 quarts of wine. For a city of big figures, by all means commend us to London.

The most frequented part of London is London Bridge, nine hundred feet long, over which passes daily about twenty-five thousand vehicles and countless pedestrians.

On the highest ground in the city stands St. Paul's Cathedral, on whose site it has been maintained stood a temple of Diana, in Pagan times. The present church, of which Sir Christopher Wren was the architect, was opened for divine service in 1697, though not completed until 1710. The greater part of the cost of construction was defrayed by a tax on coal, and the building was commenced and completed under the supervision of one architect, one master mason and one bishop. It is the third largest church in Christendom; its nave being five hundred feet in length, and one hundred and eighteen feet in width, and from the pavement to the top of the cross it is four hundred and four feet. In the church are fine monuments to Nelson, John Howard, Dr. Johnson, Sir Charles Napier, and Wellington. In a chamber behind the sarcophagus of Nelson is the hearse used at the Duke of Wellington's funeral with all its trappings.

Westminster Abbey is a fine building dating from the seventh century, in which all the British Sovereigns from Edward the Confessor to Queen Victoria have been crowned, and in which many of them are buried. Almost all the space is taken up within the Abbey by monuments and tablets, some of them very handsome, others horrible executions and designs. A peculiar inscription is upon the monument of John Gay, the poet, which was composed by himself for his own tablet:

"Life is a jest: and all things show it:
I thought so once, but now I know it."

Surrounding the eastern end are nine chapels; the centre of the chapel of Edward the Confessor was richly inlaid with mosaic work. The monuments of Queen Elizabeth and Mary Stuart are in the north and south aisles; near the former is the monument to Edward V., and his brother Duke of York, the sons of Edward IV., who were murdered in the tower, when children, by kind-hearted Richard III. In the *Poet's Corner* beside the other illustrious dead are buried Macauley, Dickens, Bulwer, and Livingstone.

The Parliament Houses occupy the site of the old palace which was destroyed by fire in 1834. They cover an area of eight acres, have eleven hundred compartments and one hundred staircases, with two miles of corridors. The House of Lords is one of the most gorgeous legislative halls in the world. It contains the throne for the Queen, a seat for H. R. H., the Prince of Wales, and the woolsack for the Lord Chancellor. The Houses were erected from a plan by Sir Charles Barry, out of ninety-seven others in competition.

Facing the throne is the reporters' and strangers' gallery. In the windows, which are filled with stained glass and lighted at night from the outside, are twelve figures, and at either end of the room statues of the barons who compelled King John to sign Magna Charta. The entrance for the Queen is at the Victoria Tower, at which she enters when convening or proroguing Parliament, and ever since the gunpowder plot of 1605, the cellars underneath the house are always thoroughly examined two hours before the Sovereign's arrival.

The Peers' Lobby contains some very elegant brass candelabra, and each peer has in this lobby his own hat peg provided with his name. The House of Commons is not so lavishly and elaborately fitted up as is the House of Lords, but in a more business-like appearance. In the central hall are marble statues of Hampden, Selden, Sir Robert Walpole, Lord Chatham, the Irish orator Grattan, Lord Clarendon, Lord Falkland, Lord Somers, Lord Mansfield, Fox and Burke.

Westminster Hall is full of historical recollections; being used at one time by the English Parliament, where coronation festivals were held by a number of monarchs, where Charles I. was condemned to death, and where Cromwell, clothed in royal purple lined with ermine, was saluted and hailed as Lord Protector, while within a very few years afterwards his body was rudely dragged from its grave in Westminster Abbey, his head taken off and exposed between those of Bradshaw and Ireton, on the pinnacles of this same Westminster Hall, where he was greeted with the "All hail, Lord Protector!" and it remained there for over thirty years, a high wind at last carrying it to the ground. Here also were condemned to death Sir William Wallace, Sir John Oldcastle, Sir Thomas More, the Earl of Essex, Guy Fawkes, and the Earl of Stafford.

The Tower of London is the next object of visitation, having a bright, cheerful record for murders done up in the most approved manner by royalty, is now a government fortress, and kept in repair as such. It is a very ancient institution, and can be traced back to the time of Julius Cæsar. It contains a renowned and wonderful collection of firearms, as also the Regalia Room for the Queen's jewels. In this tower Richard II., abdicated in favor of Henry of Bolingbroke, and the heads taken from Sir Thomas More, Queen Anne Boleyn, Thomas Cromwell, Earl of Essex, Margaret Pole, Countess of Salisbury, Queen Catherine Howard, Lord Admiral Seymour, Lord Somerset, the protector; John Dudley, Lady Jane Grey and her husband, Robert Devereux, Earl of Essex, James Fitzroy, and Sir Thomas Overbury was poisoned therein, while a very large list of celebrated personages might be named as having been confined there for the purpose of dying a slow and miserable death, or taken out to make a bonfire so that some good and noble saints might piously part their coat tails and warm themselves, while others were cruelly tortured or poisoned.

In the Tower also are the Queen's jewels, as stated, where may be seen Queen Victoria's crown, made in 1838, and containing 2,783 diamonds, and the famous *Koh-i-noor*, one of the largest diamonds known, weighing one hundred and sixty-two karats.

The General Post Office is a fine building, in the Ionic style; but let us look at a few figures, just for curiosity's sake, taken from late statistics of the Post Office business of Great Britain. In 1876, 298,000,000 book packets and newspapers, 93,000,000 postal cards and 1,019,000,000 letters passed through the mails, while in 1874, there were issued 15,100,562 post office orders, covering a sum of £26,296,441, and in 1876, the number of orders issued was 17,822,921, covering £27,516,796, and the Post Office Savings Bank had on deposit in 1875, £26,000,000, with the profits of the Post Office Department amounting to £1,894,141.

The Telegraph office is directly opposite the Post Office, and showing the advantage of the government controlling the telegraph lines; a dispatch of twenty words can be sent to any part of the Kingdom for one shilling, or twenty-five cents. The Instrument Gallery contains five hundred instruments, while in the basement is a fifty-horse power engine for forwarding messages to other city offices by means of pnuematic tubes; in 1876 the number of telegrams forwarded was 27,000,000.

An interesting place is the Royal Mint; from 1865 to 1875 there were coined in the Mint, 44,179,233 sovereigns, 15,724,945 half-sovereigns, 14,193,254 florins, 43,-275,160 shillings.

Guild Hall is a large building, which is now used for municipal meetings. On November ninth, the Lord Mayor elect proceeds in state to Westminster Hall, where he is sworn in, and in the evening gives a sumptuous banquet in Guild Hall, which is attended by the ministers of government and other public dignitaries.

At the further end of Cheapside, one of the busiest streets in London, and containing handsome stores, is the Mansion House, the official residence of the Lord Mayor during his year of office, and from the Mansion House to Blackfriars Bridge, is Queen Victoria street, one of the great improvements of London, and constructed at vast expense.

The Bank of England comes next, covering four acres of ground; founded in 1691, by William Paterson, a Scotchman, and is the only bank in London having the power to issue paper money, fifteen thousand new bank-notes being turned out daily. Its vaults usually contains from fifteen to twenty million pounds sterling, employs about nine hundred persons, and the bank receives £200,000 per annum for managing the national debt which amounts to in the neighborhood of £775,348,686, and it is estimated it would take £40,000 per annum to cover the forgeries practiced upon—principally by shrewd Yankees—careful as the bank officials are.

U

London Bridge was of course visited, if for no other reason than to see how far violators of their oaths as Knights of Submission might have to fall. It was designed by a Scotchman, the lamp-posts of which are cast of metal of French cannon, captured in the peninsular war. Close by is the monument erected in commemoration of the great fire, which destroyed four hundred and sixty streets and over thirteen thousand houses and churches.

Then we take a walk through Billingsgate, the great fish market of London, where refined and choice language are a main feature, so much so that it is as renowned for that as for its fish.

While walking along Victoria Embankment, a new and beautiful drive and promenade, constructed at a cost of over £2,000,000, we saw them putting in place the Egyptian obelisk from Alexandria, otherwise Cleopatra's Needle. This famous obelisk was presented to the English Government by Mohammed Ali, and taken to England by the private munificence of Dr. Erasmus Wilson. It measures about seventy feet in height, and is eight feet at the base, and weighs about two hundred and twenty tons.

A very interesting visit may be made to the office of the *Times*, spoken of by our lady friends *en route* to Paris; about twelve thousand copies can be struck off in one hour; the continuous rolls of paper with which the machine feeds itself are each four miles in length, and of these about thirty are used daily.

Trafalgar Square is a beautiful place, dedicated to Admiral Nelson, with a handsome granite column rising from its centre, crowned with a statue of the hero of the naval battle of Trafalgar. On one side is a scene from the battle of Aboukir, with Nelson wounded in the head, declining to be assisted out of turn by the surgeon who is dressing the wounds of a common sailor, and below the death scene of Nelson; on another side is Nelson's last command, " England expects every man will do his duty."

The Albert Memorial is a magnificent monument to the memory of the late Prince Consort, erected by the English nation, costing £120,000, half of which was defrayed by voluntary contributions. On a spacious platform, to which granite steps ascend, on each side rises a basement, adorned with reliefs of marble, representing artists of every period. On one side are poets and musicians; on another, painters; on another, architects, and on the remaining one, sculptors. Four projecting pedestals at the angles support marble groups, representing Agriculture, Manufacture, Commerce and Engineering. At the corner of the steps leading up to the basement are four pedestals bearing magnificent allegorical representations, sculptured in marble, representing the four quarters of the globe—Europe, Asia, Africa and America.

We cannot possibly go over all the ground, the Royal Exchange, Corn Exchange, Coal Exchange, Blackfriars Bridge, the Temple, National Gallery, Kensington Museum, Buckingham Palace, Hyde Park, Regent's Park, Zoological Gardens, British Museum, as the two latter alone would fill one or more such volumes as this, not to speak of the thousand other places of interest in London, not even mentioned in this volume.

A few brief facts in connection with London and we are done with that city. There are over fifteen hundred places of worship within the metropolitan limits; about four hundred Wesleyan and other Methodist places of worship; the Baptists have about three hundred, the Congregationalists about half as many as the latter; the Roman Catholics have about one hundred, the English and other Presbyterians about twenty-five, Unitarians about twelve, the Jews have twenty synagogues, with the number constantly increasing, and numerous other miscellaneous places, chapels, &c.

The Temple Church near Temple Bar, consists of the Round Church and the choir, and was formerly used as a place of worship by the Knights Templar, and no more interesting work can be read than that of Mr. William Longman, who gives a detailed history of all the religious work of London, in his "History of the Three Cathedrals," dedicated to St. Paul of London. The total number of charitable institutions in London is over one thousand, and their united computed income about twenty-five millions of dollars per annum.

While in London an unfortunate thing occurred to one of our party, poor fellow, now deceased, and we tell it as a warning to all visitors to "Merrie England" to be on the look-out for gentlemen with "freight bills" and "old acquaintances," &c. It seems our old friend, Dr. Wm. M. Herron, was sitting in front of the hotel in London, enjoying one of Elton's fragrant William's Havana cigars at a dollar a piece, in company with our rather elderly friend from the adjacent government of New Jersey, who carried a very elegant and valuable chronometer, chain and Maltese cross. Dr. Herron had occasion to go into the hotel for a moment, and on coming out found the old gentleman had also vacated his seat. After a while he turned up, large drops of perspiration standing on his forehead, and thereby hangs a tale. It appears a prepossessing-looking and elegant-talking gentleman approached our friend, engaged him in conversation somewhat thusly: "Pleasant evening," etc. "Why, you're a Knight Templar, aren't you? Happy meeting; belong to that fraternity myself," said Mr. Smart Alex, examining at the same time the honorable gentleman's cross and chain. Mr. S. took out his time-piece at the same time, and smiled that hearty smile peculiarly his own. Mr. Smart Man examined the $450 watch, &c., and loosened it from its guard, remarking that "he had a very ancient and valuable Masonic ring in his room, which he would just go and bring for the Judge's examination," taking, however, the time-piece with him, the unsuspecting Mr. S., no doubt, feeling elated over his newly-made friend from his own country. Were it not for the fact that we had seen Mr. S. in America, since his return from the "Crusade," and that he has since made his long last pilgrimage, we would be prone to believe our friend was still patiently waiting the return of the fine-looking gentleman who was a Knight Templar; and here we would take occasion to plainly say to all readers, beware of all men who by means of any emblems of any order, no matter what it is, would desire to display them for business purposes, they are neither Odd-Fellows, Masons, Knights of Pythias, or anything else, and may properly be condemned and looked down upon as being neither consistent members of the order they claim to belong to, nor are they in common terms, honorable men. A man who will display an emblem of any order for a purpose. other than that for which it is intended, can generally be marked down either in the books of the craft themselves or by outsiders as being N. G. or D. B., which being interpreted meaneth "no good" and "dead beat" in vulgar parlance.

The same will also hold good in cases of men whose hands are full of grips, as they choose to call them, as a general rule and with very rare exceptions, are imposters, practical paupers, and below the dignity of either members or non-members of any secret organization, and in saying this we mean those who would make a business of it, or who think they can accomplish an end by such means, they could not otherwise obtain.

THE RETURN OF THE WANDERERS.

We were now prepared to turn our faces homewards, towards the setting sun and our own fair land, though inwardly we had some premonition a bad case was ahead for us, which afterwards turned out to be only too true; alas! how true, for oh! how "Carlisle" suffered none can ever tell, it makes us actually sea-sick to even think of it, and notwithstanding frequent crossing of the Atlantic, "Carlisle" for about three days was the sickest, most disconsolate and let-down mortal that ever stepped aboard a steamer, and as we have told the doings of some of our party in preceding letters, perhaps it would not be the fair, square thing to allow "Carlisle" to pass by without giving him a good solid dig between the ribs, for he had his enjoyment over the poor unfortunates who made the chants and responses, and yelled "New York!" in gurgled tones on board the fine British and North American Royal Mail Steampacket "Russia." But we are very happy to say the Doctor was just as bad as "Carlisle;" but from some peculiar faculty he bears, the Doctor is by all odds the most unmitigated lively sick man, when he is sea-sick, we have ever seen. He may wriggle around on his fourfeet-six stilts, looking or making for the wheel-house, but he'll go thither and take his position at the ensign staff in the rear of the wheel-house, the vessel pitching and rolling round, a soda cracker in his hand, and expectorate at the "blarsted" country he has just left, and smile a broad grin of satisfaction through it all, but we know that it came only from sheer inward satisfaction that "Carlisle" was sticking closely to him, assisting him nobly to "Hold the Fort."

Accordingly at 12 o'clock, midnight, August the 9th, we bade farewell to our friend, Mr. John B. Main, who was to remain in London for a few days longer, and were soon safely quartered in a handsome Pullman sleeper on our way to Liverpool, from thence to embark for home; and we can assure our readers, though our "Crusade" had been one of unalloyed pleasure, the friends and acquaintances we had found and made while "strangers in a foreign land" had been unspeakably kind; the sights we had seen had been interesting, instructive and grand; yet it was with light and joyous hearts on that night we took the train for Liverpool, knowing that, with each revolution of the ponderous driving-wheels of the engine drawing our train, we were constantly nearing those we loved, who were now anxiously awaiting our return from a foreign shore. Yet, if we could only have played "Rip Van Winkle" for about three or four succeeding days to that night—oh! we would have given, well—we would have given enough to have saved John Sherman the trouble of issuing those "Baby Bonds," and we wouldn't have cared one solitary cent whether the poor in America had still had their "surplus" tied up in a stocking and buried 'neath an apple tree in the garden or not, for somehow or other "Carlisle" had an intuition he was going to be deathly sea-sick going home, and, when seated in the car, we ventured to state our inward feeling to the Doctor, who sympathized with us to the extent of saying, "He prayed heaven we would."

You see we didn't need to tell this on ourselves at all, but as each of the "Crusaders" going over who were sick, awful sick—particularly the Doctor—whenever they have seen "Carlisle" since coming home, have stated they have each a ten-column article ready for every paper in the country on "Carlisle's" indisposition, did we fail to tell the whole truth and nothing but the truth; and as we are *alleged* to have tormented the life out of all going over, we "give ourself away," which will be considerably nearer the truth than for a lot of infuriated Modocs seeking revenge to do.

Sleeping soundly until 8 A. M., we were awakened in Liverpool, and, strange to say, the feeling was stronger than ever that we were to pay our tribute to Neptune—the old *Coroner's Convention*—which name qualifies his standing better than any we can at present recall.

During that Saturday morning we wandered round the city, it raining in torrents all the time, seeing all we could of the principal seaport of England; but through it all "Carlisle" still brooded over his inevitable fate which he felt was sure to come. Everything went wrong that morning from the start; we had a surly waiter bring our breakfast, in our coffee floated a couple of roaches taking a warm and early bath; well of course we had a fuss with Mr. Waiter. Liverpool is a city of about 500,000 inhabitants, and from its busy appearance resembles more an American than an English city. St. George's Hall is a very handsome Corinthian building, with columns forty-five feet high. It is a city abounding in schools of various kinds, and charitable institutions, and having fine public bath-houses, wash-houses and drinking fountains. The splendid docks of Liverpool, along the Mersey, including those of Birkenhead, a little town opposite Liverpool, cover four hundred and four acres, and extend five miles on the Liverpool side and two on the Birkenhead side. The amount of capital invested in the docks is about $50,000,000, three-fourths of which is held in Liverpool proper. Nearly one-half of all the exports from England are shipped from the port of Liverpool alone. The total number of vessels that enter the port a year is about sixteen thousand, and representing a tonnage of about seven million tons in round numbers, and equally divided as to sailing vessels and steamers. In 1874 the registered shipping tonnage belonging to the port was 1,866 sailing vessels of 990,867 tons, and 563 steamers of 412,464 tons. The improvement of the approach to the river was to be completed in 1874, but the landing stage, the most magnificent structure in the world of the kind, was burned July 22, 1874.

Of course as we wandered round, and having appetites of which we had no cause for complaint, we became hungry, and it is astonishing what fools persons can make of themselves preparatory to embarking on an ocean voyage, and the Doctor and "Carlisle" were booked in the foregoing party. We wandered into a restaurant and went vigorously to work on some jam tarts, which, of course, are capital for one about to be sea-sick; then the Doctor, the deep schemer, under the guise of friendship and a lavish freak of generosity, hunted up an apple woman, of whom he purchased some *alleged* fruit of the orchard, and gave them unto "Carlisle," and he did eat of them, which was a wonderful addition to the good ready we were then getting on for a day or so following. We will never be convinced of anything else than that we ate about a dozen sixteen-ounce cannon balls shipped from the United States for the Muscovites to kill a few more Turks with, for these good people at that time were enjoying themselves with United States guns and ammunition, and plenty of men to practice on, and we actually presumed them to be apples.

At 3 P. M. we were on board the little tug and steaming out to the "Bothnia," then anchored in the stream, and shortly after were on board that steamer, and we felt sick then sure. We can say that the "Bothnia" is as far ahead of the "Russia" in everything about her as the "Russia" is ahead of a decent canal boat, for no other line running from New York to Liverpool *dare* keep such an affair in their trade as the "Russia," save the line that owns her. Still, we object also somewhat to the "Bothnia;" while she is a very fine boat, staunch and very nicely fitted up, we object to going down to sleep in the cellar at nights, and we won't take any more "Bothnia" or "Russia" in ours. Those who want safety can take it, and have all they want; but if we have the Atlantic to cross again, we'll take a mighty big risk if that were so, in a common White Star, Inman or Anchor Line boat, though the latter-named companies are not companies of long name and many initials. Of Captain McMickan, commanding the " Bothnia," we will say a more efficient and gentlemanly officer treads no deck anywhere than he; he is an excellent disciplinarian, and his officers, every one of them, are thorough and efficient in their duties, and everything moves like clock-work.

But, in the language of the famed orator, Mr. Hughey Dougherty, "we are wandering from the paths of literature," "we are straying from the subject," so let us get back for fear we still neglect to chronicle the fact of " Carlisle's " bed-riddenness.

About 4 P. M., we heaved anchor, (we heaved, we are sure, half-a-dozen far larger ones than the one which held our ship,) and soon were steaming away towards Queenstown, and half an hour later the " Wyoming," of the Guion Line, pulled up stakes and followed suit.

It was a lovely moonlight night, the water smooth as glass, not a " ripple on the wave;" but from all the calmness of the surroundings, we could not drive away this continual inward remembrance that our doom was approaching. The vessel was crowded. Old folks toddled up and down discussing this subject and that, gentlemen with their wives linked arm in arm looked lovingly upon each other, the Doctor and " Carlisle " trod manfully from stem to stern, and from rear to front;

and between seeing those married couples, as we said, looking lovingly upon each other, and this confounded inward feeling saying to us, "Carlisle,' you're a gon'ner," to repeat the oratorical Dougherty, "It was healthy." We imagined we were sick then; however, at about 10 P. M., we found our way to our room, and save for the then continual beating of the engine, we would n't have known we were moving, and so had a good night's rest. The following day, (Sunday) we were anchored in Cork Harbor, to await the arrival of the mail at 4 o'clock, and as we had four hours there, the look of dry land and the spacious "Queen's Hotel" was too much for us, we said to our friend, "Doctor, I'm going to be sick; I know it—I feel it in my bones plainly. Just let us go once more on to dry land and get a good square meal at the 'Queen's' before we sail." We struck the right chord that time. The fact was, the Doctor felt he was going to be ill also, but would n't acknowledge it. We went ashore on the tug and made for the "Queen's." It was Sunday, and the strict observance of that day there forbade their setting out a decent meal, so all we could get was cold meats, some Irish fruit (potatoes,) and lots of grass and hay—otherwise salad. Returning to the steamer, we again heaved anchor, and were about starting "out on the ocean wave." The "Wyoming" came up to the mouth of the harbor and lay-to there—we do n't know what for, only from pure "cussedness," as we will shortly show.

Being out of the harbor an hour or so, then—Jerusalem! there came up a blow, and the bow of the vessel began to bow most gracefully to the United States ahead, while her stern began to resemble a donkey when some one is getting too familiar with his tail; and thus it went for an hour or more, when we noticed the "Wyoming" bearing down on us rapidly, every dip of her bow lifting tons of water up and around her, and scattering it in spray, and soon she passed us, just as though we had been at anchor.

'Twas about this time—the clouds becoming thicker and blacker, the sea becoming rougher—huge waves came rolling and breaking against the strong sides of the steamer, giving her the "Boston dip" badly, while the waves she scooped up at her bow came rolling over her spacious deck, and then "Carlisle" had a dreadful feeling that his pockets had been picked. His hands moved in the vicinity of his watch-chain; it was not gone; the buttons, too, were all on his vest and coat, but there was an awful feeling of fullness in that section. We observed, also, that our good friend, the Doctor, had a bad attack of imitation about that time too; he was evidently very nervous about whether his clothes fitted him correctly, or that he had taken an overdose of our friend Stackhouse's garden vegetables, the cucumbers, and they had not agreed with him. Consolingly we looked at each other, sympathetic glances were frequently exchanged; we inwardly took back all we had said to and about any of our fellow

"Crusaders" going over; we secretly turned our eyes heavenward and said, "Never—well, ha——very seldom we mean, will we ever again poke fun at any "Crusader," or any other person, if only forgiven for the past, and let off from this approaching 'onpleasantness."

In our deck-chairs, huddled all up, sat we two poor weary pilgrims, feeling as though a Krupp gun had poured its contents against the second lower vest button, and had there failed to perform its terrible mission of death. On either side of us were fellow-passengers who but a short time before were all pleasant smiles and joyful conversation, who had now the appearance of having had a severe Caudle lecture—husbands and wives looked as if they were on the "outs," bachelors and maidens as though a telegram had reached them telling them of some loved one gone, while occasionally—no, not occasionally, but very frequently—some idiot would rush to the side of the vessel to look for the "Wyoming," when that boat was long before out of sight, and then because they could n't see her, would get mad foolishly, and expectorate at the innocent sea.

It was 5:30, and the preparatory dinner bell rang. We remarked to the Doctor; "say 'Doctor,' what's the use of giving way this way? Let us brace up and work this thing off." That remark and resolution was fatal. "Carlisle" went down to "prepare" (prepare is good,) and no sooner had we reached our room than that settled it—we dashed up the stairway like a madman pursued by a million demons." The vessel was pitching and rolling terribly now, and we made for our friend the "Doctor," and announced our "preparation" to go to the wheelhouse, and asked the "Doctor" if he also was prepared? He replied, "Carlisle," I'll never leave you; we've stuck together thus far, I'll stand by you now." We never saw a more accommodating, self-sacrificing man than the Doctor, never—nothing mean about the Doctor, I tell you.

Linked arm in arm we moved toward the wheelhouse, and to the rear of the same, too, rather more rapidly than gracefully, each with a handkerchief over his nose and mouth, as from our tender natures we feared the severe sea breeze would give us a severe cold, of course, but we arrived there only to find all the available railing space occupied, and a ticket up "Standing Room Only." A few miserable people in the way did n't make any difference at all; everybody is aristocratic when sea-sick. We transacted such business as called us there, in a highly satisfactory manner, as Old Neptune can file his affidavit to, upon application to his office in that vicinity. It is just about at the point where a remarkably intelligent and all-wise young man of our party said he saw the track of a vessel that had crossed our course during the preceding night. We retired to our deck-chairs well satisfied with the manner we carried out our part of the programme; we seated ourselves, and then the dinner-bell rang. Now, there is nothing on earth or ocean will make a man sicker than he ever was before than to hear the abominable dinner-bell when he is laboring under a state of "un-com-for-ta-ble-ness," and see a lot of healthy-livered gentlemen go down and come up, puffed and gorged, and saucily pick their teeth, and laugh a hearty guffaw!

We saw all this, and again took a promenade to the vicinity of the ensign staff, to rehearse our Knights of Submission ritual and signs in secrecy; but most of the passengers presumed we belonged to some terrible dark lantern society, and had the unmannerly and vulgarly presumption to come poking around just when we wanted to be alone, and though we gazed out longingly at the turbulent waters and quoted poetry, the passengers on board that vessel insisted on coming where we were, and standing round against that railing, and not one of them had their backs to it, and strange too, all were weeping—at the eyes, nose and earthly tabernacle of the mouth, particularly the latter. We felt sorry for them all, for the sad and solemn sight was more than we could possibly withstand, in fact we were weeping harder than any of them ourselves. Oh! if we had only been just then on the "Kaiser Wilhelm" going up the Rhine, or we would willingly undergo an initiation in the K. of S.; and then we just reckoned that, being now about fifty miles out from Ireland, we *only* had about *thirty-one hundred and fifty more* to go, and that thought was a pleasing one.

Finally we retired to our little cots in the cellar attic, and soon were sound asleep, oblivious of all we had just passed through. Of course, our readers will

v

never infer that we were sea-sick. We fear we may have given the impression now that we have written it, that from the frequency of our visits to the British ensign, we strayed thither with the intention of making ourselves and the ship lighter and the ocean fuller; but we beg not to be mistaken or misunderstood, we only went there to compare that horrible red flag to our beautiful starry blue field and its stripes—the most beautiful flag of the grandest nation on earth.

Through the still watches of the night we had the cheerful habit of getting down from our shelves and gazing intently at the fearfully and wonderfully made and soldered tin pails. We could see no patentable improvement that could be placed on them, and so retired, only to awaken to find the vexed question still troubling our minds; and it was certainly strange that the same thought came upon us both, and singular that we both came down to examine the inner side; and from the manner in which our minds were troubled on that night, we are still satisfied that somewhere or somehow we could have made an improvement on them, had we continued to devote our time more steadily to the study thereof. For three days such were the proceedings; one day we were all sitting up in a little place we had christened the "Rookery," looking as though our lower jaws had dropped in some unexplainable manner when we heard a crack, and over the ship's bow, smokestack and all, came about a ton or so of water, and we received a bath which laid the Colonel's on the "Russia" completely in the shade. They had on board some very fine ginger snaps, and one day we overheard the Doctor say, "Steward, bring me a few ginger snaps, will you, please?" He brought him t—w—o, (2,) and we heard the Doctor, as he lifted the two innocent little snaps, say "Yes, that's the kind; the samples are all right, now bring along your stock."

But all things have an end; long and weary seemingly as was our homeward passage, we had a pleasant time of it, with pleasant people on board, and the first three days of our voyage over, we had the remainder truly delightful.

The "Wyoming" had arrived and preceded us up to New York city, and disembarked her passengers and baggage some twelve or fourteen hours prior to us. Here, through the courtesy and kindness of our friend, E. M. Jenkins, Esq., we were met by a young man sent by him to help us through the Custom House, and without any detention we were passed and going it alone to the Pennsylvania Railroad Depot. And twenty-four hours after our arrival in New York we were with our friends and families in the good old city of Allegheny, and the "Second Crusade of Allegheny Commandery," so far as we were concerned, was finished.

We take great pleasure, before closing, in annexing hereto a letter received from our Captain-General, who, with some ten or more separated from the main body of the Commandery at Geneva, and compassed what was known as the "Italian Section," they, under the care of a guide proceeding from Geneva and Swiss scenery, going over the Alps into sunny Italy; and the following letter, condensed as it is, gives some slight idea of the beauties of that land of the fig and olive. It is addressed to two Sir Knights who preceded him home, and though perhaps a breach of faith to produce it all, yet we believe always in telling the whole story.

Letter No. 9.

Extracts from Letter written by the Captain-General, W. C. Moreland, Esq., while doing the Italian Section, with part of the Crusaders.—Description of Scenery and Art.

FLORENCE, ITALY, September 2, 1878.

My Beloved Companions:

I AM in the heat, under the sky, and surrounded by the fruit of Italy. With all these luxuries I do not forget the pilgrims of the west. The Colonel, Fullerton and Clinton are quietly reposing around me, looking for all the world like the "Three Graces," while I, sober and wakeful, sit down to tell you at least that we are not dead.

The Colonel insists, however, that after a person has written up an "Itinerary," to prepare which he must work all night, he ought to have some little rest. He insists that his is the hardest part of the task, and this morning reported that the work had been completed up to twelve o'clock last night. He says his hardest work was in Venice, arising from the fact that all the streets being water he found it somewhat difficult to walk around. I can assure you, however, he accomplished the duties devolving upon him. He is now engaged in his leisure hours in studying the history and biography of the streets of this " Queen of the Adriatic." It puzzles him to know whether they belong to the Romanesque, the Byzantum or Rennaissance style; or whether they are not a style of their own. He insists the town has never been laid out "on the square," or in any other special way. I have implicit faith in the Colonel, and know he will yet solve the problem; meantime he rests like a lamb and snores like a virgin.   *   *   *

I can assure you the compass of sight-seeing, pleasure and enjoyment has been completely boxed by us. Sober, steady and sedate we have gone about the work and mission of the trip, regardless of all side issues and those little things which are the annoyance of *small* minds. (He here alludes to the Doctor, undoubtedly.) Pensive and particular we wander about, as pure as lilies and as meek as bare-footed monks. Disdaining all concealment we move to our allotted business with precision, regularity and cheerfulness. We are as choice and select in our habits and tastes as a band of vestal virgins. We run the risk of being called haughty, and proud and selfish; but what of that? Doth not a good thing suffer persecution? And are we not all good and correspondingly happy? Methinks I hear thee smile at the base vanity. " Smile on, ye scoffers at the pure and the good!" If you do wonder at crime, think not that we are base plebeians and low-born serfs. Nay! by my foot, rather are we " Cook's men," loyally and lovingly following the noble duke " who leadeth us." Fortune favors the brave and fortune favors us. We scoff at the poor and lowly ones who suffer on in an eight by ten, whilst the chosen ones roam the broad world o'er. We pity the poor. (We do not know what the writer of this letter had against the Doctor, to peg away at him in that style.)

But, my beloved and devoted companions, you will wonder what all this has to do with a trip on foreign shores, and how you are to extract any benefit from this nonsense. More seriously addressing myself to the business on hand, let me say I have sighed for an hour in which to write you a note. We have thought of you, and talked about you every day since parting company, and at each stopping point I contemplated writing a word, but found almost every moment engrossed by special business.

I need hardly say to you that our trip has been as a "feast of fat things." I do not think it possible for persons to have more pleasure and profit on a trip than we have had. At each place of moment we have been able to secure a good guide, and as a result have seen every point of interest in the places visited. Our journey through Italy has been a succession of delights. This land of the fig and olive deserves all the praise, poet and painter have given it.

The plains of Lombardy and Venezia are a panorama of beauty—wide extending, level and fertile—you are greeted at every point with rare and rich charms, and besides this it teems with a history that seems like a romance. Its lakes are charming, picturesque and inviting. Como, Lugano and Maggiore are complete. The calm, blue waters, the commanding hills, the exquisite foliage, and the beautiful villas and villages, make a landscape of rich variety and profusion, and to add to the luxury of the physical you have a sunset of gorgeous magnificence. The impressions made upon my mind are indestructible and wonderfully sweet. Then, too, you have the cities, full of life, activity and culture, and with that wealth which gives an air of easy independence.

To crown this, antiquity and the present join in contributing the wealth and very prodigality of their genius to these great cities, to make them the wonder and admiration of mankind. Here art, science, literature and labor have made their offerings, and found their homes. Amidst the decay, the struggles, and the vicissitudes of the past much still remains to mark the glory and renown of the past. It is impossible to contemplate these homes without a veneration which amounts to a passion.

I have ceased to marvel at the people clinging to their homes, although the very act means for them toil, labor, often penury, without the hope of reward or independence. There is so much to lure, charm and soothe that toil loses its pain and labor its aching. Besides all this there is a history complete and wonderful of this Latin race. The fairest fields have ever and anon been plowed up with fierce contention. Grim visaged war has been a companion through the centuries. Ambition has held high carnival, and the worst passions of men have found Italy a home for freest indulgence

Solferino and Arcole are but mile posts indicating the march. From the day when Hannibal met and defeated Scipio, down to the day of the peace of Villafranca, Italy has been the home and empire of war. Is it not strange that all hope, energy, liberty, literature and art had not long since quitted her fields? And is it not a wonder that in the face of this bitter and relentless warring, there should remain a single vestige of her past glory and the brilliant achievements of her sons?

Yet, so it is. With all this bloody past, Italy is still the guardian watcher over the arts of the past, and the precious productions of the ages. Music, painting and statuary have made their home in this fair land, and embellished it with all that taste and culture could do.

I have been absolutely enraptured, as I have been privileged to walk through the galleries, and visit the homes sanctified by the cultivated genius of the past. Then, too, I have felt an admiration for the "old church," such as I never had before, as the absolute fact presented itself, that amidst all that decay, debauchery, licentiousness, and wrongs of her past history, she alone has been the friend and custodian of art. Say what we please, and think as we may, yet the truth is, that but for the taste, fidelity and liberality of the Catholic Church, the world would not to-day have a trace or vestige of Raphael, Angelo, Canova, Titian, Rubens, Van Dyck or Tinterretto.

False to a thousand things, and guilty of unmeasured wrong and duplicity in the eyes of history, she has remained ever true and faithful in keeping and perpetuating these great names and still greater works. Her domes, her aisles, naves, niches and vaults are filled with the master work of these master minds. Let us remember, too, that this church not only encouraged and compensated the labor of this divine genius, but she afforded the only possible avenue for its development. Great souls will ever treasure and praise the faith, zeal, judgment and liberality which resulted in perpetuating these triumphs of the human mind, then too, the glorious splendor of the churches overwhelms the mind.

You have seen the Cathedral at Antwerp, and bowed your heads over the matchless painting of Rubens, yet that Church, with its rich treasures, is but an epitome of that which we have seen almost every day. What the Alps are to the physical world, these churches are in architectural beauty, completeness and finish.

The Church of St. Marco, in Venice, is supreme in the profusion of its stores, and the completeness of its decorations. The entire floor is one continuous mosaic. The work and wealth of a century have been contributed to adorn and beautify this structure. With her porphyry, and her pillars of pure alabaster, brought from the Temple of Solomon, her wooden work and bronze stolen from the Church of St. Sophia, in Constantinople, (the church of Constantine,) her bronze horses surmounting the dome, and her stained-glass windows, centuries old, you have a sight and a gem which dazzles and bewilders. Then comes Milan, with her towering and colossal Cathedral, and Strassburg, and Florence, each in its turn contributing to increase your amazement and strengthen your admiration.

Another thing is, they indicate every style of architecture known to or devised by man, just as the paintings which they contain mark the progress or decline of art, and faithfully represent the style and characteristics of each school. But I might write you for hours in this train, and it would only result in increasing your desire to see without really interesting you as to what I have seen. But what a grand thing it is to be privileged to travel a little; my trip has been water to a parched tongue. Doubtless it will increase my interest in studying and reading, and will largely embellish what I have read. * * * * * *

In Venice we had the great pleasure of visiting the palace of the Doges; the prison, the senate, the rooms of the Council of Three and Ten, and then the "Bridge of Sighs." For hours we wandered through this strange, terrible building, and recalled the gloomy history and the bloody deeds wrapped in the walls of a building which had once been the home of men who were "faithful among the faithless found."

From this point we started on a general tour, visiting the home of Lucretia Borgia, Tasso, Othello, Desdemona, the office and warehouse of Shylock, the tombs of Canova and Titian, the palaces of the rich, the furniture of Marie Antoinette,—stucco work unsurpassed for elegance and completeness—the grand Canal, the Rialto, and a hundred other points about which I hope we will be able to talk when "Johnny comes marching home."

From Venice we came here, on our way, plowing through the Apennines and crossing the water shed of the Adriatic and the Tyrrhean seas, and having withal an elegant ride. To-morrow we expect to leave for Rome, when we anticipate a grand time roaming round the "Ancient City," amid its antiquities and arts. * *

I have written you this letter jointly because of want of time to write you separately. I hope it may be acceptable to you as coming from one who is
     Faithfully yours,
        W. C. MORELAND.

The Italian Section of the Commandery were some four weeks longer out than the others, and sailed from Liverpool on September 28th, arriving safe, hearty and well in New York on October 6th, thus completing, with this party finally home, the entire programme as laid down for Allegheny Commandery's Second "Crusade."

Conclusion.

BEFORE concluding this work, humbly as it is done, and hastily prepared as it has been, allow us to look over hurriedly, our party, our work, the success of the "Crusade" and the admirable arrangements made for us, and under which we have traveled.

First, let us remark, that any mention of any of the party of '78, made in any of these pages, has been in the very best and kindest of spirit and humor as towards each individual member of the "Crusading Pilgrims" without one single exception, we hold no other thought than kindness and good feeling, and if mentioned herein, the intention is far from any motive to jeer or wound, but as stated in the full intent of kindly feeling.

Of Eminent Sir Lee S. Smith, the Eminent Commander of the Commandery during the pilgrimage, he is so well known to the citizens of Allegheny County, that no word of ours can make him the better acquainted with our home readers. We can cheerfully and honestly pay to him this tribute, a heart full of sympathy, encouragement and good will, a character sterling in all of its qualities, a companion in travel, social, jovial and genial, without a trait of doing away from home that which he would not do while at home, and in him was the authority of conducting the "Crusade" justly placed, as its Eminent Commander, fitted in every way for the high position he then enjoyed.

We shall never forget our handsome, stately new-made friend Eminent Sir John Amsden, of Versailles, Kentucky, the Generalissimo of the "Crusade." A friend first, last and all the time; affable and pleasant, a merry twinkle in his eye and always a cheerful good word for every person; and, although old Father Time has slightly powdered his hair with the frosts of sixty winters, yet we trust many, many years will our good friend be spared to think over the "Crusade" of '78.

Our Captain-General, Sir William C. Moreland, a gentleman whose name is as familiar to every one in Western Pennsylvania, as is the President of the United States, with a reputation wide-spread over the entire good old Keystone State, in whose company we were closely allied on our tour, is a companion whose gentlemanly bearing, kind-heartedness and scholastic requirements shall ever be remembered with the greatest pleasure. Nothing was proposed but in what he would most heartily concur, and all his actions utterly and totally debarred from anything appertaining to the selfish. With his ever ready flow of unexcelled language and oratory, with his beautiful metaphors and full rounded periods, carrying the hearts of all his listeners with him, did he reflect great credit upon the party, and we are sure a never-to-be-forgotten share upon himself. His companionship will be remembered always as one of the most pleasant features of the pilgrimage.

Two better, truer Sir Knights or gentlemen never entered an Asylum than Sirs William Fullerton and Edward F. Clinton, of Black Hawk, Colorado. Meeting as entire strangers their many good qualities endeared them to all, and we are certain the impression made by these two gentlemen will be long, pleasant and bright in the memories of those who were their fellow travelers.

Need we refer to our life-long friend Em. Sir Wm. H. Slack, the worthy Prelate of Allegheny Commandery, a gentleman we can almost remember from infancy, and with years of intimacy and friendship passing over our heads, we have never either by thought, word or deed known him to be other than a genuine man, the highest title possible to be given to the highest work of God's creation. Neither by word or action have we ever known him say a solitary unkind word concerning anybody, but a good word for every one, behind their back as before their face, which in the seeming perversity of to-day, is a rare exception. Our years of intimacy and friendship were to the writer only more and more enhanced by our fellowship on this tour, and our sincere trust is that he may long continue to go in and out of Allegheny Commandery, as well as in his private walks of life, a worthy citizen, an honorable gentleman, cherished by all that know him.

We take special pleasure in referring to Sir J. D. Landis, of Coatesville, Pa., on his first European trip, and as our first acquaintance commenced with this "Crusade," with abundant opportunities to prove a man as the old saying is, " by living with him for a while," we think of him as a sterling young man in every particular, every word betokening him a thorough gentleman and genial friend.

As happy a recollection as we have of any in the party is of the person with whom perhaps we never would have become acquainted, had it not been for his " bath at sea," a person to whom everything the opposite of true manhood was an utter stranger, one in whom every reliance could be placed, one in whom every action was cool and deliberate; one in whom the instinct of a gentleman was plainly written on his countenance; one in whom was straight-forwardness; one in whom was honor, bright, pure and simple; one in whom the many admirable qualities he possessed were frequent marks of admiration, and one whose continuous affability, geniality and true friendship will ever be remembered as an evening star in the constellation of happy events, daily occurring on our " Crusade "—we refer to our friend Colonel Samuel McConihe, of the United States army, with a record as bright in his country's service as his social qualities on such a furlough as this; and we do not say one word here for the mere sake of saying it, but from personal inquiry at the proper place, the fountain-head of reliable information, and for this reason we take special pleasure in paying this little tribute to one well deserving the name of man, soldier, friend.

We can speak only in the kindest of terms of Sir James C. Rafferty, who, poor fellow, suffered fearfully on our outward passage, not from sea-sickness so much as from general debility, and when leaving the steamer at Ireland, was a perfect skeleton, but thanks to good care, kind friends round and about him he was soon made hale and hearty, and no better person was enrolled on the Roster of the Commandery than the young gentleman we have just named.

Most agreeably surprised were we in our worthy Sir Knights J. Fred Beilstein and James Milliken, who proved to be the most agreeable of traveling companions, ready at all times to lend their aid to anything conducive to the pleasure of others, and better hearted men have yet to tread this earth than these two Sir Knights.

We can speak with pleasure of Sirs George S. Eyster, O. H. Brusie, Robert J. Baxter, A. O. Baker, Jesse L. Stackhouse, (now deceased,) Edward L. Schroder and George S. Haines; all agreeable and pleasant, though but one was really a member of Allegheny Commandery, the remainder being from foreign Commanderies, that is, foreign to Allegheny County.

Em. Sir Robert Morris, L. L. D., is well known all over the United States as a writer and poet of note, his Masonic lectures and writings being almost in every library in this country and British domains.

We were never more agreeably surprised, nor did we have more pleasure, than when our old time friend William M. Herron, M. D., was booked with the "Crusaders" for the European pilgrimage, though he made up his mind within only twenty-four hours of the departure of the Commandery from home, which necessitated considerable lively telegraphing to secure him and his two daughters accommodations with the party. Our acquaintance with Dr. Herron dates back with that of Prof. Slack, to earliest remembrance and infancy, and aside from his skillful hand at many times bringing us through the days of illness, his own social and sterling qualities would endear him to any who may have the good fortune to claim his acquaintance. We have ever known him as a friend, and going away from home almost a total physical wreck from overwork in the pursuit of his profession, at which he has the honor to stand at the head, none hailed with more true and sincere delight, that return of good health and physical rebuilding, of which he stood greatly in need, than do we, and we are certain in the thought that his trip to Europe was simply taking a re-lease for an extension of life. No better man lives than our good friend Dr. Wm. M. Herron.

Another member of the medical profession with us was Dr. A. Dudley, of Salem, Mass.; a gentleman though we had never had the pleasure of meeting before, was one we were pleased to meet then, and we shall always remember our *vis-a-vis* at the table on board ship, who stood by the Colonel, the writer and one or two others, when all the rest of our comrades had deserted their posts.

Pleasant corners in memory's room have been made for Messrs. William E. Corey, E. W. Parker, Jacob Laucks, Frank Heath, and H. C. Levis, of whom we have the most pleasant recollections.

We may be considered guilty of most ungallant acts in going over the names of the gentleman portion of the roster first, but we always hold our best card to the very last in all things, so now let us speak for a moment of the female portion of the body, the roses and flowers of creation—the ladies of our party, ten of whom accompanied the Commandery on her pilgrimage. It would seem almost incredible, but it was none the less the truth, that from the time of leaving the Union Depot in Pittsburgh, until the time of our separation, moving rapidly as we did, up in the morning early, making close connections with trains and steamers, not one single moment of detention to one or any occurred through or by one of the ladies; never from one came a word of complaint as to weariness or being tired, but from one and all in the morning came a happy smile and a cheerful "Good morning," while at night came as cheerfully a pleasant "Good night," and to each one individually of the ladies, as well as collectively, do we attribute much of the pleasure enjoyed by us while in their company.

If we have spoken in words, sincere as they are, praiseworthy of the gentlemen, we can not say too much of the lady portion of our little band. More kind persons than our fellow citizens, Mrs. William H. Slack and Mrs. E. C. Rafferty, could hardly possibly be found, who were ever as ready with needle, thread and buttons for us, as though under the protecting wings of our own dear mothers, while any little headache or other trifling ailment were as carefully asked for as though at home, and now we claim we have about half a dozen mothers, which is we think highly preferable to having none.

As we write these pages, the cheerful smiles of the good-natured Mrs. Mifflin and her beautiful and charming daughter, Mrs. Frohock, are as distinct in our mind's eye as though we were shaking hands with each, and saying emphatically, "How do you do?" "How are you to-day?"

One of the most indefatigable travelers and tourists we have ever had the pleasure of seeing—for we delight in seeing a good traveler, particularly a lady— was our pleasant and entertaining young lady friend, Miss Ella M. Carr, of Jersey City, who evidently left home, not for the empty sake of saying on her return, "I have been to Europe," but for a visit of profit, pleasure and instruction. Though she knew not, carefully we noticed her mind ran not upon things present, dress and gossip of the day. We cannot recall an instance of overhearing the latest sensation in Jersey City, the newest romance of some belle or beau, but we did observe she had the knack of seeing everything worthy of seeing on such a trip, and none would return home with more knowledge of historical places and things, that will prove interesting to her friends, and a pleasure and satisfaction to herself, than would Miss Carr. She went to *see*, not to talk; was not thoroughly posted in everybody's business, but knowing her own fully, she profited every day by laying away in the granary of the mind some fresh grain of thought that will always prove fresh and useful. Such a person it is a pleasure to meet and to see. In like manner might we also speak of Miss Susan M. Leverich, whose mind was a perfect storehouse of historical knowledge; for having never before been to the European side of old Atlantic, from her book knowledge of its topography, its castles, its origin, its date, she appeared as familiar with the ground over which we had trod as though it were her daily walk in former years.

Mrs. Schroder, upon her bridal tour is pleasantly associated with others, and we shall particularly remember her for one remarkable thing in a lady, a precious gift we are prone to call it, that of silence on points belonging to herself, and proves silence to be golden. This will appear all the more remarkable that though on her bridal trip, married but a day or so prior to leaving New York, so completely was the fact ignored by herself and husband, that not for several weeks after our leaving home was the fact of a bridal pair in our party known, and then it became known only through the merest accident. This of itself will speak more for the good sense and character of the lady than words we might choose to state here in reference to her. She and her good husband have our best wishes for many years of pleasant association, and may the fire built upon the altar of connubial bliss, started when Allegheny Commandery made her second European Crusade, ever burn brightly in the fireside of happiness and prosperity, the flames constantly fanned by the power of Love, with the date of July, 1878, as the time the spark commenced to ignite the fire which shall ever glow mildly upon the hearth-stone of their wedded career.

Three young ladies in our party, merry and sparkling, full of the sunshine and beauty of youth, were the Misses Mary and Nannie B. Herron, and Miss Lillian B. Patterson, each of whom, with their pleasant natures and beaming countenances, contributed in a large degree to the pleasure of their fellow companions. As we trod the deck of the steamer, sat down with them at the tables of the hotels, as we sat with them in the same places of worship, or as we gracefully as possible lifted our hats to them upon the streets in foreign climes, we were constantly reminded of home, and what is true of the others, is true also of them; nothing but a pleasant countenance from each greeted all with whom they were acquainted. And since we arrived home, one of the young ladies has become the loving and estimable young wife of a most estimable young man; we consider it one of our greatest pleasures in this place, as a fellow-traveler and " Crusader," to extend to that young lady our sincere and hearty congratulations upon her entrance into our ranks, viz: among the married portion of society, and from our heart we earnestly wish that the very smallest portion of earth's sorrows allotted to poor humanity, may be the share of she and her husband, that having kissed the morning of happiness by the advent from the days of maiden, into the more responsible years of wifehood, that her happiness shall be bright, pure, clear and sparkling as the rivulet, flowing from its cool mountain home, and as the dew-drop upon the leaf glistening in the glad morning sun, which shall never dim nor fade away is the true and heartfelt wish of "Carlisle." Having spoken thus of our traveling companions, let us look for a moment at the admirable arrangements under which we traveled while on our "Crusade."

TRAVELING ARRANGEMENTS FOR THE PARTY.

As stated in the very earliest portion of this work, our arrangements were made by E. M. Jenkins, Esq., a fellow frater of Allegheny Commandery, a gentleman of large experience in traveling matters, who through hard efforts built up one of the most gigantic tourist agencies ever seen in the United States, whose business with one railroad in America amounted to hundreds of thousands of dollars per annum, to him we are largely indebted for the completeness and successful carrying out of the programme laid down at the start, now let us see what this embraced and what a convenience his system for us was. Stepping into his office we pay our expenses for the tour, which covers everything, from the commencement to the end of the Crusade. We carry no tickets; on our arrival at Queenstown we were met by Mr. C. P. Cooper, who was to be our guide in Ireland; we were spoken to by no person, never handled our baggage, paid no attention whatever to it, and it was a singular thing to us at first on our arrival at the Victoria Hotel, in Cork, to be asked by the Hotel manager, "what is your name, sir?" "Carlisle, sir," we replied. "Show Mr. 'Carlisle' up to No. 68, John!" the clerk would say, and being shown thither, there on a little table stood our baggage, all ready to be unlocked, and the same proceeding would occur on leaving the Hotel; simply turning the key in the lock, we would go away, never speaking of baggage to anyone, and that would be the last we would see of it until the next place was reached, when would come the same question, "your name, sir?" "'Carlisle,' sir!" "Show Mr. 'Carlisle' to No. 71, Mike!" and there in No. 71 stood our baggage again, the same as ever. We could not understand this for quite a little while, but the *modus operandi* is this: the hotel proprietors are all furnished with printed lists of the party, with the date the party will arrive there, whether single or married, and each name assigned to a room, so that immediately on entering a hotel and hearing your name he knows precisely where to locate you. Then you have no bills to pay, you walk into your room, to the table, and out from it, and no one says, "whither goest thou?" You have no bickerings with hotel proprietors as to the size of your bill, and extortionate charges. One most fortunate thing, and we think the greatest blessing in it all, was the fact of having nothing to do with porters, particularly in Ireland, and we looked on with the most intense satisfaction conceivable, at the poor fellows lugging around immense Saratogas and two-story mansard roof trunks, knowing we had not to give them a solitary cent.

Speaking of Mr. Cooper, we may say, and in which we will be heartily seconded by anyone and all of our party, that in every respect he is a thorough gentleman; never out of humor, understanding his business thoroughly, no troubles under his supervision occurring, nor confusion existing under his care; at least, if any did occur, none save himself ever knew of them. He cared for all in general, saw personally to every little wish and comfort, and made every, if any dissatisfaction occurred, clear and smooth, and we pledge him the word of a Knight of Submission, that if he will come out and see America, "we will make it pleasant for him." It was the handiest possible kind of arrangement, to go in and out, paying no bills, simply picking up your cane and umbrella, putting on your duster and leaving the town, only to proceed to the next, where it was ditto, ditto. No rail road conductor to bother you; no shouting in your ears "Tickets! tickets, gentlemen!" but just follow your leader.

At every railway station were in waiting for us waggonettes, or jaunting cars or omnibuses, in which we were conveyed to and from the hotels and depots. It would be a particularly fine convenience for ladies traveling alone, unaccustomed to the usages, language and moneys of foreign countries, if only for the one thing of avoiding the pestering and abominations of the most consummate begging to be seen anywhere in the world. If a man lifts his hat, nods, winks at you, moves your satchel an inch or so, it is expected that from a sixpence to a half-crown will be forthcoming at once. But if a person makes the trip two or three times, they become thoroughly hardened to the pitiful wailings of these scoundrels, for by some instinctive means, we think, by the use of some one of the five senses, or all combined, they just know when to let a man alone, or for how much they can bleed him.

By the arrangements, also, we had ponies in waiting for us, to convey the party through the Gap of Dunloe, while the party taking in the Italian section of the tour, had ponies and donkeys in waiting for them wherever necessary. Not one fault could be found in any of the arrangements, so completely and admirably prepared by our friend, Mr. Jenkins.

We do not think this work would be complete without the including a letter, received by the writer, showing how the order of Knights of Submission had taken deep root in the mind of, at least, one of our fellow-countrymen, subsequent to the publication of its noble principles and precepts. This we give verbatim, and the answer given to the same. It is dated:

BREAK NECK, Butler Co., Pa., February 10th, 1879.

Deer Sir:

i hev red ynre letters by Mr. carlisle, an liked Them very Mutch, espesily the last One givin an Account of That one hundreth Degree. i hev always wanted To join the masons But hev not done so fur 2 Reasons,

1st. they Charge two Mutch and i Am poor.

2d. my Folks are All covenanters and u. p.'s, and they are All Opposed to cecret OrganisaShuns they Cant get in.

3d. i hev Always been affraid They wouldn't hev me. Every time they hev got an organisashun in Imitation of The masons, I hev sed thot i would Try and get In, but hev Always Put it off Till they got Started, then they charged 2 Mutch, and Black Baled 2, so i Am still out.

Ever since you Spoke of The new order last month i hev ben anxis to join, and Ben wating for The next number of youre Paper to see All about it, and After readin' All about it, i think It Is just The thing i want.

As you dont sa whoo is grand mogul Now,—whether That big Night Mr. lee, or who—an As you hev the Biggest milatery Title, i write to you fur infurmation; an You will Oblige me 2 Anser The following questions:

1st. Who Is the officers Now, an do You intend to start uther Branches of the order.

2nd. how Mutch do You charge fur 1 or more; an would The 1st wun be the grand Mogul Of the new Branch?

3rd. how would we hev to do—Come to allegheny to Get the degrees, Or would yure grand Mogul come Out hear if We paid him.

4th. do you hev a Printed Book 2 Tell How 2 initiate Persons into The Order, and how Mutch are they?

5th. What hez thot Itinery Of corporal mcConihe's to do with the Order—is it Instrucshuns to Persons wantin' 2 Enter The order.

6th. would you requier All Cash, or Part on Time. if It Is not to Mutch trouble i wish you would Rite me All About It, or Hev. mr. carlisle do it.

we are all well, an hopin' you are enjoyin' the Same Blessin, My wife Sez she is anxis for Me to Jine these men so i Can be Buried with there onors.

Yours Ever
SAMUEL CAROTHERS.

p. S.—i think Cornel Smith ot 2 Feal Proud at Bein the first grand mogul and give it 2 us Free.
Yours, S. C.

The above was duly received, and from the orthography contained therein is an evidence of intellectual advancement in the superlative degree, still our mission as an humble member of an order, recognizing only the good of humanity, made us feel it our duty lay as plainly in the direction of placing this man on the right road as we would the most aristocratic prince of royalty, so we gave him the following full information which was as explicit as we could well convey:

ALLEGHENY CITY, PA., February 15th, 1879.
SAMUEL CAROTHERS, ESQ.,
Break Neck, Penn'a.

My Dear Sir and Fellow Mortal:

In reply to your very interesting letter of the 10th inst. we take pleasure in saying—

1st. Sir Lee S. Smith, for the same reason of his first election, that of taking the office by force, thereby teaching us the beautiful point of Submission, is the present Grand Mogul, simply because we are unable to depose him, and Major William C. Moreland, of Pittsburgh, is the Deputy Vice-Mogul. By our constitution and charter we are prohibited from instituting more than two councils in any one county.

2d. Having no poor people in our order, it being strictly confined to the *wealthy*, our charges are "steep," namely, one hundred dollars for each degree, and three degrees in the order; that is for one person. When giving them to a dozen or more, we give them at wholesale prices,—a very liberal reduction of 25, 20, 15, 10, 5, and 5 and 2½ per cent. extra off for cash. The first man placing in "Carlisle's" hands one hundred silver pieces bearing the engraving of the English Buzzard, he shall be the First Grand Mogul.

3d. You would necessarily be compelled to come down to Allegheny to receive the degrees at present; still the three highest officers would not object to going up to Break Neck ten times, provided there was any amount of "root of all evil" in it.

4th. In answer to this question we would simply whisper a kindly word of advice in your ear; go and have an hour with your pastor and spiritual adviser, perhaps he can tell you of the awful death which once upon a time befel a man named Morgan, an alleged member of those pagans and dark lantern heathen called Masons. Oh! no, we have no printed books. We can take our own life, if necessary, before our allotted time expires for usefulness on this mundane sphere, without sending out special invitations for some one to come and do it for us.

5. The "itinerary" of Colonel McConihe is a little degree of of his own; we know nothing about it, no one can ever enter it without the Colonel's permission. However, we will give you his address; perhaps you may obtain the desired information by addressing him personally: "Colonel S. McConihe, Camp Douglas, Salt Lake City, Utah."

6th. We hardly know whether to treat this question as ignorance or insult, but through charity will treat it as the former. Our terms are positively and strictly cash on the spot. At any time you desire the committee will assemble, and will repair to your town of cheerful and pleasant name and institute your branch of the order.

Oh! my no! it is *no trouble whatever* to answer a few such questions as these, our time is not valuable at all; all we have to do is just to sit and answer such questions—only when you have an entire catechism to propound please ask us but one or two questions a month or so. Yours truly, CARLISLE.

P. S.—Please disabuse your mind of any such expectation as Col. Smith coming up to give the degrees "free."

Thank you, we are all well. CARLISLE.

We never heard another word from Mr. Carothers on this subject, and can only surmise some of his anti-secret friends seized upon him and scared the poor fellow from joining our ranks.

We have as nearly as possible in this book endeavored to follow as accurately as possible the doings; the sights and daily incidents of the Commandery as a whole, and of its members individually; we are aware much can be found fault with, but it will at least serve as a slight momento of that happy pilgrimage, condensed as its history is, and if we have spent an hour pleasantly in your company we are fully satisfied and amply repaid.

Wishing every member of the Crusading party of '78, in business—all prosperity; in health—all blessings; in life—all joy; in death—a calm and peaceful rest, and as the inveterate foe of all mankind, relentless in his visitations, old Father Time in his inevitable and unerring flight, strikes one Crusader here and another there; as he touches one by one with his cold and fatal hand of death; should he by blind and unreasoning chance pass us by for a little while longer, there is not one who will ever be forgotten by "Carlisle," and with this he bids you each and every one "Farewell" and "Farewell."

✠ In Memoriam: ✠

"IN THE MIDST OF LIFE, WE ARE IN DEATH."
We are called upon to perform the melancholy task of chronicling in these pages the death of a worthy Sir Knight, who was numbered with the party on the Crusade—

Sir Jesse L. Stackhouse,

OF EMILIE, BUCKS COUNTY, PA.

On the Evening of July 1st, 1879, seated round an elegantly spread banquet table, celebrating the First Annual Reunion of the Crusaders of '78, were a large number of the Pilgrims, merrily chatting over the pleasant memories of the tour; at that table sat JESSE L. STACKHOUSE, Esq., who had come all the way to Pittsburgh that he might be present with his fellow fraters and companions on that occasion. Little did any of us think, as we sat and ate, and drank, in the midst of mirth and merriment, that even then the dread Angel of Death was hovering near. Little did we surmise, as we shook hands with Sir Knight STACKHOUSE, that never more would we see him here in the Asylum on the earth below.

Arriving at his home on July 4th, hale and hearty as customary, suddenly and ruthlessly he was stricken down by the Dread Destroyer on July 10th. Gentle as a child, with a spirit as meek, Sir STACKHOUSE was called from his work here; having fulfilled, indeed, his long and weary pilgrimage on earth, he was taken on the last, long pilgrimage of Death; and we know that he has simply gone with those who have gone before, and is peacefully at rest in the great Asylum beyond, where sooner or later we must all go, our lamented Sir Knight and Crusader only preceding to give us all the grand welcome; and we trust, though it is so sad to part from dear friends, we may only go peacefully to sleep here, to awaken in the world beyond, with the glad greeting from our late worthy Sir Knight, "*Pilgrim, I greet thee!*" And we trust that in the great future Temple, not one chair will be vacant, not one face be missing; that there every Crusader of '78 shall meet and hold a reunion that shall never have an end.

To the friends of Sir Knight STACKHOUSE, we extend the heart and hand of sympathy, in the bereavement with which they have been overtaken.

www.ingramcontent.com/pod-product-compliance
Lightning Source LLC
Chambersburg PA
CBHW031421230426
43668CB00007B/393